OVER 20 YEARS OF DISASTER

Michael Kevin Moore

Lightning Fast Book Publishing, LLC
P.O. Box 441328
Fort Washington, MD 20744

www.lfbookpublishing.com

LIGHTNING FAST
BOOK PUBLISHING

The author of this book tells a biographical story of living the street-life, and the all-encompassing realities and consequences. The literary offering provided is non-fictional and derived from the experiences of the author. Some names that appear in this book have been changed for anonymity. The intent of this work is to give readers an entertaining read, while encouraging a law-abiding and positive lifestyle. In the event that you use or enact any of the material in this book, the author and publisher assume no responsibility for your actions.

The publisher, Lightning Fast Book Publishing, assumes no responsibility for any content presented in this book.

ISBN-10: 0-9994653-0-9
ISBN-13: 978-0-9994653-0-1

Dedication

I dedicate this book to my parents, Melvin and Lenora Moore. All you ever wanted was for me to finish college and for me to use my life as a vessel to help other people. Well, I graduated from UDC in 2011 with a BA in Computer Info Systems and am currently working on my MBA. I also dedicate this book to my three grand kids: Omari, Marlie and Knox Moore. The three of you are now a part of my legacy.

This is a book depicting of my life in the streets. It is the story of how I entered into a life of crime, drugs, and mayhem. I made a lot of mistakes in my 25 years in the streets, and I pray that by reading these pages, the reader will use my life as an example and choose a totally different path...

Acknowledgements

First, I must thank God almighty for my health, strength, and mind; without my religious and sports upbringing; I wouldn't have had the tenacity to finish this book.

I would like to thank my brothers and sisters for giving me tough love and not enabling me. I know you all gave up on me, but I still love you and appreciate all your assistance throughout my life.

Thanks to my children, Laricka Coty and Michael Moore Jr. I know I've been incarcerated for most of your lives, so I wasn't much of a dad. I pray that someday we can get past our differences and have some type of relationship. Thank you also to my kids' mother's for being both mom and dad when I was away.

"I am not a mechanism, an assembly of various sections. And it is not because the mechanism is working wrongly, that I am ill. I am ill because of the wounds to the soul, to the deep emotional self and the wounds to the soul take a long, long time, only time can help, and practice, and a certain difficult repentance long difficult repentance, realization of life's mistakes, and the freeing of oneself from the endless repetition of the mistake which mankind at large has chosen to sanctify..."

D. H. Lawrence

TABLE OF CONTENTS

Chapter 1

The Beginning

I was born August 7, 1964 in Washington, DC, at George Washington Hospital Center. My parents are Melvin C. Moore, born February 8, 1921, and Lenora B. Jones, born December 15, 1920. I was the seventh child of their union.

I was what you'd call a mid-life baby; both my parents were in their 40's when they had me. The sibling closest to my age was Ronald R. Moore, who was born December 10, 1950, and died October 3, 1985. Ronald was killed by a Mr. John West on Sheriff Road in Fairmont Heights Maryland. Ronald was fourteen years older than I.

My sister, Judy Moore Davis, is fifteen years older than I. Then there is my brother, Donald E. Moore, who is seventeen years older than I. My oldest brother, Melvin L. Moore, is twenty years older than I. Jean P. Moore is twenty-one years older. My oldest sibling is Lenora Moore Daniels, who is twenty-three years older. There is a considerable age difference between me and my other siblings. They were more like my other parents, and my older brothers and sisters took on the responsibility of raising me.

Out of my other six siblings, I believe I was closest to Ronald. In all actualities, because of Ronald's drug usage, he wasn't much older than

I in terms of maturity. As I got older, I found our roles in life changed, and I became like his older brother. Because of his drug use, Ronald was alienated by the rest of our family. As I got older, and especially after my parents died, I also was alienated because of the choices I made in my life. I haven't spoken to a few of my siblings in over 10 years

To put it plainly, our family is like America before 1955: we are "separate but equal." Too bad *Brown v. Board of Education* didn't affect us.

Today we are still separate. How can a house divided stand? Can you imagine the success a strong, intelligent, educated, black family could achieve as one unit? Maybe after reading my book, we can finally open our eyes and see the truth. I pray the cut that separates us is not too infected to heal.

Growing up, I was a fat kid, Momma's baby and Daddy's pet. Since my parents were older, and more established when I was a kid, they really put a great deal of time into planning for my future.

Don't get me wrong, they wanted the best for all their children. My father wanted his sons to get college degrees, but let's face the facts of life: not every child is college material. At the age of twelve, my brother Donald hit himself in the head with a hammer while building a club house, then chased all the other kids out of the woods with the hammer. As an adult, my brother Melvin helped my brother Ronald with his grade school homework, and Ronald got every answer wrong. I'm not taking anything from the achievements of my brothers, for they are both successful in their own rights. They both are at the age of retirement or past it now, and they both own their own homes. Technically, I am actually homeless, so again I thank my friend Nancy for accepting me as a part of her family, and making sure I have a warm place in the winter and a cool place in the summer to lay my head.

The point I'm trying to make is that not everyone is college material. My parents and my sister Jean sent me to a private school, DuPont Park Seventh Day Adventist School, for I was ahead of all the other children in my neighborhood that went to public school. Deep down inside, I believe some of my siblings hate me because of all the extra attention I got as a child. I believe if you continuously project negative energy in a certain direction, you can sabotage a person's life. The mind is a strong organ, and man doesn't know 90% of its capabilities.

A great deal of the indifference between the siblings in our family towards one another can be blamed on our parents. My parents were young when they married, nineteen years old. Young people make mistakes. The Christian Bible states "all have sinned and fall short of the glory of God." Simply put, we all make mistakes. The biggest mistake my parents made was favoring one child more than the next. When you show favoritism in anything, this brings about hate and deceit. When you have a team of any type, you have to treat all its members equally. My mother, had been adopted by her aunt, and her aunt showed more attention to her own children than to my mother and her sister Rosie. My mother therefore exploded every time my father showed favor to any of their children. My father, being an only child, didn't know any better. My parents never read any child psychology books. A little diplomacy between my mom and dad, nine times out of ten, would have created a better living environment for me and my brothers and sisters. We all make mistakes in life, like we spill milk. The trick to the game is to accept the mistake, get up and brush yourself off, and go on with your life. When you dwell on bad things, they fester in your mind, and we are the type of people that hold on to grudges for decades I remember at the age of 40, beating a guy up for stealing one of my hot wheels cars when I was 7. I held on to that hate for more than 30 years. My father always told us to never get mad, but to always get even. I guess this is why we are so dysfunctional.

As I mentioned earlier, I was a fat kid ("Baby Huey," sixty lbs. at two years old) and I got a lot of attention from both my parents.

My mother made it her business to always keep me clean and dressed in the latest style of clothing. When I say the latest style, I mean the latest style in the Sears or Montgomery Ward catalogs. Back in those days, in the '60s and '70s, a lot of blacks had credit accounts with Sears and Montgomery Ward, thus they did most of their shopping using their catalogs. I grew up in an environment with pimps and big time drug hustlers; therefore, I wanted clothing from Cavaliers, Woodies, Lewis & Thomas Salts, and Raleigh Haberdashery. That's one of the main reasons I started robbing and selling drugs: to get clothes that would impress girls. I just had to have a pair of reptiles; if not reptiles, they had to at least be amphibians.

My parents simply were not going to buy me clothing with other peoples' names printed on the back pockets. My father was so cheap he would buy second hand clothing from Salvation Army or Value Village and then tailor them to look like new. I guess that was smart, for when he died, he had a considerable amount of money in his savings.

I remember when I was six years old; my father brought me a brand-new five-speed bike from the Sears on Bladensburg Road in N.E. Washington, D.C. On the side of the bike was written in big words, "SCREAMER ONE." That bike had a small wheel in the front, a big wide wheel in the back, a five-speed gear shift, hand brakes, and goose-neck handlebars. It looked like a Harley-Davison chopper. I thought I was the shit. I never let anyone else ride that bike. I was too afraid they would ride off with it and never come back. I remember one Sunday I road my bike to the Highs convenient Store on Kenilworth Avenue to get a Chilly Willy in the summer time. Before I could lock my bike to the pole an older kid from Kenilworth busted me upside my head and took my bike. I couldn't have been more than 10 years old at the time. I ran all the way home and told my father and my older brother what had happened. My dad told me to take my ass back around that corner and get that bike. My brother told me we don't have punks in our family, and if you don't go back and fight for that bike I had to fight him. I was always a thinker, so I had to figure a way to get this bigger kid off my bike. Behind my mom's house was a stack of 2 x 4's from an old shed we had torn down. I went back there and picked out about a 3 foot piece of wood. The problem was the board had a nail in it. I walked back around the corner to the spot where my bike was snatched, and to my surprise this fool was still there doing wheelies with my bike. I waited until this guy raised my front wheel in the air again, timing it perfectly, I took board and smacked him right across the forehead. I hit him so hard the small nail that was in the piece of wood stuck directly in the guy's forehead. When he hit the ground, I jumped on my bike and road home as fast as I could.

About an hour later, the guy I hit with the board, and his mom came to my mother's house with the police. They asked where I was, and when I came down stairs, the big white cop put hand cuffs on me. They took me to Prince George's Hospital for a psychological evaluation. I still remember the room they took me too: room H300. Once inside, I noticed there were about 12 other kids there sitting at a long table drawing pictures. A pretty, blond headed white lady was the doctor. She sat me down at the table and gave me a pencil and a piece of paper. She told me to draw a picture of something I wanted to see. I immediately noticed all the other kids were drawing pictures of trees, ponds, and animals. I drew a picture of a gun, a knife, and an open door. When the white lady looked at my picture she turned blood red. She asked me to explain my picture. I told her I wanted to see the door open, and I needed a gun and a knife to get it open. They let me go home that night, but I remember the doctor telling my father that I was destined for the penitentiary.

To be honest, after that incident, I started going over in Kenilworth and steeling some of their bikes. I think I always had a streak of bad in me, even though I was smart in school. In 2002, after my father died, we put the bike out along with my old sled. I had those items for thirty-two years, so either I'm a pack rat or anal as hell.

Not having any siblings around my own age, I sought friendship from the neighborhood kids. Our neighborhood was called Beaver Heights. We were between Kenilworth and Fairmont Heights. Believe it or not, neither area would accept us as part of their own. Our neighborhood only consisted of three blocks: Eastern Avenue, R Street, and North Addison Road, which was where I lived. Our address was 4320 North Addison Road. This was the biggest house in the neighborhood. The house had once been owned by Judge McColor. My father purchased the house from the Judge in 1962. I live in that house thirty-eight years, on and off, between college and jail visits.

Growing up in Beaver Heights in the 60's and the 70's, our neighborhood was a village. Everyone looked out for everyone else's kids. It was nothing for me to get my but beat on the next street over for doing something wrong Unlike the kids today, I better not go home and tell my parents that my neighbor whipped my ass. If I did, I had another ass whipping coming from home. People weren't as crazy back then as they are now either, for we slept with our windows and doors open in the summer time.

Also, as kids, we went outside and played sports. Our football field was a 14 foot wide, and 50 feet in length patch of grass in the front of a steel mill called Ceco. We played basketball either in my back yard, behind the Catholic Church on R Street, or in the Hemphil back yard; so most of us were in pretty good shape. We had no video games to sit home and play with. We built club houses, made go carts, and explored the woods near beaver dam creek. The girls learn to cook and take care of the home and as boys we cut grass in the summer and shoved snow in the winter.

Our fathers didn't make as much money as they do today, so they taught their sons how to use their hands to paint, and to fix things. When I got 12 years old, my mother made me work with a different tradesman each summer. I learned how to work on cars from Mr. Thompson; I learned how to use a hammer from Mr. Hemphill, and how to lay brick from Mr. McCloud. So, I was given a work ethic at an early age. I think the best friend I ever had was Jo-el McAbee. Jo-el was my next door neighbor on North Addison Road. We were both the same age, and Jo-el never stole from me nor hit me.

Jo-el, as we called him, competed with me in every sport. Basketball was always my love because my older brother Ronald was a star in High School. I always wanted to play like him. Jo-el and I also battled in football, and track. The majority of the time, he won. My older brother Melvin used to be our quarterback when we played one-on-one in football. I felt bad losing to Jo-el when my brother was the quarterback. Thank God I did win some of the games.

As we grew older, I got a lot taller than Jo-el, so I did have an advantage in basketball. He still won his fair share of games. We loved to watch the Washington Bullets; many nights, we played one-on-one, pretending to be Kevin Porter and Phil Chenier. We both had backyard basketball hoops, and we took turns playing in each other's backyard.

Jo-el grew up to be a successful man. He graduated with a degree in Business from Bowie State University. He also worked at the Department of Labor for a while. The last I heard, he was a missionary in Africa.

Jo-el's dad, Hank McAbee, was both Jo-el's and my best friend. He took us to a lot of Bullets Games and a few movies. He also took us fishing when he wasn't working. My dad, being retired, also took us places in the summer. Places like Sandy Point Beach to fish, Haines Point to swim and play golf, and Anacostia Park to skate and play basketball.

My first Bullets game was the Bullets verse the Atlanta Hawks; it was during Bill Willoughby's rookie season. Bill Willoughby was the first black to come directly from high school to the pro's. The game was on Christmas night, and they gave away free basketballs. My brother Ronald and Burt Hill took me to that game. Ironically, I'm writing this story from the Maryland Department of Correction — my brother was on a furlough through the work release program at the Southern Maryland pre-release center; which was also part of the Maryland Department of Corrections when he took me to that game.

When I got to be around thirteen years old, I started to rebel. I wanted privacy and space, and I was tired of all the babying from my parents. As they say, "I was smelling myself." The biggest rule I disagreed with was that I had to be in the house when the street lights came on. I'd be in the middle of a street football game, within eyesight of my house, and my mother would yell my name for me to come in. The other guys gave me holy hell for that.

Also at that time, I was playing football for a boys' club team in Palmer Park Maryland. Back then, your weight determined what team you played on. I was always big for my age so I played 125lbs team. The coaches' name was Mr. Ross. It was my first season playing organized football, so I had to play defense. I was a defensive tackle. My father used to drive me to practice every day in a 1974 Lincoln Continental Mark IV. The guys on the team also gave me hell for that; Palmer Park is a low-income section in the State of Maryland, and they thought I was a little rich kid. I had to show them very early on that I could fight, so I didn't have too many problems.

I went through a lot of embarrassing moments as a youth, but now that I think about it, I was quite fortunate. None of the other kids' parents gave them that much attention. My father wanted everything for me. I just wish he had moved us outside the beltway so that we lived near people who felt the same way about their children as he. My brothers and sisters didn't raise my nieces and nephews in the type of environment where I grew up, and they turned out to be doctors and law school students.

I don't blame anyone but myself for my misfortunes. I made bad choices and decisions in life. But I can say that peer pressure did play a big part in my development. Now that I'm older, I realize why they wanted me in at dark; I later learned some crazy things after the sun went down. As I sit here in this cell, I wish I'd listened to them.

When I got to be around the age of fourteen, I started sneaking out at night. That's when I learned all about the criminal life. I used to buy Newport Cigarettes just to have them in my pocket and pass them out to the older kids. I was worried that since I came from a good home, people would think I was scared or a punk. That was the beginning of my problems; I felt that I needed to prove I wasn't scared.

I think my first love was Harriet "Peaches" Bowes. She was the most beautiful girl at Beaver Heights Elementary School. Today, that school is a women's shelter. Peaches never gave me the time of day. At that time,

I was a fat boy. In the '70s, thin was definitely in. I had a great deal of disappointment with girls back then. When my parents decided to take me out of public school and put me private school at DuPont Park S.D.A. School, the problems with girls still existed. Let's see: at DuPont, there was Lorraine Armstrong Walden, Liza Ferguson, Ivy Randall, Audrey Hudson, Claire Smith, Yvonne Dunlap, Crystal Hogans, Jackie Lind, and Sherrie Blevins. I think the hurt I felt from being rejected by these girls carried on into my adulthood.

As I grew older, my luck with women changed, but I never totally committed myself to woman since. I'm forty-two years old, and I've never asked a woman to marry me. I bet you ladies didn't know you had such an effect on my psyche. I'll go deeper into the subject of love as the chapters go on.

When I got to be fourteen years old, I had my first sexual experience. I'm not one to kiss and tell, so I'll just call her BJ. She was about four or five years older than I and was in college. She became pregnant as a result. I didn't want to mess up either one of our lives, so we had to raise some money to get her an abortion. She wasn't working and neither was I, so I committed my very first armed robbery to pay for the abortion.

I had two great teachers: Fat Anthony and Black Mike. They've both spent many a year in prison for armed robbery. They gave me a BB gun that looked like the real thing and took me over to S.W. Washington, where there were a lot of gay clubs. I was to catch some poor unknowing gay guy coming from the club, put the gun on him, take his money, and run back to the getaway car. I caught two guys leaving the club, brandished the fake gun, and took their money. I knew both Mike and Anthony were older than I and thought they were slick, so I took $300 out of the wallet before I got back to the car.

When I got in the car, I threw one of them the wallet and hid in the back seat. Mike and Anthony told me there was only $60 in the wallet. I know there was more, but I never said anything. They gave me $20. If the two of you are reading this book, I bet you didn't know I took mine off the top.

I never Shoplifted, I never stole cars, and I never broke into any houses. I did sell a little reefer and commit a few robberies. My main motivation was trying to impress women. I didn't get into selling narcotics until I was eighteen years old. Mind you, all of this was almost thirty years ago, so the statute of limitations should be up. If you are reading this, you can't get a reward from Crime Stoppers.

When I left DuPont Park School, I went to Woodson High School in N.E. Washington. I used my sister Jean's address to get in. Since I was in private school from fourth through ninth grade, I was way ahead once I reached high school. I breezed through Woodson in two years. I was sixteen years old when I graduated from High School, in a rush to go nowhere. I was on a quest to be grown. That quest got me in a lot of trouble. If only I could do it all over again.

CHAPTER 2

RONALD MOORE

Before I get into the actual years of disaster, I must give homage to the older brother who introduced me to world of narcotics. This is a world that most normal people don't realize exists. They don't know about the poverty, the filth, the degradation, the violence. From the point of view of a participant, I pray my children never have to experience this part of our society.

As the youngest of four boys, I looked up to all my older brothers. Two of them were functional alcoholics, and Ronald was a drug addict.

As I sit here in prison today, I realize the mistakes I made in my life. My biggest mistake was to follow people that didn't know where they were going — the blind leading the crazy.

I was never taught drinking was wrong. In fact, at age six, I developed my love for beer. My sister Jean used to give it to me. She said it would help my hyperactive ass sleep. As I got older, it wasn't anything to go to either one of my older brothers and get a beer. Hell, they figured if I wasn't using drugs, I'd be ok, especially since they were functional alcoholics themselves. They had jobs, they had homes, they had wives, but most of all, they had problems. I think they drank the way they did to try and forget those problems. As I've gotten older, I've learned that drugs and alcohol don't help you forget problems; they give you another problem, one that is twice as hard to get rid of.

I guess you can say I had a messed up introduction into the life of narcotics as well. I was never taught "Don't get high on your own supply." Most of the dealers I knew sold and used.

Ronald was my ghetto hero. He was the one that conquered prison, the one that I thought wasn't afraid of anything, the one that was Fairmont Heights High School's basketball star; the one that could sell sand to a desert; he was the hustler, the rustler, the all-around slick dude.

Ronald Richard Moore was the baby of the Moore clan for fourteen years until I came along. My brother Donald once told me that when I was born, Ronald stopped being the center of attention in our family, thus went to drugs in attempt to fill the void, another statement that has weighed on my psyche.

Ronald started using drugs in high school, and was in and out of jail my entire life. The same woman that introduced Ronald to heroin was the lady who sold me my first sixteen-ounce bottle of PCP juice. Ronald once told me that he and his friends used to sit around after school and drink wine, and this woman, who I won't name, told him to spend a dollar and get real high. In the 1960's in Washington, D.C., you could buy a pill of heroin for $1.00. They used to call them "buck action." I think that how a great number of kids started using heroin; it was so cheap. In my days, the 1980s, the cheap drug was crack cocaine.

My older brother Melvin was the first athlete in our family, amongst the boys. My father must have been some athlete himself in order to have such athletic sons. Melvin's sport was baseball, and he was a pitcher. My father once told me that he used to sit in his car near

Watts Branch Recreation Center in North East Washington and watch Melvin hit home runs over the fence. Melvin also played for Spingarn High School in Washington, D.C. He played trumpet in the band and pitched no-hitters. Melvin once told me a scout for the New York Yankees viewed one of his games and told my father that Melvin was too small. If he could get some weight on him, the scout said, they might consider giving him a try-out. I guess with the problems my father was experiencing just trying to raise six children at that time, he put the scout's statement on the back-burner. I believe Melvin still blames my father today for deferring his dream by saying get out of my pots and pans. Big brother, that was over forty years ago — please let the anger go.

Melvin was also the one who taught Ronald basketball. I guess some people just have a gift. They can do things that seem unnatural. Well, Coach Freeman, you never mentioned Ronald Moore in your memoirs, so society never got a chance to know his history. I want to share a small piece of his story.

Ronald played point guard at Fairmont Heights High School from 1965 through 1968. He probably could have started anywhere else in the country, but he was a 6th man there. Even though he was 6th man, he still was named one of the top High school 500 basketball players in the country in 1968. His team won the state championship every year he was there.

Ronald's court antics just about drove Coach Freeman crazy. For example, every time Ronald got a fast break, instead of going to the basket for a lay-up, he would shoot a forty-five-foot set shot from the half court circle. 95% of the time, he made the shot. He used to go to the local college and watch old NBA and college basketball films. I did the same thing when I was in high School. I remember playing in a pick-up game at the king dome n and hearing some old man on the sideline saying, "Wow, I haven't seen that move in 40 years." Ronald was a player before his time. If he was graduating in the class of 2004 or 2005, he would have gone straight to the pros.

Fairmont Heights, whose team was name the Hornets, had a picture of a bumble bee painted in the half-court circle. I still remember people like Ty Thomas, "Jit," and Burt Hill telling me how my brother used to shoot from the bumble bee. Mind you, Ronald had a complete game; he just liked the feeling of seeing the entire audience rise to their feet when he made that shot. I've also felt that feeling; it's a feeling of euphoria that comes from the inside. The feeling is sometimes even better than sex and is equally addictive. You would have to experience it for yourself in order to fully understand the feeling. There are many ex-ball players using drugs trying to feel that same euphoria.

After high school, Ronald didn't receive one scholarship for basketball, but he did receive an academic scholarship to West Point. How can one of the top players in the nation not receive a sports scholarship? It was because of Coach Freeman. Coach Freeman didn't like Ronald. He once told my father that Ronald wasn't the best basketball player he ever had, but he was definitely the smartest.

That arrogant attitude kept Ronald in trouble with Freeman. My father taught us to have self-esteem and a feeling of pride, so statements that might offend or belittle the next guy didn't affect any of us. During the years 1967 and 1968, Fairmont Heights had one of the best teams in the state of Maryland. Every young kid in Prince George's County, Maryland dreamed of playing on that high school basketball team, and my crazy brother quit the team. I remember reading a news article in the Washington Star from my brother's scrapbook that read, "Ronald Moore Turns in Tennis Shoes to Coach Freeman." After Ronald quit, the team lost two straight games. The next article read, "After two straight losses Freeman asks Moore to Return." Ronald thought he was a pro in high school, but Coach Freeman had the last laugh; he told scouts that Ronald had a drug problem, so no colleges pursued him.

My father spent a great deal of money trying to keep Ronald in college. My dad knew the importance of a good education, and dad dreamed of having one of his boys finish college. He had figured that if he could get my brother Melvin to stay in college, the other boys would follow suit. My dad put Melvin in Bowie State College, but Melvin's mind was on girls, not school, and he eventually quit. Melvin once told me my dad put him in college late, like around October, and he said he was too far behind to catch up. Then my father made Melvin read a book all the way from our home in Beaver Heights to Bowie State every morning, and read a different book all the way home every evening. When Friday evening came, Melvin would disappear until Sunday evening.

My father sent Ronald to Kent State first and then on to Glenville State in West Virginia. Ronald eventually left both schools. When it came time for me to attend college, I was on my own. I did get some help from my sisters Jean and Judy, but mainly I got loans and grants.

I remember Ronald being put out of Glenville State for pushing a white kid in a wheel chair down a flight of stairs. As the story goes, it was in West Virginia in the 1970's, and they were still having race problems. It seems that the white kid, who was wheelchair-bound, spit on Ronald because Ronald didn't get out of his way fast enough. Ronald grabbed the back of the wheelchair and pushed him down a flight of stairs.

As the kid was rolling down the stairs, he yelled, "This nigger is trying to kill me."

Ronald had said, "Shut up, cracker. Dead people can't talk."

To top things off, the white kid had an extensive Michael Jackson collection in his dorm room. Later that day, Ronald broke into the kid's room and smashed all his records against the walls. I guess that is one of the reasons why Ronald eventually ended up in prison; he was crazy. That incident got Ronald expelled from Glenville State University in West Virginia.

I remember Ronald teaching me how to hold a basketball, how to bend my knees when I shoot, and how to follow through with my hands. I always dreamed of being half as good as he. I dreamed of being this great basketball star, but I just didn't have the dedication that it took to be a great ball player. In fact, I was lazy. I always took the easy way, and as a result, somewhere along the way I lost sight of my dreams. Today, I wonder what I could have been.

It amazes me how much I remember about my brother's life. I was too young to remember Ronald before he started using drugs, but I do remember the years after he was released from the Maryland Department of Corrections. I remember my brother Donald getting him a job with Page Airways, a private plane corporation at the national airport. I remember Ronald buying a New Volkswagen Beetle and getting an apartment in Dutch Village. But most of all, I remember his relationship with Barbie Cleaver. I always thought Barbie was cute. I actually had a crush on her. I used to follow the two of them around like a lost puppy. The last time they were together, they took me to see the movie Car Wash.

Barbie had a white Buick Skylark at the time, and she used to wash it every day. She still lives on Nash Street in Chapel Oaks Maryland. I think about Barbie every time I pass her house. I wish Barbie and Ronald would have worked out. I think he kind of gave up on life after their break-up. Sad to say, I did the exact same thing when I broke up with Carol. I wonder if there is some sort of Nash Street or Chapel Oaks curse.

It all started out back in82,
When my big brother taught me all he knew
About selling drugs and getting bank;
It took many a year before that ship sank.

Chapter 3

1982

The year was 1982; it was a good year for me. I had recently purchased a brand-new 1982 Chevrolet Monte Carlo. I was working for MACRO Wholesalers in Capital Heights, Maryland. I was attending Prince George's Community College full time, studying Information Systems Technology.

Even though I seemed to have a good life, I wasn't happy. I wanted more money, more fame, and I didn't want to achieve them the right way. I wanted instant gratification.

In 1982, my brother Ronald had recently been released from the Federal Penitentiary in Lexington, Kentucky. Lexington had a co-ed drug treatment program there, and my big brother was sent there to address his heroin addiction. Lex, as they called it, had a crew there from D.C. I remember seeing a picture with guys like Smut, Sonny, and

Jerald Andrews in it. There were also some women there from D.C., but I can't recall their names.

After Ronald completed the addiction phase of the program, he was given a job in the prison infirmary. There, he cleaned up after patients while secretly stealing the medication from cancer patients. I remember asking him, "Why did you take the cancer patients' medicine?"

He told me, "Hell, they're dying anyway; I need it more than they do." Thus, Ronald never actually stopped using.

The first thing Ronald wanted to do when he got off the Greyhound Bus from Kentucky was to try this new drug they had in D.C. called "Love Boat." He said he'd heard about the drug on the news. So we borrowed Judy's Volkswagen and made a beeline to the Ebony Inn.

The Ebony Inn is on Sheriff Road in Fairmont Heights, Maryland. It is owned by a man that grew up in the neighborhood, Tommie Broadway. Tommie also has a Bail Bondsman agency. There is a liquor store, a night club, a tourist home, and the rib pit. They sell beer, wine, liquor, and soul food. Their specialty is Barbeque: ribs, chicken, minced beef, and pork. It is a family owned business, and I'm proud to say that I am a personal friend of the family.

The area around the Ebony Inn is known for having lost women and plenty of narcotics. Mind you, there are many people from that area that never fell victim to drugs, but since there are so many people who have fell victim there, the Prince George's County Circuit Court labels everyone born in that area as a derelict. The Broadways have done their very best to clean up the area around the Ebony Inn, but the drug culture is engraved in the street.

Ronald and I brought two sacks of Love Boat from one of my brother's longtime friends, Burt. At the time, Love Boat cost $15 per sack, but Burt gave us two sacks for $20. We rolled four joints out of the two sacks. We smoked one of the joints before we left the parking lot of The Lodge Apartment complex, which was directly behind the Ebony Inn.

The trip back to my mother's house took us about 30 minutes, although we only live five minutes from the Ebony Inn. I guess the drugs had me hallucinating, for I thought I was traveling faster than I actually was. In fact, I was only going 2 MPH. I had traffic backed up from Nash Street & Eastern Avenue all the way to Eastern Avenue & George Palmer Highway. I actually liked the way the love boat made me feel. I felt powerful, and I actually thought I was in control. What a fool was I!

Once Ronald and I got to North Addison road, we lit up another joint. This one did the trick, for once we got back to my parents' home, we both almost fell down the basement stairs. We took a seat on the basement couch and watched *The Car. The Car* was a movie about a black Lincoln that was possessed by the devil. This car went on a killing spree through some small, western town.

We were sitting there on the couch watching this movie, which looked to us like it was in 3-D, and all the sudden the car jumped through a family's house and killed the mother. We actually thought the movie was happening in real life. When the car jumped through the house on television, Ronald and I dove off the couch to the floor of our house. We were so high that we actually thought the car came through the television set and almost hit us.

My father was also sitting on the couch, and he looked at the two of us as if we were crazy. My dad knew we were high, so he told us to go for a walk and get some air. This was the very first time I'd ever smoked PCP, and the only reason I did it was to show my brother that I wasn't scared. Boy, do I wish I had taken a stand and not smoked it at all, for the effects of PCP would bother me for many years to come.

We still had two joints of Love Boat left, so we decided to walk down into the Kenilworth Projects. In the Housing Project, there was a building for the mentally-ill, disabled, and deformed. In the past, my brother would go down to the Crazy Building, as we called it, get high with them, and trip off these funny-looking people.

We started smoking on our way there; once we reached the apartment building, we were really out of it. Ronald knocked on their door, and to our surprise, a man with only one eye opened the door. The eye was in the center of his forehead; he looked like a Cyclops. When Ronald saw this, he took off running. He ran all the way back to our parents' home, hollering and screaming all the way. I was laughing so hard that my sides started to hurt. I tried to catch Ronald before he got back to our parents' house, but I couldn't. This fool ran up the front steps, past my father, and straight through the front screen door.

My father was outside watering the grass, and seeing Ronald run through the screen door almost gave him a heart attack. Dad asked who in the Hell he was running from. I explained to my father where we were, and how the man looked like a Cyclops. My dad said both of us were nuts for going down there in the first place. "I told you two stay away from those people," he said. The guys that lived in that particular house were known to have been conceived through incest, so there was no telling what else we might see in that house. I didn't smoke boat for a while after that.

The area behind Ebony Inn was an apartment complex call Fairmont Gardens, or The Lodge. It was a low-income housing project and the crime center of Fairmont Heights, Maryland. The entire apartment complex has since been destroyed. It is now a vacant lot.

When I was first introduced to the area, I'd never seen such poverty. There were people sleeping on top of each other, two and three families living in one household while no one in the household worked, and most of the residents were on Public Assistance. My brother used to call them "once-a-month millionaires" Since they lived high on the hog for the first three or four days of the month, and after that, they suffered. The children went without clean clothing and regular food for days at a time. The mothers received food stamps, so the children should have had regular food. The ones that didn't sell all their stamps to buy drugs brought things like Oodles of Noodles and hot dogs which the children had to eat every day of the month unless an unsuspecting fool like myself felt sorry for them, and brought them a decent meal. Even though I looked out for these people, instead of being thankful for my help, they looked upon me as a fool. I was even call Michael Moron behind my back. Since I was from a middle-class family, I'd always had a meal on the table, clean clothing, electricity, water, heat, and air conditioning in the summer. I couldn't fathom that people in the United States of America actually lived that way. Mind you, this was over twenty years before Katrina in New Orleans, but we don't live in a third-world country, so I thought.

Not all families became stuck in this cycle. Some of these women took advantage of their low rents and assistance from the government, and they went on to become homeowners. But, you can count those who did so on two hands. Miss Nadine was the resident manager, and she did the best she could to keep a roof over these families' heads, but sadly to say, you cannot help everyone.

I became infatuated with the area because the young ladies were beautiful and slow, or so I thought. The kind of women I'd been looking for all my life. I always thought that with a little love and grooming, I could maybe turn one of the ladies into the perfect woman. Boy was I wrong. My father once told me that you can't change a woman; her mother has already raised her, and you just have to accept her as she is. The older I get, the more and more I see truth in that statement, and I wish I'd listened to my dad. These people had been living from hand to mouth for generations, so they knew every trick in the book.

Since I had a little common sense and a little money, I fit right into the hustling culture of Fairmont Heights Maryland. I think I started off selling marijuana. I used to buy it by the pound and half pound. After I got it, I'd package it into $5 and $10 bags. I made money, but the process was slow. Some nights, I had to stay out all night to make $200. I think I sold weed for about six months. Trying to work, going to school, and taking care of my brother's drug habit simply wore me out. I ended up having to hire someone to help me sell the drugs. That's when I met Anthony "Colby" Freebee; this kid thought he was as slick as Ice Berge Slim. He thought he was a pimp, an armed robber, and hustler, whatever was needed at the time. All he had to do was change a hat, and change hats he did.

Colby was a piece of work. Little did I know at the time, but he had his own gang, "The Chapel Oaks Crew." The Chapel Oaks Crew consisted of names like: Beady Top, ET, Hank, Da-Da, Poo-Jay, Little Lucky, Tommy Hearns, Gator, Poochy, and Pops, just to name a few. They were some really talented musicians, and eventually formed their own band: Quality Band and Show. I know if drugs had never come into the picture, they would have been more successful. They opened for Rare Essence and for Chuck Brown on several occasions. They simply spent too much of their band proceeds on drugs. Today, Jeff is considered one of the best drummers in the city. He plays a lot with Familiar Faces. I see him here and there, because he also does deals in real-estate. He's in the find, fix, and flip business. It's nothing to cut on Facebook and see one of his video's on rehabbing a home.

These kids weren't into any heavy crime; they just a group of neighborhood kids that all hung out, cut school, and smoked weed with each other. They did get involved in a few fist fights and an occasional shoot out against other youths from Washington, but no murders. Eventually, both Chapel Oaks and Northeast Washington all got to be companions in the drug game. The Chapel Oaks, Fairmont Heights, Seat Pleasant, and Beaver Heights neighborhoods were only one block from the district line. There was only Eastern Avenue to separate them. When we finally saw the profit in being on the same team, that's when we all started to make money.

Colby and I worked together with the marijuana, but I soon found a drug that was even more profitable: PCP. We could take a quarter pound of marijuana and add ounce of PCP juice, creating Love Boat. With it, we'd make about $1,600-worth of $100 packages. A $100 package of Love boat, if broken down was the equivalent of about $200 in $10.00 sacks We could sell the $100 packages to all the up-and-coming hustler wannabes, make a profit on our investment, and cut down the potential risk of hand-to-hand combat. I thought this was ingenious, but Colby and I broke the first rule of hustling: we got high on our own supply.

I really started tripping. I started watching old gangster films and actually tried to pattern my life after the Scarface movie. Colby wasn't much better; he started acting out films himself.

Colby introduced me to the club portion of the Ebony Inn. The building has a bar, and behind the bar was a dance floor. On Friday and Saturday nights, the club was the place to be. The Manager of the club's name was Miss Louise. She was a beautiful, light skinned lady with a very big heart. From the moment she met me, I think she knew I didn't belong in that atmosphere. I talked different, I dressed different, and I had totally different mannerisms from the other occupants of the club.

Her years of experience told her that that place would be my downfall. She was well acquainted with my brother, and she had witnessed his demise. She even tried to warn me, but my mind was clouded with the money, the girls, and the PCP, so I didn't pay too much attention. Again, and Burt Hill if only I'd listened!

On these Friday and Saturday nights, I got a chance to meet the neighborhood girls, especially the ones that lived on Nash Street and in The Lodge apartment complex. I think the first girl I noticed was Catty Lewis. She was pretty, young, and wild as hell. At that time in her life, she was as slick as goose grease. She was working a couple of guys, but the thing that impressed me the most about Catty was that she knew what she wanted. She wanted a good life, and she was willing to do what it took to achieve her goal. I was in college and didn't know what I wanted. I was simply going through the motions. Catty and I were only friends, and eventually I had a child by her sister, Carol.

Then there were the Mancaster girls, nine beautiful women all under one roof. The ones I came in constant contact with were Annette, Bev, Mary, Ne-Ne, and Poo-Poo. I had a thing for Poo-Poo. Actually, I think she was my first girlfriend in Fairmont Heights.

Poo-Poo's father, Pee Wee, and my brother Ronald were very close friends. I met Poo-Poo's brother, JD, on the basketball court, and we became instant friends. I think the fact that I was selling the majority of the PCP in Chapel Oaks had something to do with it. I guess you could call me a free high.

Ronald and my parents fell instantly in love with Poo-Poo. Poo had an Oscar-winning personality back then, and since my mother was raised poor, she understood Poo-Poo's situation and wanted to help her.

My father didn't allow any of his sons to have female visitors in his home overnight, but somehow Poo-Poo softened his heart. She was so cute at that time, and my dad used to love to look at her. Ronald actually told me to marry her and get her out of the Fairmont Heights environment. Poo-Poo had one son at that time, Chokey, and there was more to her than the eye could see. She really looked upon me as a rich kid that could help her, but her heart belonged to Zay.

Then there were the Hare sisters, Poogie and Marie. They had a very nice mother, Miss Liz, who would let me and Slick Stand camp out there from time to time. There were also the Towns sisters: Becky, Nick-Nick, Monnie, Tootie, and their beautiful hairy mother, Ms. Eddy. There were more Towns sisters, but the others were younger than I.

I've never had any romantic dealing with either the Towns girls or the Hare girls. We were all simply friends. They were fun to be around. I never had a sister around my own age, so I learned a lot about women from watching them.

There were two more women I spent time with: Kale Henderson and Cyntria "Cina-Bun" Coleman. In my own way, I was infatuated with them both. Cina-Bun is Colby's niece. I think she was only concerned with what she could get from me. She was another one of the girls that my father allowed to stay over. I remember her being downstairs one night and my father storming in on us. We were sitting on the couch when my father busted in, and she just smiled at him. He looked at her, said hello, and went back to bed. The next day, my dad asked me where I got that pretty girl from. He said she was just too cute to put out. Cina was light-skinned with beautiful features. In all actuality, she could have been a model. I still say that environments play a big role in shaping children's lives. If Cyntria had been raised by an upper middle class family in Montgomery County, her goals and aspirations would have been totally different.

As it was, Cyntria's primary objectives were to take care of her daughter, Erica, and to keep her head above water. Cyntria, like Poo-Poo , had a child at an early age. I truly believe she wanted to get Maried and have a family, but her then-boyfriend, Eric Walker, had other things in mind. I think when a woman is hurt, her heart become cold, and Lord help the next guy in line. I do believe Cyntria got Maried, and had other children. The last I heard, she was doing alright.

Kale Henderson wasn't from Fairmont Heights. She was actually from Simple City, a neighborhood in South East Washington. She and her close friend Linda would catch the bus to the Ebony Inn on the weekends. I think she was infatuated with the fact I had an unlimited supply of drugs and a brand-new car. We really became close. I truly think I could have made a difference in her life, but at the time I was playing about seven other women and couldn't commit to anything. When she saw I wasn't serious about our relationship, she started messing with my close friend, Timmy Gordon. In 1986, Kale had a baby girl name Reeka. To this day, I still believe that child is mine, but in 1986, I was totally distraught over my brothers' death. Therefore, she put the child on Timmy. Timmy died in 1992, and I haven't seen Reeka since. I'll make it my business to try to locate Kale and Reeka once I reach society.

Colby and I used to go to the bar every evening. We even had our own table. Our favorite drink was the Singapore Sling. The Ebony Inn had a special formula for the drink, and I think theirs was the best I've tasted thus far.

I think the biggest mistake I ever made was to allow Kevin "Slick Stand' Sims into our fold. Colby introduced me to Slick Stand, and at that time he was the most ambitious person I've ever met. Slick was from Washington Heights, a low-income neighborhood in Landover Maryland. I met Slick when he was seventeen years old, and he already had two children: Erica and Little Kevin. At that time also, Slick was on the run from the police, so he was staying in the lodge. When I say staying in the lodge, I mean that he lived with about six different families. I kind of felt sorry for Slick, and I really tried to help him; but I truly believe Slick took my kindness for weakness. Once he got on his feet and I started using drugs, he treated me like I was a piece of shit.

Slick has two younger brothers: Keith "Keedie" Voreen, and James "Tag" Evans. They were totally dependent on their older brother. Slick wasn't that smart in school, but he had an uncanny amount of common sense. He could figure out how to pull a dirty trick on someone at the drop of a hat. That type of knowledge comes in handy when you're trying to run a small-time criminal enterprise. Now, more than 24 years later, he no longer goes by "Slick" and owns a home improvement business.

Even though I went to college and thought I had a pretty good head on my shoulders, I learned a considerable amount from Mr. Slick Stand. Slick introduced me to new line of criminals, the Seat Pleasant Crew. At that time, they were led by the infamous Mango Quick. Mango was the best leader I've ever met. He's been incarcerated numerous times for things that other people did, and he always held his water. He is a better man than me; because I would have hit that hot-ass nigga Teddy in the head for turning state evidence on me, not once but twice.

Mango now and owns his own home improvement business too. He has a beautiful religious wife that keeps him on the straight and narrow. I guess he and his wife, Jenny, have prayed about the situation, and they have moved forward.

Slick also introduced me to Evans Grill, a club in Forestville Maryland. Slick's brother Tag's father owned the club, so we got free admission. That's where I met people like Shannie "Black" Richardson, his brothers

Fats and Timmy, John and Arthur Mcginnis, Kevin Ford, Sticky Fingers, Man Vest, Lefty, Danny Man, Zay, Ted, Herc, and the infamous Scotty Briscoe. These were some of the slickest men I had met, and they were all hungry. When I say hungry, I mean they wanted money, and badly. I think you never realize how good you have it until you see someone that doesn't have anything.

In 83, he said be all you can be,
Live high on the hog, as high as a tree,
But like a soldier jumping out an airplane,
I was smoking that BOAT; steadily going in sane.

Chapter 4

1983

In 1983, I stepped my game up a little. Instead of wetting down Quarter Pounds of weed, I started wetting down pounds.

My main girl at that time was Liza Pruitt. She used to live on Polk Street in N.E. Washington, D.C. I met Liza when I was hanging out with a guy named Kevin Williams. Kevin introduced me to the entire Polk Street crew, including We-We, Kenny, Zeke, Alan Johnson, George, Ant Man, and the Brown family.

One Brown in particular, Baldy, truly helped me take my next step forward in the drug game. He introduced me to Slime and Irving. I think they actually took a chance on me because of Baldy, because they don't like to deal with new people. But everyone in Washington knew my brother Ronald, and my name was ringing in the streets for being Ronald's ambitious little brother.

Baldy was a piece of work; I think he dropped out of elementary school, but he was extremely intelligent. He was another person with an uncanny amount of common sense. At that time, Baldy was a used car salesman, and he was doing quite well. I think Baldy could talk a hungry cat off a fish truck. Even though he helped me tremendously, he also tricked me out of $1,600, but I wasn't mad at him. Knowledge is costly, and we either pay now or we pay later, but we pay. We used to take rides to Baltimore, he drove, and I read the street signs. We picked up a lot of girls, and increased my gift of gab. After a few months of hanging around Baldy, I had the articulation to run for mayor.

In 1983, I still had my dream of being a basketball star. I wanted to keep my skills intact, so I practiced on the weekends with high school superstars. I grew up with these guys and I took a piece from each of them to clone myself into a "beast". People like Darryl McLain who played for Dunbar, Darryl Alexander that played for H.D. Woodson, Phillip Diggs that played for Fairmont Heights, and John "Wild Man" Stewart who also played for Fairmont Heights Each one of these guys could have went professional, but we didn't have all the camps the kids have today. We were self-taught, and still great in our day. I loved the game, but my time was divided between going to college, selling drugs, working, and chasing women. I didn't know it at the time, but I was actually multitasking.

My problem was I wouldn't commit to one thing. But after taking numerous business classes over the years, I have learned that specialization is the way to go. Today, I do one thing at a time, complete it, then go on to the next venture, so now I am considered a completionist.

The truth was, I was still searching for my place in this world; and most of all, I was afraid of responsibility. I remember listening to my father telling me stories about his working with the Navy Department for over thirty-two years. My dad hated that job, but he had eight mouths to feed, so he had to endure the bullshit. Even though my dad lived a long, respectable, profitable life, I know deep down in my soul he hated what he did. My father wanted to explore; he wanted to play his trumpet in a big band setting. He wanted to see the world, but the responsibilities of having a big family deferred his dream. By the time I was old enough to take care of myself, he was an old man. My dad was a dreamer; he was the kind of man that brought the buggy and never got the horse to pull it. He attempted to start his own band; he had guys at our house practicing every night of the week. He printed business cards, but he never got one single gig. Don't get me wrong; my dad was an excellent provider, and I never went without a meal, but I think he had no sense of business.

I have read numerous books over the years to get an understanding of our history as black people. If you don't understand your history you are destined repeat the same ole mistakes. It seems that around the late '60s and '70s, the baby boomers started believing they were free; free to explore, free to love, free to be loved, free to experiment, free to forget their responsibility to family. This new sense was given to us by the white society. That was the only way they could conquer us. They had to divide us. They also convinced the black woman that she didn't need a man. That we were more of a hindrance than a help, but a woman cannot teach a boy how to be a man. They also locked up over 200,000 black men from Washington, DC alone in the 1980's. They justified these arrests as trying to conquer a "War on Drugs". Actually what they did was to give all young black males Criminal records, and knock us out of the job market. Without a job, how were we expected to take care of our families? How were we expected to be providers? Then they flood the streets with cocaine. Cocaine the Government got in trade from Iran for weapons. They then sell us the cocaine at a cheap price, so we were seeing astronomical profits. Since we were making a profit on our investments, we were now labeled kingpins, and as a result the FBI was allowed to take everything we had and put us in dungeons for decades at a time. I truly believe that's the main reason we have so many single parent families.

I did learn a lot from watching my Latino brothers on how to start a business of my own. Today people are lazy. They don't want to do anything for themselves. All I had to do was to offer a service, and do it to the best of my ability. That way I could feed myself without having to throw a brick at the penitentiary.

Those of us that were afraid to get into the drug game were running around doing everything to forget the realities of life, indulging in drugs, sex, and alcohol without knowing that these escapes would someday bite them in the ass. I realize the mistakes I have made, and this book is my way of correcting my mistakes. I plan to change the thinking of as many people as I can. This is my gift to society.

The "Big Mamas" are dead and gone today, thus the children have to raise themselves. That's why a great deal of them don't have morals and values. Morals, values, and principles are passed down through the generations. Our ancestors set standards for us to follow. Somewhere, we forgot where we came from. Those who didn't ran to the other side of the beltway to escape the black masses. Besides, it only takes one bad apple to ruin a whole bunch. So I've heard, and so I've seen.

In 1983, I was living high on the hog, not paying any rent, driving a new car, eating out every night, shopping whenever I wanted, and screwing every pretty female ass that moved. I thank God I don't have AIDS as a result. I definitely have a guardian angel. I know God has a purpose for my life, because I should have been dead long ago. I'm on what you'd call "borrowed time." I If I can help anyone from the writing of this book, I'm just paying a debt that's long past due.

Also in 1983, I changed jobs. I got a job at Best TV. I was a route manager. Best TV rented out electronic appliances, such as televisions, stereos, etc. They loaned these items on weekly or monthly bases. Can you imagine paying $25.00 per week for eighteen months for a television in 1983? If you do the math, that adds up to around $1,950 for a 19 inch television.

This company took advantage of poor, uneducated black and white consumers. My job was to collect the weekly or monthly fees. Boy, was that a job. Can you imagine going to poor peoples' homes and asking for money for an item they were paying triple for? I even sat down with some of the people and explained to them the enormous fees they were paying. I told them to apply for an account at Sears or Montgomery Ward, and that it would lower their cost considerably, but like most poor folks, their credit was shot, so they had to do business with places like Best TV in order to have the appliances they needed.

When it came time to collect the fees, I heard every excuse in the book. I remember the last day I worked for Best TV. I was having problems collecting in the Shaw neighborhoods of N.W. Washington, so my supervisor, Frank, decided to ride along with me to show me how collecting was done. Frank was a few years older than I; I would guess he was about 22 years old at the time. He was a preppy white kid from an upper middle class family that really hadn't had any experiences with poor black folk. All he really knew was what he'd learned in his Marketing and Economics classes at the University of Maryland. Boy was he in for a surprise.

Connie, I'll call her, had a floor model television delivered to her home in December; it was June when we visited, and she'd only paid two of her payments. The problem I was having was that Connie was never home, or she just hid from me like I was a Jehovah's Witness. The law prohibited us from going into people's homes without their permission, even to claim our merchandise.

On that particular Saturday morning, Connie was home. It was hot that summer day, so the screen door was open. When Frank spotted the open door, he just walked right in. He introduced himself as the supervisor from Best TV, told Connie about her lapses in payments, and SAID that we needed a payment then or we would have to take the television. The television was in the middle of the living room, and there were about ten kids around it watching cartoons. Connie said, "You aren't taking shit out my house. You all cheated me in the first place — a TV don't cost that much."

I walked into the living room when Frank was unplugging the set. He called me to grab the other end of the set, but before I could get there, all those kids jumped on Frank's ass. While they fought, their mother yelled out instructions on how to whip Frank's ass. She yelled: "Bite him, Molly! Scratch him, Johnny! Kick him Toney! Billy, go get Mama's knife."

That's when I ran straight through the screen door. By the time Frank got out of that house, he was beaten up something terrible. His shirt was torn off, and he had scratches everywhere. I asked, "Man, are you crazy, trying to take a TV from all those kids? I wouldn't have gone in there in the first place without the police."

He asked why I didn't help him. I said, "Man, you don't mess with a momma bear when she's protecting her cubs. And especially not a black woman with a knife." Best TV had to pay for the screen door I broke, and I wouldn't let them take the money out of my paycheck, so they fired me.

The next job I got was with Capital Messenger Service in Beltsville, Maryland. The owner's name was Don Cross, and he had a henchman by the name of Mike Matters. I think Mike was such an ass hole he got on his own nerves. He was the type of unhappy individual that got a kick out of belittling the slow and uneducated. I'm surprised that even during the short time I was there, no one punched him in the mouth. Most of the people that worked there had inferiority complexes, or were recently released from prison, so they need their jobs.

Capital Messengers was a typical Redneck establishment. The secretary and bosses passed gas in the middle of the office area without saying "excuse me," and they had a large poster with the cast of the TV sitcom *MASH* on the wall in the main office. Each one of the employees was named for a cast member of *MASH*. Since there were no black male characters on *MASH*, I never got the privilege of having my name scribbled on the poster.

The job seemed like a graveyard for ex-government workers, especially the ones who had been fired or laid off for having drinking problems. While working that job, I developed a taste for vodka, especially since most of my coworkers drank their lunches.

I remember names like George "Poor Boy" Monk and Oliver "OJ" Jones. These two taught me how to steal. These guys were middle-aged and reminded me of what I didn't want to be in the future. Yet later on in my life, after I'd experimented with crack-cocaine, I was so low that I had to look up to see the curb. It's amazing how the tables turn. I used to look down on those guys because of their adversities, but my life ended up twice as bad as theirs.

In 1983, people like Fats, Kenny Boo, Little Tim, Eddie Wilson, Little Robert and his brother Bo, Reynard, and Michael Fray, were the people to know in Kenilworth. They each controlled their own areas, and they were given the utmost respect. Today, I still admire Reynard because he had sense enough to get out of the game before he lost. Hustling is a game, similar to golf; it can be played, but never actually won. Someone always loses. Either you go to prison or you ruin the user's life completely.

In 1983, we still had hustler's balls at different hotels and at the Masonic Temple on 10th and U Street N.W. Washington. We all looked forward to potentially being the hustler of the year. Since I was hustling on a small time level, I was never invited to any of the balls. That's another thing I should thank God for, because little did they know the Feds were often at these places, taking notes and pictures. A great number of young men saw the inside of the Youth Center at Lorton and numerous Federal Penitentiaries because of these balls. Most of them were there because of greed, and many were trying to live out stories from movies like Scarface and the King of New York, The dream of coming from nothing and achieving everything.

In 1983, Slick Stand and my brother Ronald got me in the habit of beating up the people that ran off or messed up our product. They taught me that in order to be in charge of an organization, you needed fear and respect. If people didn't fear or respect you, they wouldn't pay you; if they don't pay you, you can't eat.

Slick used to box, and he taught me a lot of moves. I learned to step with my punches and to throw my punches from the hip. Slick was maybe 150 1bs back then, but he had the heart of a lion. I wasn't a violent person, so I picked up my aggression from watching him. When I was using drugs and Slick had gone off to prison, some of the people I'd beat up got their revenge on me. Eventually, I got them all back again.

I believe Slick was mad at the world because he didn't have a lot of luxuries as a youth. His mother, Ms. Rebecca, was a single mother that did the best she could under the circumstances. I think I created a monster when I taught Slick the drug game, for he always wanted more. If he had applied that same mentality in business, he would have been the black Bill Gates. Slick was never satisfied with anything, and he spent money like the world was ending tomorrow. He wasn't the cutest dude in the world, but once women got wind of his spending habits, you'd have thought he was Wesley Snipes. I used to call him the black Johnny Carson because he paid outlandish costs to be with women.

Slick never had a drug problem, but he definitely had a tricking problem. I guess you have to pay to play. I remember telling him more than once, "Pussy don't cost that much." But Slick did have some women you'd write home and tell your mother about.

Colby thought he was a pimp. He wouldn't give a woman a dime. He used to hang up on 14th street with his uncle Ernie, and he had firsthand knowledge of the world's oldest profession. It wasn't anything for local pimps Shaky or Hollywood to drop Colby off from a night of uptown life.

Colby had this older girl, Elaine Profit. She was a beautiful girl but slow as hell. She had an apartment in the Lodge, and Slick Stand, Colby, and I thought the place was our Honey Comb Hideout. We stayed there whenever we wanted. I think Elaine was happy just to know where Colby was. Elaine, her two daughters, her sister Lisha, their brother Tom, and Lord knows how many other kids lived there. Most of the time, there was never any food, so I brought a lot of chicken boxes. I just couldn't stand to see a child hungry.

We also had some Virginia girls that we met at the Evans Grill: Virginia, Gullet, Magi, and Angie. They all were from Alexandria, Virginia and attended T.C. Williams High School. At that time, we didn't know Alexandria was a ghetto too, so we thought we really had something. We used to rent an apartment from Elaine's sister, Mopsy, in District

Heights to entertain the girls on the weekends. We spent a lot of money on those girls trying to impress them.

I used to mess with Angie. She got jealous of my being with other women, and once, while I was in my mother's basement with another girl, she and her friends painted my car. I still thank God today for Doug Vines, a close friend who was killed later in the 1980s. I guess Doug had had something similar happen to him, so he knew how to get the paint off. We just went to a 7-Eleven and brought some fingernail polish remover. That stuff took the paint right off. I still had to wash and wax the car when we finished, but I was relieved that I didn't have to get a new paint job.

Colby also had another girlfriend, Carol Lewis. I ended up stealing her from Colby, but Carol was one package I wish I'd left in the store. Sometimes I think I lost my mind over Carol, but I won't get into that now.

There is one thing I will say; never sell your soul for anything or anybody. I put too much of myself into people, drugs, and the streets, so much of myself that it was hard to regain my sanity afterwards. When you give too much of self to anything other than God, you run the risk of becoming nuts. People leave you, people lie to you, people hurt you. Today, I trust in God, not people, and certainly not drugs.

In 84, Ty opened the door.
He just came home, so I gave him the floor,
He put me with lemuel and leprechaun,
And in me, they grew very fond.
We made big money every day;
That's all just a part of that Palmer Parkway.

Chapter 5

1984

Ty Thomas lived one block from my mother's house. I always looked up to Ty Thomas because of his personality and the slick way he dressed and talked. At that time in our lives, Ty Thomas was just coming home off a ten-year prison sentence, and he knew people that could help me achieve my goal of financial stability.

I think the first person he introduced me too was Joseph Gwynn, a gambler, but he came in contact with a great deal of narcotics. My first purchase from him was a half-ounce of cocaine. I didn't know anything about cocaine, so I didn't want to financially burden myself by buying a large quantity. At that time, people were still buying a lot of powder cocaine. The best spot to get your coke was Hanover Street in N.W.

Washington, but the screen door, as we called it, was hot, so I could make some considerable change and save people from having to make that trip.

The first thing I had to do was learn how to cut cocaine. In order to increase your profits, you have to increase the amount of product by two or three times the original amount by adding mannitol or inositol.

I learned how to do this with the assistance of an old friend, Darryl. I met Darryl through his older brother Winston. Winston and I worked together at a company called Adams & Burch, where my brother Donald worked as well. Winston pulled orders, my brother Donald drove a truck, and I was a forklift operator. Adams & Burch is a distributor of hotel and restaurant equipment. They paid more than Capital Messenger Service and there was more room for advancement, or so I thought at the time.

After working there for about one year, I found out that the company was a family-owned business, and if you weren't a Blaylock or a Packard, you certainly weren't going to move up very far. The only blacks they gave an opportunity to were the Perry's, Neal, Tim, and Reggie.

Winston really impressed me in 1984 because he was Married to Noreen, and they had a daughter. He was actually responsible, which made me view him with the utmost respect. Yet somewhere down the road, Winston also got frustrated turned to a life of hustling.

Darryl was just the opposite of Winston. Darryl was for Darryl. I think that's why we became friends: both of us were selfish as hell.

Darryl and Winston were raised in the Landover area, in Bradley Hills and/or King Square area to be exact. Film star Martin Lawrence grew up in the same area. Once Martin got his big break, he took some of his childhood friends along with him; the Whack brothers worked in his studio, and Shawn played the character Nipsey in the hit series *Martin*.

In 1984, you could buy drug paraphernalia and substances used to cut drugs at any corner store. I remember going to M&M Munches in N.E. Washington to get my inositol and coin bags. Then I made my way to Cheverly for my first class in Cocaine 101.

At the time, Darryl had an apartment in Cheverly, Maryland; he lived in Cheverly Terrace Apartments. Darryl had what you call a bachelor pad. He used to talk a lot of shit about his sexual escapades, but his heart belongs to his childhood sweetheart, Lee-Lee. Darryl kept that place immaculately clean, and he also spent a pretty penny furnishing it. Darryl had plush green carpeting along with a sofa and loveseat to match the color. The dining room and living room furniture were both made from antique oak wood. Darryl had a large walk-in closet in his bedroom. His clothing was in perfect order: all the pants were together and color-coordinated, all the shirts were together, as were all the dress suits, the sweat suits, and the hundreds of dress shoes and tennis shoes. From the first look at Darryl's pad, you would think he had a maid.

Darryl had every illegal gadget they made, and even the legal ones were suspect. His apartment held triple beam scales, cocaine grinders, sifters, measuring spoons, film canisters, and seal-a-meal machines. In 1984, all a person had to do to obtain these items was to go either to South Capital Liquors in Southeast Washington or to Earth Works in Georgetown. These places sold everything from crack pipes to triple beam scales. You had to go to K-Mart to get a seal-a meal machine. None of the items were against the law back then. I guess the public didn't know their other uses, or they didn't care.

Darryl taught me more about the mixture of drugs than I ever learned in chemistry class in high school. First, we used a fine-grade sifter. We broke the half-ounce up with our hands, and then we placed the broken product into the sifter. We sifted the cocaine about four times. We took a few of the rocks out of the mix to add to the bags later. Most people that purchase powder coke feel the bags for rocks. Feeling rocks in a bag gave them the false sense that the product was good. At that time, stores on 14th street N.W. such as Adam & Eve and This Is It sold not only pornographic materials but also items like Bolivian Flake, Bolivian Rock, and Super Toot. These substances would numb the tongue. They often were not only used as additives to cocaine, but they were also sold by themselves to unsuspecting victims.

After we sifted the cocaine, which weighed approximately 14 grams, we weighed out 28 grams of inositol. We were putting a two-cut on the coke. We also sifted the cut, inositol, four times. Then, we sifted the cocaine in a circular motion on Darryl's' glass-top table. Next, we sifted the inositol in the same circular motion over the cocaine. We took a playing card and mixed the two substances together. Next, we placed the mixed product into the cocaine grinder, which was similar to a coffee grinder. We grinded that mixed product for about twenty minutes. If you think drug dealers don't work, you are very much mistaken.

If you hold pure cocaine under a light, you see the color yellow. The object to the continuous blending is to make the finished product as yellow as possible. If a potential buyer decided to hold your bags under a light, the more yellow they saw, would determine how successful and lucrative the distribution process would be. We bagged the finished product in $50.00 bags. I think I paid $800.00 for the 14 grams of powder cocaine; and I got about $3,200.00 in $50.00 bags. That's a very profitable flip, if I do say so myself.

The next step was selling the $50.00 bags. Mind you, drugs sell themselves. If your product is good, word of mouth can make you thousands of dollars. Before I left Darryl's apartment, he shared a couple of joints of some freshly mixed Love Boat. I guess in 1984, Love Boat was a cash crop for a lot of hustlers. We smoked the boat and then snorted a few lines of the coke, and then I was off to the Ebony Inn to start the distribution process.

You can plainly see that, I was a functional addict. There was no way in the world you could have told me I had a drug problem. I had money problems and women problems, but drugs were the last of my problems. I never realized I had any kind of problem with drugs until several years later, when I didn't have a large supply and actually had to go out and look for the drugs.

My timing was perfect in obtaining the cocaine, for it was the first of the month, and everyone seemed to have a check. I might have sold $3,000 worth of coke in an hour. I had never made that much money so fast in my life. I got addicted to selling cocaine. It gave me a feeling of power. I had something people needed, not wanted, so I could play God, in sense. The stuff was so good that I kept everything else I had for my personal stash; it was something to trick with. It has always amazed me how poor people put money together to buy drugs. They spend money like there's no tomorrow.

Female addicts are smarter than most male addicts. An old female addict would play victim to a young dealer but would take an older male addict for all he had. They would use an older male addict's kindness to support their habits. In most cases, there's a promise of sex in the end.

For many men, cocaine decreases the sex drive, in other words the male can't get an errection, Thus, once they've spent a couple-hundred dollars getting high, they don't have the sex drive to get the pussy in the end. Can you image spending your entire pay check getting high in hopes of something you can't get? People were really fools!!!

During that year, I also came into contact with three men for whom I came to hold the utmost respect: Lemuel, Leprechaun, and Monkey John. They were all from Palmer Park, Maryland. Palmer Park was put on the map in 1976 when Sugar Ray Leonard won a gold medal in the Olympic Games. Boxers Andrew Maynard and Curtis Peoples also brought recognition to the area, but there was money in Palmer Park long before Ray.

They had a club there, the Club LA Barron, which hosted a local band at least four times a week. The club was the spot to be on the weekends. They featured bands such as Rare Essence, E U, and Chuck Brown and the Soul Searchers. A lot of fly women came out of Palmer Park.

As far as money is concerned, the first names that come to mind were the Harris brothers. These dudes owned homes, a waste removal company, and a construction business. They were in the process of building a shopping mall on Nannie Helen Burroughs Avenue in North East Washington when the oldest brother, Poochie, was arrested. Aside from the Harris family, you had names like Petty Eddie, Winfred, Marshall, Dogg, and Heartbeat. Each of these dudes had their day in the sun.

Lem drove a white 5-series Mercedes, lived in a high-rise apartment, wore a mink coat, and spoke like a Harvard lawyer. And they say money doesn't make the man. The way Lem handled himself; you could tell he had some formal education in the field of business. I won't go into any of our financial transactions because he's presently fighting a conviction in court, but I will say, that if he's ever released, I'd let him run my company.

If many of the hustlers in the 1980s had the chance to operate a Fortune 500 Company, we would have made financial history. We had hands-on experience with life's challenges the legal system, and the criminal element. Can you imagine spending all your life's savings on some bad product? You would have to use marketing, economics, and salesmanship to get rid of it or starve. College students don't have that kind of hands-on experience. We were taught ghetto economics at a young age and learned how to make a dollar out of fifteen cents. The prisons are full of financial geniuses. America gave Martha Lewis another chance; how's about one of us?

I remember riding through the Kenilworth Projects on a Sunday afternoon in 1984. It was summertime, and I'd just washed a waxed my car. I was smoking a joint of Love on my way to Parkside Recreation Center to play some b-ball when I noticed this girl walking down Quarles Street: she was walking with a girl I knew by the name of Letty Harper. Letty was my childhood buddy, Steve Edwards' girl at the time. The girl with her reminded me of Irene Carol. I almost had an accident watching her walk.

I stopped the car and asked Letty to introduce me to her friend. Letty, along with a lot of the girls from Kenilworth, thought I was a little rich kid, especially since I went to private school and my parents lived in the biggest house in the Beaver Heights neighborhood. Eventually, I found out the young lady's name was Juanna.

I did a great deal of talking, but I eventually convinced Juanna to allow me to drive them home. Once she got in my car, I totally forgot about basketball. Juanna lived in an apartment building at the end of Quarles Street. She lived with her two sisters, Donnisha and Neicey. Their mother had died a few years before, and Donnisha and Neicey were both sisters and surrogate mothers. Believe me, it took me a while, but I eventually gained both their trust and respect. I still consider Donnisha and Neicey my sisters today.

I think I was infatuated with the fact the Juanna was a virgin. I worked double-hard to get into her pants; but once I finally achieved my goal, I lost interest. Remember, I was a hustler, going to college, worked full time, and had about seven other girlfriends. Juanna was just too much work. The only woman I actually loved at that time was Liza Pruitt. She held my heart completely. If her God-sister, Noreen, hadn't told me about Liza's infidelities with an older guy named Fellow; I would have Maried her. I never knew Juanna's middle name, her favorite color, anything. If she told me, I never paid that information any mind. My only concern at that time was getting in her pants.

Juanna got pregnant that year. She told me she was going to have an abortion. I thought she would realize that we didn't have a relationship; but that's what I got for assuming. I had to learn the hard way that problems don't just go away; you can't hide from them. You have to nip them in the bud, like my father used to say. The last time I saw Juanna in 1984 was around Thanksgiving. I didn't see her anymore until around June of 1985. When I saw her again, I had a beautiful daughter named Laricka. Juanna is a strong woman; she went through the entire pregnancy alone. Today, I wish I had been there. .

I eventually had to break the $50 bags of cocaine down to $25 bags for economic reasons. I figured I could sell twice as many $25 bags because most of my customers had to get a half partner to come up with $40.00. I would feel sorry for them and take the short money. I think that's the main reason I could never be a successful drug dealer — I had a conscious. You can't have a conscious and sell people poison.

In 85, all my dreams died
Right at the point when I'd arrived
Along with my brother Ronald Moore,
And ever since then I've felt poor.
About myself and those around me;
To this day, it still astounds me...

CHAPTER 6

1985

In 1985, I stepped my game up; I started dabbling with the distribution of heroin. "Ain't no money like dope money!" Heroin creates a physical addiction whereas cocaine produces a mental one. If a dope fiend doesn't get his or her dope, their bodies go through extreme physical pain. The bigger the habit, the bigger the withdrawal. I've seen addicts actually die while going through withdrawal. The human body is a strange instrument; it can endure almost anything and then repair itself. Drugs tear a body to pieces. I've also seen addicts use drugs for decades and function normally, but when they stop using, their bodies fall apart. I think some people's bodies actually adapt to the drugs, and when they stop abruptly, they shock their systems and their body shuts down. Whenever I stopped using for any extended period, I'd have pains like I'd never experienced, when I was using. Mind you; this is just my analogy, and I am in no way a physician, but I can say, I've experienced my share of withdrawal pains.

In 1985, my brother Ronald introduced me to the fast pace of uptown living. We hung out in spots like 7th & T Street N.W., Georgia Avenue & Park Road, 9th & U Street, and 15th and Swann Street. The people I came in contact with looked like zombies walking aimlessly through the abyss. At that time in my life, I'd never seen so many sores, abscesses, and swollen body parts. I couldn't fathom what would make human beings do this to themselves. My brother was a heroin addict himself, so I got a bird's eye view of the interiors of oil joints and shooting galleries.

The insides of these places were gross, with all the blood and hypodermic needles everywhere. I saw people with arms, hands, feet, and legs the size of watermelons. They had holes everywhere on their bodies, and infection ran rapid. I even met this guy, Jimmy, whose legs had no skin on them; you could actually see the inner workings of his legs. Jimmy's legs were so infected that Howard University Hospital gave him maggots to put inside his legs to eat up some of the infection. He called them "good maggots."

I learned terms like "speedball" and "piggy-back." A speedball was when a dope fiend mixed cocaine and heroin together and injected them both into their veins at the same time. A piggy-back was when they used two separate needles, one for the dope and one for the coke. They put the needles into two different veins and inject the dope to go down and the coke to go up. This process is extremely dangerous and could seriously damage the heart. I was a snorter since I've always been afraid of needles. Except for the time when I crushed both my legs in a car accident — I couldn't wait for a shot of Demerol.

I've met entire families that used dope, from the mother to the youngest child. I've even met one brother that got his dog high. I think he put the heroin in the dog's food. How sick can you get? Even though these people used drugs, I still respected them as human beings. Besides, I used drugs also; all addicts are the same. It doesn't matter how you put the drug in your body. Either way, you are still consuming poison.

The reason I wanted to sell heroin myself was because of how much money people spent on that stuff. Some of the folks I met had up to $500–a-day habits. I figured if I could get just six regulars that spent at least $100 a day, I'd be rich in a year's time.

In order to acquire the knowledge, I needed to successfully run a heroin business; I picked the brains of Ronald and a few of his dealer buddies. They had me buy coin bags and the cutting substances: Bonita and quinine. I already had sifters and measuring spoons. After I got everything I needed, I was ready for my first class in Heroin 101.

I purchased one tablespoon of Heroin. It cost $300 at that time, but it took an 8. When I say it took an 8, means you could put 8 times the weight of the heroin in cut. I didn't want to extend myself too far my first time out. Second, you can't trust an addict. A spoon of dope is a party for an addict, and I was determined not to let them screw me in the cutting process.

The cutting of Heroin is a lot more sophisticated than the cutting of cocaine. If you make a mistake, you can ruin a whole batch.

I sifted the inositol and cocaine four times each, mixed them, then put the mixture in a cocaine grinder for about ten minutes. With heroin, I had to sift the bonita and quinine five times each, mix the two together with a playing card, then sift that mixture five time. After that, I would sift the bone (heroin) five times before mixing it with the bonita and quinine. The heroin usually comes in a rock form, so you have to break it down into powder before you could mix it with your cutting substances. The last step is to mix everything together, and sift it ten times. Other people might cut their dope differently, but this process has always paid off for me.

Once or twice, when I was having the product tested, the dope jelled in the needle. It happened because the bone had been cut before I cut it. In that case, I had to remix the entire batch with vitamin C, or vitamin B and start the entire process all over again.

When you purchase heroin in quantity, you buy it by the number of times it can be cut. For example: If you get some bone that can take a seven; that means the dope can stand six times the weight of the dope in cut. The bigger the number, the more money you can make. In 1985, if you were lucky, if you could get a ten. The Nigerians had bone that sometimes took up to a fifteen, but it was almost impossible to find a Nigerian connection. Today, you'd be lucky to get a three, so people use substances like Morphine, Fentanyl, and sleeping pills to cut their dope in hopes of increasing their profits.

I paid $300 for the spoon I brought and bagged up $2000 in ten-packs. A spoon of dope is the equivalent of three grams in weight. Once the completed substance was ready for packaging, I used a 1/8 measuring spoon to make my bags.

In 1985, a bag of dope sold for $25 today, they sell $5 bags. The young generation ruined both the dope and the coke games. Somewhere down the line, drugs were made too accessible. Now, you have more dealers than addicts. When I was growing in the drug game you couldn't buy raw heroin unless you knew someone. Today, they sell raw on every corner; especially in Baltimore. That's why you have so many kids selling and using it.

In order to sell the freshly packaged dope, I had to hire runners. I paid them $5 off each bag they sold. Most of the time, I gave them two extra bags for themselves so they could get high plus make a little money. From that moment on, I became a night watchman. I had to watch for the police; watch for the stickup boys, watch the junkies I had working for me; and make sure I never had too much money on me. I didn't want the police to catch me with a lot of money and take it, and I didn't want to get robbed on a humble.

I had a buddy named Murphy who taught me a lot about the dope game. He was my age, but he'd been dealing heroin since he was a kid. Murph, as I use to call him, knew all the tricks of the trade, and I made it my business to soak up all the knowledge I could from him.

I stacked a great deal of money in 1985. I was so successful I was able to take a leave of absence from my job, pay my car off, and set up a workout schedule so I would be ready to play basketball on a college level in August of that year.

I had my heart set on playing for the Virginia Union Panthers. They had a center by the name of Charles Oakley and a flashy, small forward named Jamie Waller. I just knew I could fit into their program. They were the reigning CIAA champs, and I was determined to be a Panther.

My workout partner was Randy Doggett. Randy and I both played ball at DuPont Park and had been friends since elementary school. Randy had played the year before for Prince George's Community College and wanted to take his game to the next level.

In Washington, D.C., there are two men that are responsible for sending more kids to college than the Negro College Fund. These guys were Fluff Parks and Mr. Bateman. These two gentlemen were college recruiting agents. They even got ball players that couldn't pass the SAT into prep schools to get their grades up.

I met Fluff Parks at Turkey Thicket Recreation Center. He was working with a few college-bound athletes. His son Stacy was also there.

Randy and I scrimmaged with the other guys, and I guess Mr. Parker liked our performance because he offered Randy and me a chance to play for a junior college in California, West Hill. West Hill was just starting a sports program and was looking for ball players to fill their roster. A lot of guys from D.C. went out there to California and were disappointed. I had my sites on Virginia Union, and I wasn't about to lose a year of eligibility playing for another junior college.

I think the brightest point in 1985 was when my daughter Ricka was born. She looked just like my mother and me, so there was no denying her. She was both beautiful and smart. My mother fell in love with the child from first sight.

I just wasn't ready to accept the responsibilities of being a father. I had saved my money to go away to college, I wasn't in love with Juanna, and I was determined to have a better life, one that didn't involve poverty, drugs, and crime. My father had been denied his dreams and he was miserable the majority of his life. I was determined I wasn't going through the same heartaches my father had. Don't get me wrong, I do love my daughter; she is the light to my darkness. I know today that I made one of the biggest mistakes in my life by not being around to see her grow up. I missed so much about her life, her personality, her likes and dislikes. Today, I don't know anything about my child, and that makes me feel awful. I guess we never bonded as father and daughter.

Contrary to what I'd expected, Juanna had no problem with me going away to college. She has always been intelligent, so I guess at the time, she figured it would be best for her child if I had a college degree.

Liza Pruitt was also ok with the idea of me going to Virginia for college. She knew I wouldn't be that far away; plus, I had spent more time in the streets in the last couple of years than I did with Liza. She knew how dangerous the streets were and figured I wouldn't be subject to jail or death while in college.

The only woman that had a problem with me going away to college was Carol Lewis. Now that I think about the whole situation, I believe both Juanna and Liza had other boyfriends and were glad to have the freedom that came with my leaving. Carol might have been the only one of the ladies I was dealing with who actually cared about me. I guess I'll never find answers, but today I can finally stop beating myself up for doing Liza and Juanna wrong.

I don't think at that time in Carol's life she could even fathom the importance of a college education in today's society. She was already two years behind in high school and on the verge of dropping out. She would have been happy for us just to have a nice apartment and a couple of dead-end jobs.

I had no business messing with Carol in the first place. She wasn't on my level mentally, socially, or educationally; but she had the cutest smile, a beautiful body, and an Oscar Award winning personality. Those are the things I should have been weary of, but like 90 percent of the male population, I fell victim to a big butt and a smile.

For some strange reason, my brother Ronald never liked Carol. He really liked Poo -Poo, and he had reason to believe that Carol and her family had a cake baked for me. I never saw the slickness in Carol until years later, and by that time I was too involved to walk away.

Carol wasn't the only one unhappy about my going away to college; Slick Stand wasn't too fond of the idea either. Colby had been arrested earlier in the year for a robbery gone badly, and since that time, Slick and I had gotten close. He was my lieutenant in my drug business. He did most of the leg work while I worked out for college. I had been Slick's meal ticket for the past three years, and he didn't want to lose his bread and butter. He came up with every scenario in the world for why I didn't need to go, and when none of those things worked, we had our first fight. Slick even involved the entire Seat Pleasant Crew. The actual beef didn't bother me at all, for I had plans for bigger and better things. My main purpose in life at that time was to escape that ghetto prison, the one that so many people can't seem to get out of; the one that has taken more lives than AIDS, the one that keeps its participants continuously spirally down towards the abyss. I didn't speak to Slick again until after my brother Ronald's misfortune.

I left for college in August of 1985. My sisters Jean and Judy and my nephew Brian drove me to the college. My sister Jean actually pulled some strings to get me into Virginia Union. She also had dreams of me being a successful, productive individual. Judy and Jean helped me with supplies. They were so particular that when they saw the mattress on my dorm room bed, they wouldn't let me sleep on it. They took me directly to Sears and brought me a mattress. Jean gave me $500 in cash and $500 in traveler's checks to start a bank account at the First National Bank of Richmond. $1000 was a lot of money in 1985, and I will always be in her debt. I still definitely hope to pay her back. Jean always thought she was my mother, especially since she never had any children of her own. She probably had been saving that money for years explicitly for my college education.

I felt bad about leaving my brother Ronald when I went to college. He had always been my hero, and I'd also been his meal ticket for the past three years.

I remember when I first started selling heroin; I gave him two ten-packs of dope for $100. At that time, dope sold for $25 per bag, thus, he had $500 worth of bags. When it came time to pay me, Ronald only had $80.00. I told him I wasn't going to give him anything else until he went and got that other $20.00. The incident happened on a Sunday, and I happen to be spending the day with Carol. For that entire day, Ronald peeked continuously in the room on us. I was determined I wasn't going to give him anything else until he had the full amount. I guess it was about 8:00pm, and the peeking in had gone on since 11:00 am.

Carol asked me to pretend like we were asleep just to see what Ronald would do. I kept the dope by the bed in a little box, along with some acid. I kept the acid just in case the police came, for in no way did I want to endanger myself or my parents. Usually, I never kept anything in my parents' house, but the place I'd kept it before had been burned down. I was in the process of paying someone else to hold the drugs, and they wouldn't be back in town until Monday morning.

We cut out the lights in the room and pretended to be sleep. About three minutes later, I noticed the door crack open; it was Ronald and his buddy Billy. My mother had told Ronald to leave us alone, so he had Billy had been watching out for my mother. Ronald tip-toed all the way up to the bed, and peeped at us to see if we were still sleeping. Once he felt we were asleep, he tipped over to the box. As soon as he put his hand on the box, I jumped up and turned on the lights. The quick-thinking fool put his arms straight out as though he was sleep walking and walked back to the door. Carol and I laughed so hard, I ended up giving him some more dope anyway.

That was just one of the tricks he used to pull. When I left for Virginia, I had about a pickle Juice Jar full of Love Boat left. I gave it to my brother, free of charge. I know there had to be about $4,000-worth left in that jar. I prayed he would at least make enough money to keep himself up.

I remember coming home about three weeks later to check on my mom. I went to Chapel Oaks, looking for Ronald. The first thing that seemed strange was all the drunks on the corner had on new Fila tee shirts; then when I walked through the Lodge, all the old ladies were eating crabs. I finally found Ronald in the Ebony Inn at the bar. He looked good, but he'd messed up most of the money. That's one thing I could say about my brother, he had a heart of gold.

Virginia Union is on North Lombardy Street, in nice middle class section of the city of Richmond. The school is one of the most prestigious black Universities in the country, with alumni including Douglas Wilder, Walter Fauntroy, Max and Randall Robinson, and Superior Court Judge Henry Kennedy.

I stayed in Huntley Hall, Room 108. My roommates name was Charlie MayBerry. Charlie was pledging Omega Phi PSi (Q-Dogg), and was also on the tennis team. He was one of the slickest country boys I've ever met. He was from Suffolk, Virginia, and he wore his hair in a high top fade. He was even messing with one of my home girls, Tanya.

The buildings at Virginia Union were old; some were built in the 1800s, right after the Civil War. The school was small, so the place had a family atmosphere; everyone knew everyone else. The dances every weekend in the multipurpose room were one of the highlights of my stay there. There were women there from all over the city of Richmond. Richmond wasn't the nicest city in 1985, for their murder rate was climbing; not to the extent of a Washington, D.C., but you had to keep your eyes open. They had projects there just like they have in Washington: Church Hill and Jackson Wall. Two of the guys that played on the basketball team were from those areas: Ray Neb (Jackson Wall), and Jerry Hargrove (Church Hill).

The women there were beautiful beyond reason. I still kick myself today for not hooking up with one of those intelligent, strong willed and strong-minded women. I remember ladies like: Bernadette, Thomasema, Wendy, Cynthia, Tanya, Kya, Mel Cat, Jocelyn, Dianna and Daisy. . These ladies went on to be successful in their fields of choice. There were so many women I could list names for hours

I should have been enjoying the females on campus, but my mind was on my studies and basketball, during the week, and Carol seemed to show up at the Greyhound station in Richmond every weekend. I guess Carol was just keeping a close eye on her investment.

I learned a great deal at Virginia Union because I was around prestigious black people from all over the country. These were people with goals and aspirations. They were all leaders in their own right. They knew exactly where they were going in life. They also knew the sacrifices people had made in order for them to get such a great education, and they appreciated the effort. I wish I had taken total advantage of the situation. If I make some money off this book, I'll go back to Virginia Union and get another business degree. Hopefully, my daughter Ricka will come with me. I truly wish we can someday be father and daughter, but as of today, we are strangers.

The date was October 3, 1985. I was playing in a pickup game at the Barco Arena on the Virginia Union campus and having the game of my life. I got a fast-break dunk, and on my way back to play defense, I got a strange feeling in my stomach. It was a feeling of loss. Five Minutes later, my roommate, Charlie, ran out on the court and told me to call Carol immediately. He said something bad had happened at my home, and I needed to call right away.

I ran all the way back to the dorm to use the telephone. When I got through to Carol, she was crying. She told me my brother Ronald had been shot and that she thought he was dead. At that moment, my entire life with my brother flashed before my eyes. I remembered him picking me up when I fell, him wiping my tears when I cried, him teaching me how to play basketball, our good times and our bad. I was speechless on the phone for at least ten minutes, and when I came out of my trance, Carol was hollering my name. I hung up the phone and called my family.

My father answered the phone. He seemed upset that Carol had called me. He said the family had planned to come down to Richmond on Sunday night to tell me what had happened. He eventually told me that Ronald had been shot five times and had died at Prince George's Hospital Center. My dad said, since Ronald didn't have any veins, they weren't able to get an IV in him in time to save his life. He also said, "The family would be there Sunday to bring me home. It was Thursday then, and I had no intentions of waiting until Sunday.

I felt light-headed when I hung up the phone with my dad. I didn't even have enough money on me to get a bus ticket home, and the bank didn't open until the next day. I was determined to get home then and there. I needed air, so I took a walk to the 7-Eleven to get a Slurpee. While in the 7-Eleven, I saw a guy with a wallet full of money. Instead of getting a Slurpee, I got a large bottle of vinegar. I waited out on the parking lot for the guy to come out of the store. When he got to his car, I held the bag in a way so as to make the object inside resemble a pistol. I think I scared the man something awful, for he threw me the wallet and ran away. I went back to the dorm, gathered a few articles of clothing, and made a beeline to the bus station.

Once I got to the bus station, I brought a one-way ticket to Washington. While riding home, I had a feeling of guilt. For the last three years, my brother Ronald and I had been a team; and I had abandoned him for a better life, so I thought. Our roles in life had changed, for now I was the big brother, and he was my little brother. I remember hearing in treatment the statement, "some must die so others may live", but at the moment, I wanted to die myself. I knew in my heart that I had to avenge his death, but I was a lot of things, but not a killer. If I hated selling people poison, how could I pull the trigger and kill someone? I searched for the heart and strength I needed through the use of drugs.

The first place I went when I got back to D.C was to Skull-Murphy's house on 15th Street. I just knew I could get a pistol there. When I got there, the only person home was Murph's father, Jimmy. Apparently, their house had been raided the night before, and Murphy and everyone else had been arrested. Jimmy gave the police a fake name, and they didn't arrest him.

I left Murphy's house distraught. I walked straight down T Street, towards 7th. When I got to 7th Street, I saw Harry ducking in and out of the alley's selling dope. Instead of consoling me over my brother's death, he was more concerned with the leather hat I was wearing. He persistently kept asking for the hat; I just walked away, before I took the frustrations I was feeling out on the wrong person.

I finally caught a cab, and went directly to Chapel Oaks; where the actual shooting of my brother occurred. The first place I went was to Miss Bella's house. Miss Bella had four sons that were very close to my brother and me. I figured I could get some answers there as to what had actually happened. The first thing Miss Bella said to me was, "Ronald, they told me you were dead!" I told Miss Bella that I was Michael not Ronald, and she looked as though she had seen a ghost. I asked her where her son Brezzy was, she told me he had gone to check on Ronald. She specifically told me not to do anything crazy, and that I had a future ahead of me. I still think to this day, she called my family's house because my father met me before I could reach the Ebony Inn. He seemed really upset, so I didn't give him any problems about getting in the car. Plus, I had plenty of time to find out the truth.

My brother Melvin was driving, we dropped my dad off at home, I hugged my mother, and then while we took a ride to drink beer and talk. Mind you, I hugged my mother before we left.

Melvin told me that my father and he had been the first two to arrive at the emergency room after they found out Ronald had been shot. He told me how they had gone to the receptionist's desk to inquire about Ronald's condition, and how the receptionist had told them that they had Ronald listed as a vagrant because he had no fixed address. She also told them that Ronald was on the life support machine and that he already had an outstanding bill with the hospital. She said that if someone from his immediate family didn't come and claim Ronald, they were going to cut off the machine. Melvin said my father told the receptionist that he was just a friend. That was mainly because my dad didn't want to be responsible for the paying of the hospital bill. Melvin said he was so upset about my father's statement he just walked right out of the hospital, and my father followed. They never got a chance to see Ronald before he died.

Just hearing that my father cared more about his money than my brother's life, made me hate him. That fact weighed heavily on my soul for many years to come. My sister, Jean, came up with the ingenious idea that everyone was to put up $500.00 a piece to share the cost of my brother's funeral. My brother Donald had to get a loan from the bank to pay his portion. I was excluded from the $500 because I was in school. All of this because everyone thought my father was broke. He had retired 10 years earlier from the Naval Oceanographic Office in Suitland Maryland. The Office in Suitland moved down south was the last my dad wanted to go. He was born in 1921 and had experienced Jim Crow in the city. I could only imagine what the south was like back then. My father had over $25,000 in his bank account. His cheap ass wasn't going to mention it to anyone, so the family equally sharing the bill for my brother's funeral was right up his alley.

My dad and I eventually made up, but our relationship was never the same after that. Later on in life, when I was in jail and thinking clearly,

I came to the conclusion that my brother Melvin wasn't much better than my dad, especially since he didn't stand up at the hospital and say Ronald was his brother.

Today, I still have nightmares about my brother being killed. I feel even worse for not killing the man that killed my brother. I know today that the pain and grief felt, made me want to die, that's why I tried to smoke and snort my life into oblivion.

Later that evening, when things quieted down, I snuck away to the Ebony Inn, to get the true gist of what had happened to my brother. I saw one of Ronald's old buddies, Carl Butler; and he gave me his version of the story.

As the story goes, Ronald, Wildman, and William Lee (Carol's older brother) had been drinking iced tea cocktails all that day, and they had a gun on them. The day before, Ronald and Wildman had pistol-whipped a guy for saying something nasty to Carol. On this particular day, Gabby Hayes, the neighborhood alcoholic, was being beaten by her boyfriend John West. My brother asked Gabby's brother June to stop that man from beating up sister. June stated, "fuck her"; so my brother took things into his own hands.

Ronald walked up on West, and proceeded to whip him with the pistol. Ronald shot dope in his hands, so they would swell with the slightest of touch. Some kind of way, the gun slipped from Ronald's hands, and there was a fight between Ronald and West over the weapon. Mind you, while they fought, there were at least twenty people in the immediate area. West got to the gun first and shot Ronald five times. All someone had to do was to pick up the gun and my brother wouldn't have died that day. Poo-Poo's father, Peewee Mancaster and his wife, Wimpy, tried to assist Ronald, but the gunman was just too fast. I find it ironic how a person can live by the gun and die by the gun.

The entire incident occurred on Sheriff Road, directly across from Sandy's Liquors. The Chapel Oaks Fire Department is also on Sheriff Road, not more than six blocks away. They had a qualified EMS Crew, but none of them had prior experience with heroin addicts that don't have veins. They tried for about five minutes to get an IV in place without luck. Finally, Michael Robbie, who also worked with the Fire Department, showed up and took charge. Mike did get an IV in place, but Ronald had gone five minutes without oxygen to the brain. My mother told me once that if Ronald had lived, he may have been mentally disabled because of the lack of air. She also said, "Ronald was a proud person, and he wouldn't have wanted to live that way."

After hearing the story about my brother's death, I had mixed emotions. Ronald and I were really considered outsiders to chapel Oaks and Fairmont Heights. The people look upon us as rich kids gone bad. They never really had any sympathy for either of us. Honestly, I think they thought we were fools for being in the area in the first place, just someone else to use. The actions and statements I heard from people after Ronald's death proved my point completely.

Later that evening, after having a few drinks in the Ebony Inn; I noticed Gabby walking up and down Sheriff Road, ramping and raging about her man being locked up. She also made that statement, "I'll be glad when my man gets out of jail." Then there was Horris, Spoons younger brother, who said, "better him than me." I think at that exact moment, I lost my mind. I had never felt that much rage before. I commenced to knocking both of Gabby's front teeth out, and I blackened both of Horris's eyes. If I'd had a gun that night, someone would have definitely died.

My brother's funeral and wake were both held at Stewart's Funeral Home. Everybody that was anybody showed up that day and night;

there were people that had grown up with Ronald on East Capital Street, friends of the family, relatives I hadn't seen in years, and his old penitentiary buddies. Ronald was thirty-four years old when he died. He'd spent the majority of his life either on drugs or in prison; thus, he had no life. My father took Ronald's death very hard, but since I was still mad at him, because of the statement Melvin had made about my dad "just being a friend", I didn't console him that day. I still regret that today.

The night before the wake, my dad and I were up late watching a movie. We talked for a while, and then were startled when the doorbell rang at such a late hour. We both rushed to the door to see who was there; when we opened it up, Ronald was standing there. I don't know if it was that we both wanted to see him again badly or if it was grief, but we both were seeing the same thing. My father simply said, "Ronald, you have to go back. You can't stay here — you have to go back. "Damn, Ronald was put out the house in life, and put out the house in death.

The funeral was extra dramatic for me. I had four women there, and each one of them was introducing herself as my girlfriend. At my mother's house, after the funeral was really a close call for me; Poo-Poo was walking around in my mother's bedroom slippers, Liza had her mouth poked out, Carol was sitting in a corner, and Kale and her friend Linda were sitting on the front porch. Can you believe I had to hideout behind my father's garage until the repast was over? I had my brother Melvin drop Poo-Poo off at home, my brother Donald took Liza to his house, Kale and Linda left on their own, and I drove Carol home. My brother Donald still teases me about the events that day.

The things that most affected me about the repast at my mother's was the way people boldly asked for Ronald's clothing and the amount of plates people took from my parents' home. I can see someone leaving with maybe one or two plates, but seven and eight now that's taking advantage of people's kindness.

That evening, after everything was over, I freebased for the very first time. I had a little money and Wildman and Cina-Bun wanted to get high. They told me the high would help me to forget my problems. Mind you, I had been offered freebase thousands of times in the past and never succumbed to the peer pressure. Also, my brother Ronald never told me what smoking the pipe would actually do to a person, but he always protected me when people tried to influence my use. I guess curiosity killed the cat.

Cina-Bun told me not to be afraid. "Smoking cocaine is just like smoking reefers I always thought a person couldn't get addicted to a substance you smoked. I always thought as long as you didn't inject the substance into your arms or legs you'd be alright. Boy was I wrong. . .

I went on a Love Boat and freebase binge that lasted for about two weeks. My parents thought I was back at school, but I was actually at the Holliday Inn on route 450 with Slick, Mango, and Black Shannie.

I never felt anything in life like my first hit of cocaine. I looked so crazy afterwards Wildman teased me for weeks. I had a feeling of euphoria. My entire body went numb, and I climaxed on myself. I've been searching for the last twenty years for that same feeling. I guess you only get it that one time; every time since, I've been chasing a ghost.

Eventually, I went back to school. Slick, Keedie, Gator, Sharon, Jackie, and Uncle Chuck took me back. Uncle Chuck had just received a large settlement from an accident case, so he brought a Monte Carlo, like mines, and a luxury van. We all piled into the van and got high all the way to Richmond, Virginia.

I remember Uncle Chuck having a briefcase full of Love Boat and cocaine. Chuck climb in the back of the van from time to time to get high with us. When he did, he let Slick drive. Mind you, in 1985, Slick didn't have a driver's license. I remember the cops pulling us over because Slick had been speeding. At that moment, Slick and Chuck switched seats. Chuck jumped out the van with the briefcase in his hands. I just knew I was going to jail that night. God must have been with us, because all Chuck came back with was a $100 ticket. When we arrived at the school, I still remember Sharon running through the dorm knocking on doors.

I made a great deal of bad choices in 1985. I blame no one but myself for my indiscretions. Today, I'm still living in the aftermath of the bad decisions I made over twenty years ago.

I spent the rest of the 1985 school year in a daze. I think the coaches and instructors at Union took it easy on me because they could see something was wrong with me. I wish instead of trying to medicate my problems with drugs, I would have gone to see an analyst or psychologist. I always thought that seeing any kind of psych doctor was weak, but in all actuality, using drugs is weak. It took me to complete the tedious task of writing down my entire life story to actually get to the root of why I got "stuck on stupid."

I was arrested for the very first time in my life on December 11, 1985, one day after my brother's birthday. I had come home from college during the Christmas break, and the only thing on my mind was getting high. I stopped by my parents' house, picked up my car, and made a beeline to the Lodge...

Once I got there, I picked up Gator, Monie, Bucky, and Shirley Harper. We all went to North Englewood Park to smoke some boat. While we were there, the park police rolled up on us. Gator and Shirley both hid their drugs under the back seat of my car. The Officer claimed he smelled marijuana, so that gave him probable cause to search my vehicle. After an extensive search, they found the drugs and arrested all of us.

We were taken to the Park Police Barracks in Riverdale, Maryland. The officers scared the girls to death. They told on Gator from the door. Since Monie and Shirley were juveniles, they were released to their parents. They transported Gator, Bucky, and me to Hyattsville Detention Center to see the commissioner. We were all still released to the custody to our parents. I called my brother Melvin to come get me. He didn't make a big deal out of my arrest, but he did say I was slipping. I didn't want to go to my mother's house at that time of night, so I had Melvin drop me off at Liza's new apartment on Ely Place S.E.

Liza really loved me. She stuck with me through two children and a lot of infidelities. When I went to prison, in 1988; I think that was the straw that broke the camel's back. I had also put her on the back-burner for Carol, and she hated that. She had a position at the World Bank and Carol was working at Sandy's Liquors at the lottery machine; what kind of fool was I?

When I was arrested, the officers impounded my car; so the first thing I had to do the next morning was to raise the money to get the car out of jail too. Slick loaned the money, for in no way did I want to alert my parents to my arrest.

I truly believe 1985 was the beginning to my end. I thank God I finally had the courage to fight the demons that have bound me for so many years. I've actually been stuck twenty-one years in the past. I blamed myself for not avenging my brother death, for leaving him and going away to college. All in all, I wanted to die too.

Today, I have liver cancer and am really dying. I'm having a hard time dealing with that, but after reading the Bible, the Koran, and books like the *7 Habits of Highly Effective People* by Stephen Covey, I've gained a sense of closure. Today, I can look up.

In '86,

I was throwing bricks.

When I say bricks, I mean stupid shit.

But thanks to Bo acting like a brother,

Once again I learned to love one another...

CHAPTER 7

1986

In January of 1986, I went back to Virginia Union. My desires, my goal, my plans, my ambitions had all changed. My heart and soul were dead. I no longer cared about school, basketball, or life; I just existed. All that mattered was killing the pain that lingered in my soul. I attempted to relieve this pain with drugs, money, and women, but no matter what I tried, the pain just got even more excruciating.

This time when I left for school, I took my car, my drugs and the streets. Everything that Michael Moore had built was lost to his alter ego, Mike-Mike. Mike-Mike was the street hustler, the armed robber, everything I had gone away to college to escape. I was no longer able to separate the two. Mike-Mike was now large and in charge. I no longer cared about basketball; I walked away from the team. I no longer cared about my studies; I walked away from my classes. I only did well enough to pass. I cheated, I paid for term papers, and I always played the grief card.

I was actually the one that introduced Love Boat to the city of Richmond. The locals used to call the stuff Zoom-Zoom, and they loved the effects. I remember there being lines, with up to twenty people in them, just to buy a single bag. I remember my home-girls calling the police on me because I wouldn't finance their habits. I remember the campus security kicking in my door, tearing up my dorm room, and giving me the what-for, all about a substance they had no clue

My dorm representative, Yogi, had called the Richmond Police on me, and he felt they didn't do a good enough search. They just knew I was selling heroin or cocaine; not marijuana with a chemical sprayed on it. If I had gotten caught with the quantity I had; I would have still been in a Virginia prison today. Virginia has never played with drug dealers.

I started hanging out with a home boy from Washington, Emit Spencer. Spencer had lost his football scholarship due to his involvement in a robbery on the Virginia Union campus. Spencer and two other football players from D.C. robbed the Domino's pizza man. The other two guys chose to leave school, but Spencer stuck it out. He got student loans, Pell Grants, and everything else possible to stay in school. In his heart, Spencer wanted to achieve greatness, but like the saying goes, "You can take the person out of D.C., but you can't take the D.C. out the person."

The two of us were a chemistry project gone badly. We smoked Boat and snorted coke like there was no tomorrow. I remember the two of us going to see the Tommy Hearns vs. Marvin Harris fight. We were in an atmosphere with the elite, and we smoked Boat and snorted cocaine right in front of them. We just didn't care. A few of my home-girls told me I was on a path to destruction, but I paid them no mind at all.

This path of destruction followed me all the back to Washington. If it wasn't for a family friend, by the name of Stallie "Bo" Edwards, actually sitting down and talking to me, I might be dead today. Bo talked to me about what my brother Ronald would have wanted for me and how Ronald always bragged about his little brother. He said my task in life isn't finished and told me that I was destined to greatness. He also told me that he was my older brother now, and he said if I ever needed anything, I could always come to him.

That statement touched me. I actually cried that day for the first time in a lot of years. From that day on, in my heart, Bo was my family. He had said things to me my own brothers and sisters never said. I believe deep down inside, my family wanted Ronald to die. He was an embarrassment, a drug addict, a criminal; he was everything that my family had fought so hard to get away from. Ronald was the only tarnished on the prestigious Moore name. Now that he was gone, they felt relieved. Little did they know that I was destined to be worse than Ronald. Officer Francis Barnes tried to warn them about me at my brother's wake, but the way Barnes delivered that information almost got him beat up by big Shannie Richardson.

In May of 1986, I came home from Virginia Union, never to return. It was the summer break, and I wanted to be closer to the action, closer to the drug source. That's one decision I still regret today. Boy do I wish they would invent a time machine, because I would certainly go back and get things right this time.

Carol graduated from Fairmont Heights in June of 1986. I made sure I was home to see her walk across that stage. Her school's prom was held at the Greenbelt Hilton, and we wore red and white. I brought her a red gown and rented myself a white tuxedo to match. Carol's friend Chris did her hair and makeup. The hardest thing for me was finding a pair of white shoes to match the tuxedo. I wanted a white lizard, but I had to settle for beige crocodile and had them dyed white.

We drove my brother Melvin's red Ford LTD to the prom. We took several pictures which her mother still has to this day. After the prom, I rented a hotel room. We stayed there the rest of the night. Deep down inside, I was still lost. I really didn't know what I wanted in life. I was just going through the motions.

My father once told me a strong man was like a good watch. He said, "In a watch, you have several wheels, but there is a big wheel that turns all the smaller ones. The man has to be that big wheel." I was supposed to be the one that held everything together, that big wheel. When a man becomes less than that big wheel, most women search for someone else to move the hands on their clock. Eventually, that's what Carol did. I don't blame her for abandoning a sinking ship.

That summer, I moved into Carol's mother's house on Nash Street. We had a small room with a single bed. That bed was smaller than the bunk I slept in prison. I truly believe Carol became my world that summer. I did for her, more than I did for myself. I actually think during the summer of 1986, our souls intertwined.

In the fall of 1986, I went back to school at Prince George's Community College. I realized it was a step down, but I didn't want to be away from Carol. I tried out for the basketball team, but my heart wasn't really in it. Besides, I would have to have been red-shirted. I got a co-operative education job in the computer room. My supervisors were Catty Van and Jerry Mar. They were wonderful people to work for, but my heart wasn't in the job. My mind was in the streets, so I didn't achieve the success I should have. I was mainly surviving by selling drugs. I guess that was the easy way out.

Also in 1986, Slickstand followed me down to Carol's house, and he became infatuated with Carol's sister Catty. At that time, Catty was messing with Wildman; and Wildman wasn't willing to just give her up, so he and Slick fought and fought and fought. Eventually, after several beatings, Wildman finally walked away. Catty got a big kick out of having two men fight for her hand. Slick really thought he was gaining the hand of a princess.

They eventually got married in late 1986. Slick's brother Keedie and his girl Larissa were their best man and maid of honor. I knew Slick and Catty were making a big mistake; they were too young for marriage. Second of all, they were both control freaks, and you can't have two chiefs in the same teepee. They didn't know enough about each other. They weren't compatible at all.

Slick had started hustling for Petty Eddie, a big-time hustler out of Palmer Park. He was setting it out there for Slick, and Slick was bringing home the bacon. Slick was bringing home a lot of cash. I guess Catty couldn't see the forest for the trees.

In 87, I almost went to heaven
Fooling with a dirty black dude named Kevin;
He put us with a man named Petty Eddie;
Ed tricked us out of money and was very petty,
But we still made bank every day;
That's all just part of that Montana way….

CHAPTER 8

1987

In 1987, I was still attending P.G. College and working in the college computer room. I also had a part-time job at UPS. I was loading trucks at night and loading tapes drives during the day. I was trying to at least send my daughter $50 a week. The two jobs were wearing me down to the extent that I was falling asleep in class. I came up with the ingenious idea to quit my job and hustle with Slick at night.

Boy, did I make a mistake. Slick and Ed had set up shop on Montana Avenue. They were selling ready rock. At that time, most people had to buy powder cocaine and cook it up themselves. Well, Ed came up with the idea of selling the Cocaine already cooked up.

Montana Avenue was a low-income housing project in Northeast Washington. This was the first time I had ever seen professional crack heads. These people lived for their next hits. I saw women sell their bodies for a crumb of crack cocaine. Crack was the devil on another level. Once you took a hit of crack cocaine, you were addicted in ten seconds. It reminded me of a line from the movie *Crookland*: "If God made anything better than crack, he kept it for himself."

Cocaine in the freebase form is the purest form of cocaine, but people use other substances like Return and Comeback to increase the weight. The bigger the rock, the more money you make. Return and Come back's actual use is as a rug deodorizers. The company that makes them just doesn't add the perfume to the product. That way once you cooked the cocaine and the substance together, the finished product doesn't have a strange taste. The effects of these two substances together have to have some type of long-term effect on the human body.

I learned Crack 101 from two long time users: Greg Sharp and Ricky Walker. They taught me the basic mixture of cocaine and baking soda. These two substances mixed together along with heat and water turns the powdery substances into a hard rock substance. You can also use ammonia along with cocaine to get a rocky substance, but the finished product has a nasty taste, especially if you don't rinse off all the ammonia.

I learned how to cook using cocaine and Arm & Hammer baking soda. There are several ways to cook cocaine: you can use the proper measurements of baking soda (1/3 the weight of the cocaine), or you can make what they call "whip," which is the same weight in baking soda as cocaine. With the 1/3 baking soda, on the cocaine you are guaranteed to have a good product; with the whip, you are taking a fifty-fifty chance. You will be increasing your profits, but you might get bad product that will take you forever to sell. I always liked to do this the right way the first time. I might not make as much money, but I won't have as many problems getting rid of the stuff. The object of the game is to sell your product. You can't take cocaine to the store or the bank, at least not in the United States.

Eddie Franklin, AKA Petty Eddie, was only 2 years older than I. In 1987, he owned a 560 SEC Mercedes, a home in Fort Washington, and an apartment building in Baltimore. He had the most beautiful wife, Alfreada, and a son Eddie Junior. Eddie was a very serious dude. He had a lot of bills, so he needed his money to keep up his lifestyle. I learned a great deal of logic from him. He taught me the value of morals and principles. Most people that use drugs lose all their values and get cruddy in a sense. Ed taught me that my word was my bond, and without your word you were nothing in the dope game.

Ed only had one bad habit: he wasn't afraid of anything. Fear is a defense mechanism. If you don't fear anything, you are subject to die an early death. I think Ed made a lot of careless mistakes; the biggest one was taking people for granted. He felt he could look at a person and see where their heart was. What he failed to realize is that a scared person will kill you the quickest, and at the time of his death, there were a lot of people afraid of him. I was in prison when he died. I remember reading about his death in the newspaper.

Ed started me off with an ounce of cocaine. I was selling it at the Ebony Inn and was my own boss. At that time, cocaine cost $2000 an ounce, but with a little cut, I really made a nice profit. Slick Stand and his brother Keedie were hustling on Montana Avenue North-East along with Eddie's longtime friend, Herman Epps. Herman had started smoking crack, and was nothing like he used to be. I remember Herman being a boxer, but the constant use of cocaine had diminished his weight considerably. Herman also had a lot of heart; I guess he had to if he was going into a housing project where he didn't grow up and had planned on setting up shop.

Slick knew I was smoking cocaine, and he didn't want me to mess up Ed's money, so he came up with the idea of me coming up to Montana Avenue with him. I guess he felt that way he could keep an eye on me.

I had been on Montana before; Poo Blake lived there along with Earl Blake. I had dropped Poo off several times after the club was over at the Ebony Inn and walked her to her door.

Right beside her house was the crack house. A guy name Pop ran the place. If you wanted to hustle out of Pops house, you had to pay him $200 a day. That would have been good money if he had been saving it. His rent was only $40 per month, but Pop, like a lot of people during that time was addicted to crack, so he smoked up all his profits. Pop had people in and out of that place 24 hours a day. The place was a gold mine, but it was hot as hell.

Montana Avenue was a new world for me. I thought I had seen a lot of money when I was selling heroin, but crack money was even more plentiful. As the saying goes, "One hit is too many, and a thousand is never enough.", so the addicts smoked until they simply fell out from exhaustion.

On Montana Avenue, I had an unlimited supply of cocaine. Ed had the house kilo working in three eight-hour shifts. On each shift, we cooked up a 1/8 kilo (4 ounces). Ed wanted $8000 for the entire 1/8 kilo. Slick Stand and I split any profits we made on top of that.

Ed had met a lady that had a place on the other side of Montana Avenue. Her name was Pat, and she had three kids. They were wonderful kids, and they had no business in that type of environment. I know Pat loved those kids, but she had a monkey on her back, and along with the money Ed had promised her, it had clouded her judgment.

Slick and I worked all three shifts. We went to Pats house on Sunday nights and wouldn't come home until the next Saturday night. The breaks I took were for food, clothing, and smoking.

We cooked the coke, half-ounces at a time. Since I was the one that actually cooked up the cocaine, I would stash a little of the pure cocaine out of each ounce. At the end of the day, when I took my breaks, I would steal off and either sell what I stole or smoke it. Nine times out of ten, I'd smoke it. No wonder my liver is in bad shape now. I lost a considerable amount of weight too. I would steal off with girls, let them smoke hundreds of dollars in cocaine, and the next day when Ed came, they'd tell him everything. It was like they were dedicated to pleasing Eddy. Ed didn't give a damn about anybody up there on Montana Avenue; his loyalties were only to the money he made.

Since I was away from home a lot, that gave Carol the chance to explore other men. I remember coming home early one week after I had given her a considerable amount of money to go shopping, to find out she was sneaking around on me. Carol was always the type of person that listened to what other people said. She could not figure things out for herself. Everybody that was anybody knew I was getting high, and that made Carol embarrassed. At that time, I thought of the situation as betrayal, but actually, she was looking for a better deal. She knew eventually my ship would sink, and she didn't want to go down with it.

Carol also got pregnant in 1987. I couldn't figure that out to save my life. Why would you have a child by someone you were embarrassed of? A drug addict to boot. Now that I have heard the true gist of the situation; I finally understand. Carol had a cyst on her ovaries. She felt if she didn't have a child soon, she wouldn't be able to ever have a child. I think I was just a sperm donor. Besides, she'd already had one abortion, and going through with it had almost driven her crazy. She wanted and needed someone to love, someone that would always love her, no matter what the situation was. A child was her best bet.

I got locked up three times in 1987. My first arrest that year was in the Paradise and Mayfair housing projects in North East Washington. I had left Montana early that night to study for a test, and I'd then gone to Paradise to get rid of the cocaine I had stolen. I got caught up in a drug raid. Boy do I wish I'd gone home. There was a crack epidemic in Paradise. They had dealers there from New York and Jamaica. The Jamaicans there were ruthless. I thought Ed was uncaring, but the Jamaicans were twice as bad. They would find a girl that used and simply commandeer her home. They had no sympathy for the woman or her kids. When the woman messed up money, they beat her right in front of her children.

The Jamaicans and New Yorkers had actually cornered the crack market. They were selling cocaine, three times the size the Washington dealers were, but for the same price. They sold what you called "working halves." A working half was $50 worth of cocaine that you could break down and make up too $150.00. The normal D.C. hustlers couldn't afford to do this, so it started a lot of gang wars.

In the '60s and '70s, Paradise and Mayfair were reputable neighborhoods. They were part of Eastland Gardens, an upper class black neighborhood in North-East Washington. Doctors, lawyers, grew up in this area. Once the crack epidemic hit the area, the place looked like Beirut.

First all the grass disappeared. The children could no longer play outside, and then the older residents became hostages in their own homes. There was actually a drug war going on inside this small, nice neighborhood. The crack heads ran rapid, 24 hours a day. That era definitely brought down the property value of the North-East section of Washington, D.C. A lot of the older residents refused to abandon their homes, so they were forced to live in a war zone.

When I was arrested, I was taken to the 6th District on Benning Road to be booked and finger printed. Then you were transferred to the Central Cell Block, which was called the Bull Pen. Many people have died in this cold, nasty hole-in-the-wall block of holding cells. The cells smelled of urine, and there was no ventilation at all. When you were arrested in the District, you had to endure the Bull Pen before any chance of release.

The D.C. jail was packed as usual, so if you didn't kill anyone, you were going to get out the next day. I was only arrested for a possession charge, but my case was assigned to the Honorable Luke Moore. Judge Moore knew about my family's prestige, so he tried every way he could to help me. Judge Moore placed me on urinalysis test, and that was the beginning to my end. I liked getting high, and I had an unlimited supply. I was living a drug addict's dream. , and the Honorable Judge was throwing a monkey wrench into my program. I continued to hustle and use, thus, my urines were dirty.

My next arrest was on Montana Avenue, only two weeks later. I was in the kitchen cutting up rocks when the police hit the door. Eddy had smacked a girl named Sharon in the face for telling people the crack batch we had that day was no good, so the police call was meant for Ed. Luckily, Ed had left only 10 minutes before the raid. We actually had a doorman, so they didn't get right in. I had time to throw the guns out the window and hide the cocaine in the freezer, which hadn't been defrosted in years. When they burst into the house, I sat on the couch with the other crack heads in hopes that I wouldn't be recognized as a dealer.

Slick Stand was also there. He hid in a dark bedroom under a bed. The police eventually found him and beat him in the face with the flash light. They eventually found the drugs, and an officer that had been standing outside identified my arm from when I threw the gun out the window. It was off to the District this time. They also arrested Slick, but they only charged him with disorderly conduct, a $10 fine. I was transported to the central cell block once again.

When the police officers showed me the charging papers, I saw that they had charged me as Eddie Harris. I had to have my father bring some identification to the precinct to prove that I was Michael Moore.

They charged me with distribution of Cocaine, Manufacturing cocaine, paraphernalia, and carrying a dangerous weapon. They gave me a $4000 bond this time. Slick and Ed paid the bond, and Carol and her aunt Netta got me out. I only stayed locked up a day, and that seemed like an eternity. Even though this was my first felony charge, I was facing a considerable amount of prison time.

My sister Jean loaned me $3,500 to get an attorney. We hired attorney Gene Randolph Johnson. (The Judge). He was a good lawyer, and he really tried to help me. I just wouldn't accept the fact that I had a drug problem and needed help. Mr. Johnson did his best to me into Karrick Hall, a drug program at Saint Elizabeth Hospital. I had heard a lot about drug programs, and I definitely didn't want to go to one of them. He once told me "I was the only person he had ever met that wanted to break into jail". Also in 1987, Lorton Penitentiary was a rite of passage for young, up and coming hustlers. If you hadn't had been locked up at Lorton you were a nobody… If I had to be locked up, I wanted to go to Lorton.

What kind of fool was I?

Slick and Ed gave me nothing towards an attorney. I guess they felt that with all the money I was supposed to be making, I should be able to afford my own Attorney. Little did they know, I had smoked up almost all my profits.

At my Probable Cause hearing, the officers didn't show up, so Judge Henry Kennedy actually dismissed my charge. I still had the possession charge that was heard before Judge Moore, and he definitely wanted me to get some form of drug treatment.

On September 12, 1987, Carol's birthday, I got my third arrest. This time, I was in the East Gate housing project, selling Love Boat. Gene Johnson represented me at the bail hearing and got me out, but little did I know the courts would bring back up the distribution charge they had once dismissed.

I had two felony arrests and one misdemeanor in less than five months. A blind man could see there was a problem, but not Mike. I actually thought I had things under control.

In 88, young got late.
I went to Lorton to sit and wait,
But I reamed more crimes
And I learned how to rhyme
from a dirty black dude
whose name was Grimes.

CHAPTER 9

1988

In 1988, my life took a drastic change. I was on my way to prison. After the raid on the house on Montana Avenue, I stopped hustling for a few months, but I ran out of money so I had to return. In March of 1988, I was arrested for the 4th time. This time, I was in South East Washington, at the Arthur Kaper housing project. There was a crew hustling out of those buildings from New York, selling crack in vials. They had $5 vials that could be sold for $10 in North East, Washington. I was simply trying to make a quick flip and got locked up in the process.

I purchased 25 vials and was walking back to the subway station when I was approached by a potential buyer. The lady asked me where she could get something for $20, so I sold her two of my vials and kept walking. Before I reached the train station, I was tackled by the undercover drug task force. Apparently, I had gotten caught up in an undercover sting operation.

Once again I was on my way to the Central Cell Block and the D.C. Superior Court. This time, when I went for my bail hearing, I was given a three-day hold. I was already out on three other bonds or pretrial agreements. Gene Johnson got me out once again. After this arrest, I knew I was going to prison.

My son Michael Kevin Moore Junior was born April 22, 1988, the same day his mother's grandfather was born. He was my pride and joy. I brought cigars and everything. My buddy Zay gave me and Carol a ride home from the hospital. I couldn't run wild like I use to; I had to be more responsible.

Gene Johnson talked me in to pleading guilty to one felony and two misdemeanors. I was praying I didn't get any jail time, but deep down inside I knew I was going away. My only hope was to claim to be an addict and get into a drug treatment program.

I have always had the problem of putting other people's needs ahead of my own at the wrong time. Instead of doing everything I could to get into a drug treatment program, my smart ass came up with the brilliant idea to tell the judge (Henry Kennedy) that I had lowered my use considerably. The truth was, once again, I didn't want to leave Carol. She had just had that new baby, and I felt obligated to try to stay on the streets. Well, my bright idea didn't work. After we had what they called an "Addict Exception Hearing," Judge Kennedy ruled I was not an addict and need to serve some jail time.

Judge Kennedy was also a Virginia Union Alumni, so he didn't hit my head too hard. He did give me a long, drawn-out lecture about me having had the best of everything growing up: home, family, and education. He also said I didn't have to live a life of crime; crime was a life I chose. Judge Kennedy sentenced me to twenty months of incarceration and five years of probation to follow after my incarceration. The fact that Gene Johnson gave an eloquent speech before I was sentenced also played a big part in me not getting say twenty years. I had been arrested four times within one year, and each arrest yielded a considerable amount of drugs.

I was sentenced on June 22, 1988. My son was exactly two months old. I felt bad seeing Carol and the baby crying as the marshals led me away to the Bull Pen. I had feelings of confusion, for I'd never been imprisoned for a long period of time. To put it honestly, I was afraid. I had heard the crazy stories about Lorton, but if I was going to be a bad, street-wise dude, I had to complete my rite of passage.

Prison is simply modern-day slavery. The Thirteenth Amendment clearly states: "Neither slavery nor involuntary servitude, except as a punishment for a crime wherefore the party shall have been duly convicted, shall exist within the United States or any place subject to their jurisdiction." Prisoners are packed into small living spaces, herded to chow and recreation, and forced to work for menial pay. The Department of Corrections contracts out the medical services to the lowest bidder, so you can just imagine the type of medical treatment inmates get. They give you a placebo for everything.

The only good thing about jail is the free room and board. Most honest law-abiding citizens have the wrong misconception about incarceration. The general consensus is that most people want to lock up all criminals and throw away the key. Actually, more than 75% of the incarcerated inmates will be getting out of jail someday. By the public putting up such a resistance to their tax dollars going towards college programs, and many other programs in the system: they have been cut, thus you have the same uneducated criminal returning to society. The only difference is they have been to Crime College.

Let me give you an analogy: you have two dogs, one wild, one tame; if you put the two together, does the wild dog become tame, or does the tame dog become wild? The answer to the question is the same for humans as it is for nature; Survival of the fittest; only the strong survive; the tame animal would have to become wild in order to protect itself. Mind you, some people can jump between channels, (tame to wild, wild to tame) but others, especially those that can't see outside the box, get stuck, and now instead of a petty thieves returning to society; you now have a violent armed robbers returning to the world.

My first stop on the prison train was the Modular Center in Lorton, Virginia. In 1988, the place hadn't been in existence that long, so most of the social work staff was playing things by ear. The actual purpose of the Modular Center was to assess inmates so as to determine their security levels and send them on to a prison within the D.C. Department of Corrections. I'd been through the degrading, strip-search process at the D.C jail, but that was nothing like the search process at the Modular. The Correctional Officers actually made you strip and proceeded to look up your rectum.

The living conditions in a dormitory setting were atrocious. They actually had us stacked on top of each other like boxes in a warehouse. They did give you a care package that consisted of a bar of soap, shampoo, lotion, toothpaste, a toothbrush, and a washrag. The problem was, they only gave out these items once, so if you didn't have money or a hustle, you stank. Can you image drug addicts who have burned all their bridges in society? They weren't going to get any help from the outside world. Thus, you had a small warehouse that smelled like a dog kennel.

They did have a sanitation crew, but these men only made $8 a month. They were not going out of their way to do a top-flight job. Also at that time in prison, inmates were allowed to smoke, so can you imagine a smoker with no money in a prison full of vultures. I'll just say, people were taken advantage of.

The modular facility was an annex for the D.C. jail, so we were locked in the building twenty-four hours a day, the same as the jail. We did receive one hour of outside recreation in a small 20 x 30 yards. Can you image 150 men in a 20 x 30 yard?

The modular had four cell blocks and four dormitories. Each unit was specified for a particular group. Dorms one and two were for people with open charges, probation violators. Dorms three and four were for sentenced inmates in the process of transfer. Cell blocks one and two were for intake, and cell blocks three and four were for detail workers: outside detail, sanitation, receiving and delivery, and kitchen workers. Each unit had separate recreation periods.

There were two things that made the Modular Facility bearable; one the food; there were serving lines, thus you got to eat as much as you could. Two the chapel services; God was definitely in the building. Even though there was no ordained minister at the modular, I saw more men saved there than in any other facility I've ever been in. A great deal of men turned their life around in that place. We had a choir, and an inmate by the name of Mike had a great knowledge of the word. Mike really kept things together, along with brothers like Terrence Cummings. I stayed in the modular until August of 1988. My next move was to the Occoquan Facility.

The Occoquan Facility was built in the 1800s, so the buildings were old and falling apart. In the early 1900's, when you were sent to Lorton, you boarded a boat at the pier in South West Washington, and traveled down the Potomac River to the Occoquan River; then you were marched to the prison. Occoquan was called the old brick yard. Many a drunk in Washington went to the Occoquan Facility and made bricks.

Occoquan had three sides. In 1988, one side consisted of dorms A through J; two sides consisted of dorms K through Q; and three sides consisted of dorms 1 through 7.The orientation dorms were units six and seven.They were actually a real warehouse's with beds in them.Thanks to the problem of overcrowding; people were packed in these two units like sardines. Eventually, the ceiling fell in, in unit seven, injuring several inmates, thus and both units were condemned. There were actually two lawsuits filed against the District Government in Washington, D.C. (Inmates of Occoquan v. Marion Barry 650 F. Supp. 619 December 22, 1986, and 717 F. Supp. 845 June 30, 1989), in hopes of alleviating the problem of over crowdedness. Because of the over crowdedness, along with poor medical attention and homosexuality, disease ran rampant.

There were homosexuals in Occoquan that were considered AIDS carriers. The actual disease didn't affect them, but the disease killed everyone they came in sexual contact with.The institution knew who the "AIDS carriers" were, but because of laws on confidentially, their names were never disclosed to the general population.As a result, of the institution keeping quiet, a lot of men died.

The debate on same-sex relationships has been going on since the beginning of time. Religion teaches us the homosexuality is morally wrong; I feel that not telling the men who was infected with the virus and allowing them to continue having sexual relations was just as bad as injecting them with the virus itself. I've never participated in a homosexual anything, but I had a lot of friends that were on the "down-low." These men eventually got out of prison and carried this illness home to their unsuspecting female companions.

In prison, I met men that had exceptional athletic abilities. They were naturals at their chosen games. Some of these men even benefited from their incarcerations, for they got themselves in excellent physical conditioning. When I think of boxing, the name Jerry Battle pops into mind. Jerry, better known as Young Mike Tyson, had exceptional boxing abilities. Once he was released, some of the big-time hustlers got behind him and got him a few fights. He eventually went on to sign with Don King.

I saw some of the best football, basketball, and baseball games while at Lorton. To some people, Lorton was a blessing. They never ate three hot meals every day before and they never had clean clothing to wear every day; they never had the time to exercise and take care of their bodies. Most of the convicts had some form of drug problem, either selling or using, so they never had that much time to concentrate on themselves.

One particular man, Robbie Grimes, taught me to use both sides of my brain, the logical side and the creative side. He taught me how to put my feelings to words and how to paint a mental picture through poetry.

Robbie had a 20 year to life sentence. Everything about this man was serious. He was well-read, and knowledgeable of a great deal of information that could have been quite useful; that's if I had paid total attention. I took what I wanted from our conversations, and the rest I just threw away. I did learn a great deal about the history of the black man. I learned where we originated and all the about slavery. I began to appreciate education.

My first ever poem was called "Drug Dealer:"

My heart was as cold as stone;
I only cared for what I owned;
A Mercedes. A truck, a home, and a Jetta,

If I hadn't of gotten caught, I'd done even better.
I should be rich and that aint funny,
For the streets where I hustled were sweet as honey.
I sold my product to the meek and the elite;
All you needed was money, I wasn't very discrete.
Women spent their welfare checks, and sold their food stamps, but when they ran out of money, I treated them like tramps.
All I wanted was fame and glamor;
But instead I sit here in the slammer.
I'm in a constant struggle with in my mind, because I done so much to hurt mankind.
Blacks as a whole are economically behind,
And for me to sell them drugs only added to the genocide.
Prison is a place for the ignorant and dumb;
Everything I made hustling was never worth my freedom.
Once back in society, a new profession I will strive; I'll definitely live a different life if I **survive**...

That poem was actually published in a college text-book. My second poem was called "Prison," reprinted here:

It's an unusual city behind the walls;
A concrete jungle, large but small;
The place they send us when we take our falls;
From humanity; from society; from amenity:
A place where evil dwells without mention;
Constant loneliness beyond comprehension;
I pray every day for reformation; for regeneration; for re-education; For re-invigoration.
I've taken so many losses in my life;

My mother, my father, my brother, my wife;
I'm in constant strife;
With myself; for messing up my health; my wealth;
With my education, there are so many things I could achieve.
My mother and father would never believe;
That I'm living in a jungle without any leaves;
With rapist, robbers, drug dealers, and thieves...

While at Occoquan, I worked in the academic school. I definitely used my education to my advantage. While working in the school, I got a chance to see how far behind my peers were educationally. I actually stood out like a sore thumb when it came to guys in my own age group.

I did meet a few men that were destined for greatness. One particular man was Calvin "Rock" Woodland. Rock simply had a lust for learning. Rock actually slept in unit six with me, but I didn't learn how deep the brother was until we took a Street Law class together. Georgetown University Law Center gave a class on Street Law to teach inmates their rights as citizens in the United States of America. Rock and I had some heated debates in that class. I notice right off how articulate he was. Rock was a take-charge type of guy. Today, Rock works for the D.C. City Counsel. He put his misfortunes behind him and went on to help society.

In October of 1988, I was moved to L Dorm. There were over 150 men in that dorm, and I didn't know a soul. There were a few older convicts that were familiar with my brother Ronald: Rabbit, Mike Blackwell, and Mole Face. They took me under their wings as if I was one of their own. I've always had the type of personality where I can fit in anywhere, so I never had any problems. At night, when the lights went off, we had Crime College. The older men talked to the younger ones about ways to improve their crimes. These older guys were actually quite intelligent, but their dependence on narcotics kept them from succeeding in society.

Through all the moves I made, from prison to prison, Carol and my father always came to see me.Their visits kept my spirits high. Eventually, after my incarceration, Carol started messing with Perry Grant and little Money; but she always brought my son to see me. I still remember those visits today.

My father, being older and more experienced in life; told me to forget about Carol completely; this was also some great advice that I failed to heed too. I don't know if Carol and her beautiful mother "Mousey" worked some roots on me, but I still love the two of them to this day. Even after everything we've gone through over the many years, today I'd still take her back at the drop of a hat. Now that's insanity!!!

I stayed at Occoquan until November 30, 1988. I was then moved to the central facility, called Big Lorton. My case manager at Occoquan promised he would send me to minimum security. Technically, I only had twenty months, and anyone sentenced to two years or less was eligible for minimum security. I guess the case manager wanted me to actually experience prison life so I wouldn't come back to jail. For the record, it didn't work.

Occoquan, had controlled movement, thus the correctional officers controlled where the inmates were at all times. At Occoquan, there was also an officer in each dormitory 24 hours a day. Central was completely different. The place was actually a small town. Once the count cleared at 8:00 am in the morning, you were free to explore the entire prison. There were only two units that had officers in them: Units 25 and 26 A & B; these were the orientation units. Inmates only stayed in these units until we found permanent housing on the compound.

My first day there, I saw and didn't see two guys get stabbed, and I heard about someone's bed being set on fire. At Central they, set your bed on fire if you were suspected of being hot. My brother's friend

Little Laurence really stood out. When I met up with him, he gave me a knife about two feet long. His famous words were, "It's better to get caught with it than without it.

The strangest thing I've ever heard in my life was on the day I was classified, the classification committee asked me if I was beefing with anyone inside the prison and where I was from, and they informed me that I had to find my own housing unit. I've been to a lot of prisons in my life, but Lorton was the only prison where an inmate had to be accepted into a dormitory. The classification officer actually told us to walk around the compound and see if we could find a dorm that would accept us.

Everyone in each unit was doing something wrong; that's why you had to be accepted into a unit. They didn't want anyone there snitching and ruining their business. I was eventually accepted into dorm fourteen, the Liquor store. Any given day, they sold from 10 to 20 gallons of homemade wine.

There were twenty-six dorms at the central facility, and more than half of the units had some type of illegal hustle going on. Dorm thirteen was the crack house, dorms nine and eleven sold the heroin and the sets (cancer medication) six and seven were the weed stores, twenty-three and twenty-one were the Love Boat stores, fifteen and sixteen were the regular stores, dorm twenty-four sold the sandwiches, dorm eight had the powder cocaine, and dorm one was the whore house. In dorm one, they had every type of sissy (homosexual) you could imagine.

I also saw a lot of correctional officers with substance abuse problems, and homosexual issues, which kept everything a float.

In '89, I'm still doing time,
Falling further and further back behind

Chapter 10

1989

In January of 1989, I was in the mist of my first prison riot. It seems that there was a power outage at the central facility, and both the primary and auxiliary generators malfunctioned. As a result, the entire complex was pitch-black. I mean, the place was so dark that a person couldn't see their hands before their eyes. This made the situation quite dangerous for correctional officers and snitches. Let's put it this way, a lot of dirty people got their just due that day. Mind you, there was also some senseless murder. I had a friend that attended the UDC college program with me who was actually quite bright, but it seems he had a beef with someone on the compound as a result, he was stabbed several times. The fellow whose name I won't mention later died.

The convicts took advantage of their uncommon freedom. They ran around like barbarians, looting, burning down buildings, raping officers, breaking into buildings, and clearing up old beefs. The slogan for the event was, "If you ain't with it, check in," and believe me, a lot of men checked in.

They burned down the automotive shop and the administrative building. A convict came up with the ingenious idea, since all our records were inside the Administrative Build, if they burned down the building, all the records would also burn up. Well, that idea went bust, for everything in the Administration Building did burn up: the offices, the visiting room, etc., everything but the records. They were in a steel, fire-proof safe. Thus for the next few months, we had to do without a visiting room.

The rioters attempted to burn down the church, but the Christians armed themselves with knives and protected their sanctuary. That's a good thing, because after the riot, we used the church as our visiting room.

The riot only went on for about five hours, but that five hours had to be an eternity for the officers running and hiding for their lives. There were police officers there from Fairfax, Lorton, and Washington, D.C. to patrol the perimeter. They didn't want to take any chances of even one of us fools getting out. They had the National Guard in full riot gear enter the prison in attempt to control the situation.

I remember being in the Hollow (dorms fifteen and sixteen) when the National Guard entered the prison. They came in through the motor pool, in attempts of giving the convicts a surprise attack. I know they wouldn't believe it, but the riot did have some organization prisoners had seen the National Guard coming in and watched while they organized their ranks. Before they could get into the main compound, the prisoners placed a lock on the gates separating the orientation units from the Hollow. That strategic strategy slowed down their progress for about twenty minutes. They had to send an officer to get a bolt cutter, which gave the convicts a chance to hide their weapons.

Contrary to thought, when we saw those soldiers marching into the prison, we knew we were going out on the football field, until they got the entire prison under control.

When I saw the guards marching, I went directly to my unit, dorm fourteen. I went to my locker and put on every piece of clothing I had. I think it was about two degrees that night, and I wasn't about to freeze while the officers got control of the prison.

I was the kind of youth that pull a lot of practical jokes, so when the older convicts in my dormitory saw me putting on all my clothing, they laughed. I tried to warn them that the National Guard was coming, but no one believed me. I guess I'd cried wolf too many times.

After I got fully dressed, I went over to the door and squatted down in a combat position. Boy, did that move bring laughter. A couple of guys were on the floor. They next moment, a tear gas canister came through the door, and several armed guards followed. They told everyone to come out of the building.

Since I was already positioned at the door, when they came in, I just slid out the door with my hands up. I was told to get down on the ground. I was then searched and lined up against the wall. The same men that laughed at me were beat with Slicks and gun barrels. The officers didn't even allow them to put on clothing. Some of the men were in their pajamas. I escaped the blunt of the force from the officers, because I was out the door and on the ground before they had set up their beating session.

We were all marched down to the football field and made to stay there until morning. I remember seeing my brother's best friend, Pete Brown, and a lot of other convicts I knew standing on that field in the cold. Pete and I smoked cigarettes and laughed at the antics the convicts and officers preformed. I think we were both fully dressed, so the cold didn't bother us right off.

I had another friend, Tim, who was nervous as hell. Apparently, Tim had saved an officer's life in dorm 26, and he was in fear of his life. The convicts had rushed in the unit in hopes of killing the officer, and Tim locked the office door so they couldn't get to the office. Tim was paranoid as hell. The next day, they moved him to another institution.

There were men on that field in their long underwear and shower slippers. Mind you, the temperature that night was about two degrees. I'll just say, some men got frost bite.

The Catholic Priest, Father Moore, came out on the field to survey the situation. The father was actually appalled by the cruel and unusual punishment. He actually called Mayor Barry for us.

When all the fathers' efforts were exhausted, the convicts took matters in their own hands. They proceeded to tear down the football bleachers, placed the wood in a large circle, and started a large barn fire. After the fires got to burning, we were actually warmer. The men that didn't have on too many clothes were allowed up front. I also saw a lot of male bonding with the homosexuals.

Around 6:00 am, we were allowed to return to our units. Apparently, the correctional officers called their union and complained about having to be out in that weather to watch us. They didn't have a fire with the magnitude as we did, so they were freezing themselves.

The actual riot took place on a Friday night. We were locked down the rest of the weekend, but Monday morning the prison was up and running as usual. The FBI did question several individuals about the murders, and several men were moved to federal penitentiaries, but the blunt of our punishment was the loss of our visiting privileges. Central was the only prison within the Lorton Complexes that had 7-day visiting. After the riot, we had visits on Tuesday, Thursday, Saturday and Sunday, like all the other institutions.

My father and Carol came down to see me the very next weekend. They were concerned about my wellbeing. I gave my dad and Carol some of the graphic details about the event that night, and I still remember to looks of terror they had in their faces. After experiencing such vulgarities, it would seem like I would have never wanted to ever set foot in another prison, but actually, after the riot, I felt like I'd passed the street test, for after those events, nothing ever bothered me again in life. I think I experienced some form of psychosis, for I had faced death and survived without a scratch. I had conquered the fear test.

I remember reading a book by motivational speaker, Les Brown. He made a statement in that book that has stuck with me until today. The statement was, "People prefer known hells to unknown heavens." From that moment on, I had already experienced prison, so prison was never a fear in mind again, but success was something I'd never really had, so I think I was afraid to venture totally in that direction. I understand today, the mistakes I've made, the fears I've had, and am finally ready to move forward in life, and venture through some of those doors to the unknown heavens.

I stayed at Central until May of 1989. From there I was sent to the minimum security facility. I finally got a chance to see my old buddy Colby again. I actually moved into the same dorm as he, and I became his bunk mate. I slept on the bottom, and he on top. We made our hook- ups and had our long drawn out conversations. The one thing that bothered me about the whole situation with Colby was the point that Slick Stand had come down and visited him several times. I'd been locked up only one year, but I had gotten locked up on Montana Avenue assisting Slick; I actually though we were closer than we really was.

Deep down inside, Slick Stand never really liked me. He looked upon me as someone that had everything on a silver spoon and didn't have enough sense to take advantage of the opportunities. My father warned me several times about Slick Stand. I guess he could see the evil in his eyes. I was just too stupid to pay attention.

I was given a job in the administration building as a clerk to the administrator, Mr. Link. I worked directly under Mrs. Welch and Robin. I had another convict that worked with me, Teddy Fields. We were mainly runners for the secretaries, even though I did type up a few parole and halfway-house packages. I also had my own computer and was given the task of creating a new census for the entire institution.

Colby had been down about five years, so he was eventually moved to the work training trailers. The work training trailers were for men that left the institution every day to work in society. They were men that had been down for decades, and work training was supposed to help them re-enter society. Those trailers were full of drugs and alcohol. The fence in that area was only about four feet, so you could literally step over the fence, walk to the liquor store, buy what you wanted, and be back before count. I know some guys that actually spent their Saturdays in hotels with their women. The place was off the hook back then.

I got the chance to get my civil service rating while in Minimum. The vocational instructor took us to 19th & E Street, Department of Personnel Management to take the test. That was my first time back in the city since my incarceration. I enjoyed seeing the cars and women for the first time in a while. I had a good time that day.

The vocational specialist's name was Ms. Cary Nobles. Ms. Nobles was a strong, intelligent woman that was very serious about prison reform. She actually wanted to see the ex-convicts succeed after prison. She put herself out on a limb several times for the men. It was truly a blessing to make her acquaintance.

I still remember the last visit I received from Carol. It was in the month of September 1989. She brought my son, Little Mike, to see me. We had a nice visit, but before she left, she explained to me that we no longer had a relationship. She told me that she had a new man, but I could always be a part of my son's life.

That statement went directly to my head; I was furious. For my entire period of incarceration, I had dreams of going home to my readymade family. I had plans to be a responsible father to my son and making a home for the three of us. When Carol made the statement she did, my entire world came crashing down on my head. I actually walked her and my son to the door, grabbed my son's baby bottle, and threw it into the prison yard. I got ten days work restriction for my actions. I know that was the sucker's way out, for my son never did anything to harm me; I just directed my hurt in the wrong direction.

My brother's friend, Francis Nichols, talked to me for hours. Nick was a lot older, and I respected his advice. He told me that she would eventually come around. That's another problem I always had; I'd listen to people in the street, but wouldn't listen to my father. I never looked at my father as street-wise.

Putting my hopes and my dreams in the hands of another human being was the biggest mistake of my life. While in prison, I had gone to college, completed drug programs, and became computer efficient, all in hopes of being with Carol and Little Mike once released. When the dream didn't materialize, I no longer cared about life. I looked for relief for my hurt and pain. I sort the relief through drugs.

I was sent to the Hope Village Halfway House on October 16, 1989. Hope Village was on Angle Place in South East Washington. Mind you, Angle Place was a drug haven at that time, and 90 percent of the prisoners released had some form of drug problem. I saw a lot of men and women sent back to the penitentiary for dirty urine's. Most of them, once they started getting high, they just escaped; which lead to further legal problems.

I got to hope Village on a Friday night. My brother Melvin brought me some Popeye's Chicken; my first street food in over a year. Petty Eddie, had been killed on Branch Avenue, only a week before my release. Ed had promised me a hand up once I was released, but that went sour after his death. I didn't want to mention money to his wife Alfreada, for she now had two children, and would need everything she had to take care of them.

On Sunday, October 18, 1989, I got a four-hour pass. I went directly to Carol's house. Her mother and sister Catty were excited to see me, but Carol seemed upset. I did get a chance to play with my son for an hour or so before I went to my see my mother and father. I still remember running late getting back to the halfway house. My old childhood buddy, Vincent Temple, gave me a ride back.

I eventually met up with Slick Stand and his little brother Tag. Keedie was in prison in Maryland, and Colby had about a year before he could be released. Can you believe the three of us actually went job hunting? We eventually found a job at Mash's Hams.

Around that same time, I met up with my old friend, Ray-Ray Ford. Ray-Ray had a lucrative heroin organization running on Division Avenue. Ray actually had about ten soldiers. Ray and I were also childhood buddies. Ray was from Kenilworth. Ray gave me $200 and a business proposition. The proposition was he would give me $10,000 worth of heroin in10 packs and I was to give him $5,000 back. As you may remember from the early parts of my book, I made the statement, "aint no money like dope money". Heroin was the quickest-selling drug in America. I knew I couldn't lose, so I took the deal. Besides, I did have Slick and his little brother Tag to help me.

I had the best possible situation at HopeVillage, the entire counseling staff in my house got high. All I had to do was to keep them high, and I could stay out as much as I wanted. I think I worked at Mash's Hams maybe two weeks; the rest of the time, I was at the Ebony Inn hustling. I don't think Slick or Tag worked two weeks. That job was very tiresome. We worked long hours in a freezer, preparing pork products. You actually smelled like a ham sandwich when you got off. The job didn't pay that much, but they did have unlimited overtime.

It took me about a month or so, but I finally got to Carol's heart. I still remember the last time we made love: December 9, 1989. I was so excited; the actual event didn't take that long; but the thing that stuck to my soul was the statement she made afterwards. She told me we could be together on the down-low, but she was in love with Perry Grant. I guess you could say I was a sucker, because that statement made me furious. I wanted my family back; I didn't want to play second fiddle to anyone. From that day on, I made it my business to screw every friend Carol had. When that didn't bring me anymore satisfaction, I sabotaged my own life; I started smoking crack again.

I still remember Christmas of 1989 I gave Carol my entire paycheck from Mash's Hams to go Christmas shopping. She got everyone something nice but me. I think she was upset because at the time, I was messing with Tommie Broadway's niece, LaTarsha. Carol told me Tarsha was going to bring me down. I think she feared I'd give Tarsha more than I'd given her.

I still remember coming by Carol's house on Christmas day to pick up Little Mike. She handed me a little box, and said Merry Christmas. I was ecstatic. When Little Mike and I got to my mother's, I opened the gift. Mike actually helped me unwrap it. Inside, the box was empty, all except for an old sock and three condoms. There was also an inscription:

"Use these on your new woman." My mother laughed at me for hours; she even called me a "sucker for love."

I think it actually took me more than ten years to get over Carol. I still love her, but she doesn't have the same significance to me now. Today, I care more about myself and my own feelings.

1990, a new decade;
All my dreams began to fade
Because I was smoking that pipe
And that ain't right;
I lost everything I'd gained in life.
I was looking really bad and feeling real sad;
Started snatching pocket books like a fag...

Chapter 11

1990

In January 1990, I was still in the Hope Village Halfway House. Fate finally caught up with me, for all the addicted office workers were fired. They had hired a new, more efficient job counselor. He sent a lot of dudes back to prison for not having a job. I pretty much had my paperwork in order. I was a computer wizard, so I could forge any type of document made.

About three days before this big crackdown on staff, Carol's uncle, Roger Beam, who was in charge of union local 639, got me a union job at a furniture company on Central Avenue. I was a forklift operator.

I made a decent salary, and I still had my dope business running on Sheriff Road.

The new job counselor took all my privileges. I actually went back to the halfway house, one hour after I got off work. That loss of freedom put a hamper on my drug business. I had just recently gotten a large quantity of cocaine from my man Big John. John had given me the coke on consignment, and I hadn't paid him a dime. I was in a real predicament.

Luck had it that on the very next Monday, The Early Powers Act (EPA) came out. What that meant was that anyone that was within six months of release ninety days was automatically deducted from their sentence. I only had a twenty-month sentence, and my entire sentence would be complete in April of 1990, so the EPA put me out the door.

I had probation, to follow, but otherwise I was as free as a bee. I celebrated with my old friend Darryl Dickey. Darryl, Kenny, Tina, and I all got high as hell that night. This was the very first time I'd done cocaine in over a year. I just knew I could handle the effects. I knew cocaine had completely dominated my life before prison, but my smart ass figured I was stronger and could handle the drug.

Cocaine is like a demon; once you release yourself from this demon, and decide to go back to the demon again, the old demon is twice as strong, plus he bring about three more demons to help possess you mind, body, and soul. That one hit went straight to my head. I was addicted from that day on. I know today how much I love cocaine, so there is no sense in me even trying the drug unless I want to go nuts again.

I eventually moved in with LaTarsha's mother, Bootsey, and her brothers Donald and Jay-Jay. At that time, they had a home in Cheverly, Maryland. The house was beautiful, a brick home with a pool in the back. The only problem was Bootsey was the only one in the home working.

Bootsey did have a roommate, Jean, but the two of them couldn't handle the bills of that home. Donald and Tarsha were doing their thing, getting high, and Jay-Jay was still in high school at Fairmont Heights. Tarsha's younger sister Noreen worked at the federal parole office, but she had her own apartment in District Heights. Their step-father, Britt, was a hustler and gambler who stayed on the road most of the time, trying to make his living. He did come home with money from time to time, but the bolt that held the family together was Bootsey. Bootsey was a very strong woman, but the stress of having a man on the road and two drug-addicted children was wearing her thin. To keep her spirits up she partook in the drinking of spirits.

Tarsha was recovering from a cancer operation, so she pretty much did her. I think she is a beautiful woman, but she definitely needed some psychological counseling in 1990. She was given a terminal diagnosis, so she had completely given up on life. The only thing that mattered to her was relieving her pain.

In the 80's, Tarsha had been diagnosed with cancer of the uterus. She had been through several surgeries, loss of hair, chemo therapy, loss of self-esteem, and loss of trust; by the time I was released from prison. Thus, I was now with a very hurt young lady. I still wanted to be her knight in shining armor; the man that revived her to her normal self. I learned the hard way that I couldn't achieve that task if I had a wizard, two witches, and a warlock.

When I first saw her in front of the Ebony Inn in 1989, my mind jumped back to my last recollection of Tarsha; right after her graduation from Fairmont Heights High School. She was the most beautiful cat eyed girl I'd ever seen. I guess I was still stuck in the past, because I just couldn't accept the fact that the woman that was before my eyes was not the same person I was infatuated with six years earlier. My crazy ass tried to will her to be that person. Tarsha and I had our ups and downs but we both cared for each other.

At that time, I had another friend named Karen. I used to sneak off with her from time to time. She was a Janet Jackson look alike. Her only flaw was that she loved to smoke crack. Her entire life centered on getting high. I think that's why we got along so well. We had a lot of neurotic sexual rendezvous. On one particular night, we had already gone through a quarter ounce, and she just had to have something else. I had more cocaine stashed, but I didn't want the person I had holding it to know I was getting high, so we had to go out at 3:00 am to a strip to try and find some. We ended up on C Street in South-East Washington. I didn't want to drive her car, so we called a friend named Greg to drive us.

Greg drove a 78 Datsun B210, and the car didn't start unless you pushed it. I brought him $6.00 worth of gas and a bag of dope from Lincoln Heights. When we got to C Street, I gave Greg the explicit directions not to cut that car off because I didn't want to have to go through the tedious task of pushing the car to start it. I put my 380 in my dip, and proceeded to a building to cop.

Once inside, I noticed a Jamaican sitting on the top stairs. I asked him did he have anything, and he told me to come on up the stairs. Once I was at the top step, he told me he only had $50 rocks. I told him I had approximately $49.50 and handed him the money. At that exact moment, he reached over and slapped me. I couldn't believe what had happened. His next statement was, "I told you not to come around here short again," he said. "I keep your money."

I pulled out my pistol and shot him directly in the ass. I stood over him, I know, sixty seconds contemplating killing him, but for some strange reason, I maintained my composure. I told him to give me all his money and all of his crack. He had about $3,000 in cash and about $5,000 in crack, and I took it all. I also told him that if he made a noise, I'd blow his head off.

I proceeded back to the car, and when I got there Greg had cut it off. He had a rag and a spray bottle, washing his windows. When I got to the car, he saw something was wrong, for I was sweating perversely. It took us about five minutes to get that car started. Once we got the car started, a jeep came up behind us and shot off the driver's side mirror. There we went on a high-speed get away, down Benning Road, them shooting at me, and me shooting back.

When I ran almost out of ammunition, I suggested we go to the police precinct on 42nd street and Benning Road. We made it to the police precinct; the jeep was directly behind me. I just knew they wouldn't follow us inside the precinct parking area, but they did.

I still remember the driver pointing at me and saying, "I'm going to kill all of you." We darted out the parking lot and went through a yellow signal light. A police car had pulled up to the light in the opposite direction. I guess our pursuers didn't want to chance arrest, so they didn't follow us through the light. We made a right turn at the top of the hill and went through an alley. At that moment, I remembered I had a friend named James Cleaver that lived in that alley. Finally we made it to his house, parked the car in the backyard, and raised our hood. James kept a lot of junk cars in his back yard, so with our hood up, the car fit right into the landscape.

The three of us ran to James' back door and knocked like our life depended on it. James opened the door with pipe in hand, as usual. He let us in and directed us to the dining room. The three of us were totally out of breath. There was a girl their named Fee-Fee who was on her way out. I gave Fee-Fee a $50 rock and told her that if anyone asked, she hadn't seen us. She thanked me and left out the front door. To my surprise, the jeep pulled right up in front of Fee-Fee as she started down the street. I guess they scared her to death, because she pointed back at James' house and ran.

The four men exited the jeep with guns in hand. The one with the shotgun took the butt off it and banged on James' front door. They announced, "If we were not sent out, they would kill everyone in the house.

James had just taken a hit of crack, and that statement almost sent him into shock. James immediately stated, "Moore, what did you take from those people? I've got my family in here. I've got to put you out." I pulled out the large zip lock bag of crack, and James instantly got some heart. He said, "Moore, you've got too much coke to be put out," and went directly to the phone and called 911. Within minutes, the entire house was surrounded by police. The police successfully arrested all four of our tormentors, guns and all.

Greg, Karen and I were ecstatic. After the police had gone, I attempted to give James $300 worth of crack. James insisted that we take a hit with him, so we followed him upstairs to his wife's room.

James' wife's name was Renee. She was a nice lady that worked very hard to take care of James and their two children. James yelled at her so much, so Renee's nerves were shot. James told Renee to go in the room with the children.

They both left the room at the same time. James came back two minutes later with three beers and a bucket of water. I told James the cocaine was already cooked up, so we didn't need any water; he just shook his head and left out again. This time, he came back with a hammer and nails. I pulled out my gun and stated, "James I just know you aren't up to nothing crazy. Please don't make me shoot you."

At that precise moment, James nailed us in the room. When I went towards him, he ran to the window and threw the hammer out. We stayed in that room four days. Finally, I bribed someone walking by to come up and get us out. When I left James' house, I might have had $500 worth of crack left.

Smoking crack for days had me totally disturbed. Once out, we made a beeline for Lincoln Heights and bought an entire ten pack. I had to snort three bags before I came down.

Heroin is a downer, and cocaine is an upper; in order to quickly come down off cocaine high, you have to use some form of downer. This is called speed-balling, and is very dangerous to the heart. We had smoked so much crack rocks over that 4-day period my equilibrium was off. I was paranoid, seeing things, completely disturbed. That four-day binge led to years of misery and pain.

By me hanging out and not handling my business, I opened the door for Slick to renegotiate our deal with Ray-Ray. The new deal completely cut me out, but instead of me going to Ray like a man, I sought assistance from my old friend, the crack pipe. I can't be mad at Slick; he simply handled his business.

My probation Officer at that time was Ms. Diane Pickard. She was a very nice white lady that saw all the potential I possessed. I was nothing like her other probationers as far as education was concerned, so she really tried to help me. She only required me to take a urine test once a month, so I had time to clean up my act. Cocaine and heroin only stay in your system seventy-two hours or so, depending on the amount of usage. All I had to do was stop getting high a week before I was to be tested. I never got a dirty urine test for the entire five years I was on probation.

Without the money from the heroin operation, I had a hard time financially. I was trying to keep up my image and get high at the same time. Everyone knew what I was doing; the only person I fooled was myself.

That's when I realized I had a drug habit. As long as I had an unlimited supply and didn't have to look for the stuff, I functioned normally. Now that I didn't have a supply of heroin or cocaine, I had to actually hustle to stay high. Addiction was the hardest job I've ever had. It's a lot of work staying high. Drugs are expensive, and I was living beyond my means. Trying to be discrete with my usage put me in some very dangerous areas. Kenilworth Projects was a very dangerous spot, especially since I was once a big time dealer. The other addicts saw me as free high, someone from a good home that had access to big bucks.

My family has always kept up appearances for the neighbors. We kept our problems internally, everything except Ronald's and my addictions. That's why we were outcasts, embarrassments, undesirables. From the outside looking in, you would think of them as the Cosby's with two wayward sons. People thought we had money. We were successful, but little did they know we had some deep rooted problems.

In my travels to get high, I ran across people that were once successful but had let drugs bring them down. Then there were others that had no class but sold drugs. They felt that the drugs could fill the void for all those years of a poor upbringing. I saw a lot of women lose their dignity by dealing with men that they wouldn't give a second glance to if not for the narcotics they loved. Addiction is just another form of slavery; it controls your mind, body, and soul.

I remember hanging out with one of my buddies, Dead Face. We had been up on 48th Street all night getting high. I had about a $20 rock left, so we sat in Dean Wood Park and smoked it. Once the rock was gone, I notice a lady I thought I knew walking through the park. I jumped up and ran toward her. Dead Face thought I was losing my mind. I walked up to her and asked for my money. She looked at me like I was crazy.

I thought she was the women I had given $50 to on Quarles Street, to get me some more cocaine. That particular woman never came back with my money or cocaine. I asked once again for my money. When she didn't answer, I snatched the pocketbook off her shoulder. I started to look in it, but Dead Face tried to tackle me. I was thinking in my mind, he was trying to take the money from me, so I ran.

Once I got to 49th Street, a Capital Police officer was on my tail. She had been coming out of her house and had seen the entire incident. That's when the chase began.

I ran through the back of the apartments on 49th Street, through the alley, and all the way to Eastern Avenue. Once I was on Eastern Avenue, I notice a red car following me, so I attempted to run up on the train tracks. When I got to the top of the wooded hill, I noticed that a new barbed wire fence had been put up. The officer had gotten out of her car and was looking for a way to follow me.

Since I had grown up in the area, I knew all the shortcuts. I slipped down another path and ended up back on Eastern Avenue. I ran to the top of the hill and made a left on Olive Street, then ran past a few houses and slipped down an alley. I came out of that alley on the other side of Quarles Street. Quarles Street is separated by the Dean wood Subway Station. When I came out of the alley, the officer was getting out of her car with her gun drawn. Only by the luck of God did I slipped past her and ran down another alley. I went through a yard and down the railroad tracks. I ran down those tracks until I got to the path that led to my mother's house.

I came out the path, crossed Olive Street on the Maryland side, and jumped my parents' back wall. I slipped in the back door and ran directly to my room. I took off all my clothing, shaved my head, and got in the bathtub.

I know I couldn't have been there ten minutes when the front door bell rang. It was Dead Face. Apparently, he had been caught, and they had scared him into telling them where I lived.

My mother answered the door. She had been watching my daughter Ricka while her mother worked, so my daughter was directly behind my mom. The officer stated that I had been involved in a robbery and that they were looking for me for questioning. My mother told them that I wasn't home. At that exact moment, my daughter told the police I was upstairs in my room. Without a search warrant or even consent, the officer pushed my mother out the way and rushed up the stairs.

My father was still asleep when the officers arrived, so he was very startled to see two large, white police officers in his home unannounced. They came into my room with their guns drawn. I was instructed to lie on my face. After calling for backup, I was taken to the front of my mother's home to be identified by the victim. Since I had changed my clothing and shaved my head and face, they had a hard time identifying me. They finally got Dead Face to identify me and made him a witness for the State.

The only flaw in their arrest was that they had come across state lines without being in hot pursuit. The actual crime was committed in Washington, D.C., and my parents lived in Maryland. Thus, they had to call the Prince George's Police Department to make the arrest.

To my luck, Officer Mathews and his partner were sent. Mathews knew me from the Ebony Inn. We also used to shoot basketball together on the weekends at the South Bowie Recreation Center. They knew me as a drug dealer, not as a pocket-book snatcher. They couldn't fathom in their mines me having done such a thing. Even though the District police asked them to hold me until they retrieved a warrant, they simply handcuffed me, drove me to the Ebony Inn, and released me. I still remember Officer Mathews saying, "I'm getting ready to get off. I don't feel like filling out any paperwork. If D.C. wants you bad enough, they'll get a warrant."

It only took about a week before my mother's house was surrounded again. This time I wasn't there for real. I think it took them another six months to catch me.

The thing that bothered me the most about my arrest was the fact that my baby daughter told the police I was in the house. I know at the time she was only five years old, but I still remember her teasing me about her getting me locked up. She is very smart. I know she knew what she was doing. I think that's one of the reasons we aren't that close today. I'm still holding the grudge. Now that I've had the chance to express my feelings towards the situation, I truly see how silly I've been all these years.

In November of 1990, I got a job at Joseph Smith & Sons. The scare of incarceration straightened me up for a while. The Smiths were from Forestville, Maryland. They had a large plantation there, but the place where I worked in Beaver Heights, Maryland, was a recycling plant. There, they crushed automobiles and recycled paper and every type of metal imaginable. A new kind of modern day slavery....

I was hired as a purchasing agent. I purchased every part, belt, motor, bolt, screw, and conveyor on that yard. I even picked up the lunches for the entire yard. Paul Smith wanted the yard to run 24 hours a day, so he purchased our lunches. That way, we didn't have to leave the yard for anything. That process worked during the week, but on Fridays when the men got paid, they made a beeline to the liquor store to cash their checks.

The majority of the employees there were alcoholics, ex-cons, and drug addicts. The place consisted of dirt, oil, and mud. When you left that place you were filthy. Mind you, there were a few hillbillies there from West Virginia. They stayed with friends in Maryland during the week, and went home to West Virginia on the weekends.

I had my own truck, and my supervisor made a list of all the items he needed and the cheapest places to buy them. I brought everything with cash. Every morning, I signed a promissory note for the money I needed and was on my way. There was a very sweet cashier there named Mrs. Black. She had been with the company since the beginning. Carl Smith trusted her with everything.

I started that job with the best of intentions. I lived a block from the job, so I could walk to work; everything was so convenient. Little did I know my addiction was waiting in dormant for me to get a big paycheck.

When I got my first paycheck, I went straight home and gave my father half. Then, I went around the corner to my friend Tony's house. Tony and my brother Ronald were friends. He had spent a considerable amount of time in the Maryland Department of Corrections, and I looked up to him. Tony and his sister Pat were the best hosts. They would bring you soda, cookies, and paper napkins while you got high.

Like a fool, I thought I could have some control over my crack usage like a fool. I brought a $50 rock and shared it with Tony. That rock went so fast before I knew it I'd spent $200. Once I was almost broke, Tony came up with the story about his mother being up and me having to leave immediately. They say, "One hit is too many and a Thousand is never enough", that's one statement that is totally true. You never get enough crack. They don't print enough money at the Bureau of Engraving to smoke that stuff.

The only way I could ever control my crack usage was to snort two bags of heroin before I started smoking." That's what they call speed balling. Being dual-addicted is very expensive. I was afraid of getting addicted to heroin, so I just messed up all my money smoking crack. I went home many nights feeling stupid as hell.

I guess my father thought I would grow out of it or something. He used to just look at me as though I was crazy back then. He did tell me to join the Muslims. He said they had a cure for addiction. He said if they could cure Malcolm X, they could cure anyone.

In '91, I had big fun.
Tim Gordon came home; a new dream begun.
We made big money every day,
But I was doing it in the right way.
See, I was snorting that dope,
And that ain't no joke;
My mother and father lost all hope.
I got hit by a car,
My biggest pain by far;
For the next four years, a wheelchair was my car.

CHAPTER 12

1991

In January of 1991, I was still working for Joseph Smith & Sons. The police were looking for me, so I moved back in with Tarsha and her family. They had moved from the house in Cheverly to an apartment in Landover, Maryland, Belle Haven Apartments. They had a three-bedroom apartment, so I wasn't putting anyone out by staying there. Besides I was working, and could be quite helpful to them financially.

Tarsha's brother James and I came up with the ingenious idea that we could sell crack cocaine at the Ebony Inn and on Farmingdale Street in Fairmont Heights Maryland in the evenings after I got off work, and he got out of high school. We did quite well with that venture up until Tarsha found the entire stash of crack and ran off with it. She knew we loved her, and so there wouldn't be any physical repercussions.

Tarsha could smell drugs, or she was just nosey as hell. However you may put it, she could find a crack rock in white gravel. Once again, I was putting someone else's wellbeing ahead of my own. Tarsha had been diagnosed with terminal cancer, and I was afraid to leave her. I had some crazy notion in my head that if I left her and she died, I'd feel guilty for the rest of my life, so I continuously put up with her shit.

After she ran off, I think it simply broke my spirits, because I too went on a binge. I messed up some money that Bootsey was planning to pay bills with. I felt so bad I went back to my mother's house that night so I could walk to work and borrow the money from my boss. Little did I know, the police would be waiting at my mother's for me...

I was arrested by the Prince George's County Police department, in front of my mother's house at 4:00 am. I had a fugitive warrant for robbery in Washington, D.C. Since I didn't have any charges in the State of Maryland, D.C. was given seventy-two hours to come get me. They transported me to Upper Marlboro Jail to await extradition.

Exactly seventy-two hours later, D.C. came to get me. I was taken to the 6th District Police Station to meet with robbery detectives. That particular day, there was a snow storm in Washington, so the courts and everything else closed early. I never got to see the detectives. I sat in the Bull Pen for two days because of that storm.

On the third day, I was taken to the Superior Court for a bail hearing. At that time, the city jail was full to capacity, so I was released to Third Party Custody.

Third Party Custody was a bullshit organization that was supposed to monitor people that had been released on pre-trial release.You reported to their offices twice a week, signed in, and went back to your life of crime. I reported to a place on 9th and U Street North West. It was an all-black organization, and they took money under the table. I never took a urine test the entire time I was there.

My probation officer, Diane Pickard, was totally upset about my arrest. She did say she wouldn't violate me unless I was actually found guilty.

Once I was back in society, I went back to work at Joseph Smith's. When I got there, my supervisor had my last check in his hand. I had asked my mother to call my job while I was being arrested. Apparently, she didn't think I was going to get out, so she never bothered to call. Every story I came up with for my boss, he simply batted down. Honestly, I was glad they had fired me. I had been stealing for months; and my father had scared me with talk of auditors checking the books.

I still owed Bootsey the money I had messed up the night before my arrest, so I made a deal with my father to paint his entire house so I could pay Bootsey. Bootsey sent James over to my parent's house with my clothing I had left over their house, and I paid him her money. Bootsey's husband, Brit, told me I could never stay there again.

I started hanging out on Division Avenue during the days and Ebony Inn at night. I did a little juggling, but only enough to survive and stay high. I also started sorting heroin regularly. When you smoke crack, the high only lasts for a few seconds. The depression stage lasts for hours. To keep from continuously experiencing the down, I started snorting dope. With the dope in my system, I could function normally after taking a hit of crack. Without the dope in my system, I was stuck on stupid. I simply couldn't put the pipe down.

Around that same time Timmy Gordon got out of the Maryland Department of Corrections. He had been arrested five years earlier for assisting his mother in a drug sale. When Timmy first came home, he had dreams of opening his own landscaping business, which required money and equipment. He brought a used truck, but buying all the lawnmowers was a different story. Eventually, Tim had to supplement his income, so he started hustling again.

Getting the business off the ground was hard, for his older brother Brezzy didn't want him to go down that road. Brezzy had established himself as the cocaine king of North-East, and a lot of hustlers had a great deal of respect for him. Brezzy told everybody that was anybody, not to do drug deals with Timmy.

I had a friend from Palmer Park who went by Orange Juice, and I asked him to look out for Timmy as a personal favor. At that time, Orange Juice was the man, as far as weight in the cocaine game was concerned. At that time, everybody knew I was getting high, so to keep from killing me, nobody trusted me with any large quantities of drugs on consignment. Timmy was a different story. His reputation wasn't as bad as mine; besides, everyone knew his brother was the man, so they could always go to him if Timmy messed up in any way.

I think the first large amount Timmy and I got was a quarter kilo, equivalent to nine ounces. I was in cocaine heaven again. I made a lot of money every day, but I smoked coke and snorted dope all night. I guess the ends exceeded the means, so I never had any money. It's sad to think that I sold $6,000.00 a day in drugs but smoked and snorted up all my profits. Boy, was I stuck on stupid.

During this time, Tarsha's younger sister, Noreen, talked her into going into the RAP Drug Treatment Program. It was an eighteen-month inpatient program. I prayed every day that she would get her life back in order. The problem was, I should have been praying for myself.

After about six months, Tarsha got a home visit. We made love for hours before she went back. Two weeks later, she quit the program. I guess I did something right or something wrong, because she wanted to keep an eye on me. She always had her slickness, so I knew I wasn't the only person she was seeing, but I wasn't with anyone, so I went along with the program.

Tommy Broadway Sr. opened a new restaurant in Upper Marlboro, directly across from the courts. The place was a money maker, and he allowed Tarsha and Bootsey to run the place. They did quite well, and Tarsha even brought herself a used car. That car of hers got me in trouble, because she was now able to ride around at night and look for my ass. I still remember being in the Kenilworth projects, getting high, when she paid a girl name Mira $5 to show her where I was. When she saw me come out of that house twisted, she commenced to beating me upside the head. The cat-fight went on for about fifteen minutes before I ran away from her.

When she returned to her car, someone had tried to break in it. She had left her purse in the car, and someone had jimmied the front driver's side door. They didn't get the purse, but they messed up her door pretty bad. That made her furious. She tried to run me over with the car. I eventually ducked her and made it back to my parents' house.

The very next night, October 3, 1991, the anniversary of the day my brother was killed at the Ebony Inn; I called Tarsha to say I was sorry about her car door and that I would pay for it. We had a decent conversation, but something just wasn't right. I had a bad feeling.

That night, I had been in the Ebony Inn sitting at the bar drinking a Gin & Orange Juice, when it donnish on me to call Tarsha. Timmy had left me in charge, so I didn't want to be too far from the thick of things. I walked across the street from the liquor store on Sheriff Road to use the pay phone.

After our conversation, I remember crossing back across the Sheriff road. Phonso was working for Timmy at the time, and he had all of the heroin. He was having a problem with Black Bonnie. They were arguing over a bag of dope. Phonso stopped me in the middle of Sheriff Road to ask me if he could sell Black Bonnie a bag for $15. I remember telling him that Timmy said no shorts, and the next few hours were a blur.

I got hit by a 1986 Lincoln Continental. That car knocked me twenty-seven feet in the air. I went higher than the telephone wires. When I came down, I landed on my head. The car then road up the grassy hill and hit the Animal Hospital. The car then rolled backwards, and crushed both my legs. But after the initial hit, I never felt a thing.

I do remember having an out-of-body experience. I remember seeing a man lying on the ground in a pool of blood. There were people all around him. There was an old lady across the street with a bag on her head, sitting on a bucket cursing everyone. Then at the next moment, I saw my brother's friend Jimmy Guy. The thing that bothered me was that Jimmy Guy had been dead seven years. I remember saying to Jimmy, "Who is that dude laying on the ground? He looks really hurt." Jimmy told me I was that man. He also said, It wasn't my time, and I needed to get back in that body.

I was having trouble hearing Jimmy because of the old woman making all that noise. When I turned around to say something else to Jimmy, he was gone. I walked over and took a look at the man lying in the blood, and it was in fact me. That next moment, I saw my brother Ronald walking in my direction. He had an iced tea cocktail in his left hand. The next thing I remember was him slapping me. He said, "Boy, get back in that body, if something happens to you, it would kill Momma." I woke up hours later in Prince George's Hospital.

My entire family was at the hospital. The fact of me being at the Ebony Inn after Ronald's death had them up set alone. The fact that I might be paralyzed made them even more worried. My father was the first one in the room to see me. I was happy to see him, but I was also thinking the police officer in the room might attempt to search me. I had about $300 worth of crack in my rectum. I gave the coke to my father like a fool and asked him to hold it for me. My dad made a beeline to the toilet to flush the stuff.

The next day, Faggy Brian came to see me. He said he was there when the accident occurred, and that car had jumped the curb and hit me. He also told me I was pronounced dead for a while. The next thing he asked me still has me in awe. He asked me if I saw the old woman sitting on the bucket across the street from the Ebony Inn. I told him, "Yes I did see the old lady. Who was she?" Faggy Brian told me that in the 1950s, that old lady's son had been killed by a car on that same Sheriff Road. He said the boy was her only child, and the old lady was a witch. He claimed that that old lady had placed a curse on Sheriff Road, and when you were close to death, you always saw her. That story still gives me chills today. More people have died being hit by cars on that road than on any other street in the state of Maryland. Since then, the county has widened the road and put in better lighting.

When I totally regained consciousness, I was on a gurney in Prince George's Hospital. I had lost the use of my legs. There were rods extending from my calves. I looked like a monster. I had been operated on by Dr. Willie Blair, one of the best surgeons in the state of Maryland.

I come from a very influential family, so I was given the best of medical treatment. The average drug addict that came to the hospital would have had his legs amputated.

When I realized I couldn't move my legs, I went through some extreme mental problems. I had always been an athlete, a jock, a runner, and a basketball player for my entire life; what was I going to do without the use of my legs? I would run for miles when stress got me down or at least until I got the euphoric feeling from running. The running really cleared my head. I now had no way of releasing my frustrations.

All through my life, even though I may have been strung out on drugs, my personal appearance meant the world to me. Now, I was a freak of nature in my own eyes. For the first few weeks, I had a hard time accepting my new physical impairment. I wanted to die.

I had family and friends visit me at the hospital, and they couldn't bear the sight of my legs. Carol brought Little Mike to see me, and he couldn't look at me. Tarsha and Bootsey came, and Bootsey sat at the far end of the room.

I even had a Minister, Pastor Davis, visit me and tell me "God had punished me for getting saved, and continuing in my evil ways." He said Satan wanted to kill me, but God had kept me around for a specific purpose. I have been seeking out that particular purpose for the last fifteen years. I honestly believe, through me telling this story, I will gain some type of redemption in God's eyes. Hopefully, if the youth of America reads my book and takes the subject matter seriously, they won't have to experience my pain.

I know my family dreaded the thought of having to have to take care of me. I had temporary paralysis. I needed help in doing everything. I think it was my father that snapped me out of my mental stupor. My dad told me that he was now in charge of my life, and I was now to dance to his tune. My father and I hadn't been that close since my brother Ronald's death. I know my father loved me and only wanted the best for me, but my crazy ass refused to listen. As they say, "A hard head makes a soft behind."

I stayed in Prince George's Hospital for over a month. The entire time they kept me twisted on Demerol. I never liked needles, but the pain from my accident was so excruciating that my hand stayed on the nurses call button. The high I got from the Demerol was even better than heroin, and it lasted a little longer.

The nurses tried to detox me off the Demerol, but when they did, I started hyperventilating and having seizures; so they just decreased my dosage. Too bad they didn't write that my dosage was decreased in the log book, for when the night shift came, I got my full does again.

My court date for the robbery was postponed indefinitely because of my accident. I was in such a bad condition; I couldn't make it to court if I wanted too. That worked to my advantage, for at least I didn't have to go to prison in a wheelchair. Not yet, anyway.

I did have a few friends that came to visit me and didn't give a dam about my legs. First, there was Gator and Heef, who started a crap game with the hospital orderlies. The game lasted from Friday night to Saturday. On a Saturday night a few weeks into my stay came Mr. Eddy Thompson and Duncan Hayes; they were too drunk to notice my legs anyway. They ran around the hospital with alcohol reeking from their pores, harassing nurses. The hospital was so upset with my visitors and my not having any insurance that the very next day, I was placed on a gurney, put in an ambulance, and dropped off in my mother's dining room. The nurses called my mother to warn her I was on my way. I didn't even have any clothing on except a hospital gown. My father put my bed in the dining room, and that was my new home for the next three years.

My first night home, Timmy visited me. He gave me five bags of dope and a few dollars. At about 3:00 am that morning, my father awakened me, complaining about the smell of rubber burning. I guess he thought Timmy left me some crack. I hadn't smoked any crack in over a month, and my mind wasn't on the drug, but my father's constant bickering made me want a hit of crack some kind of bad.

In '92, my man Tim was through,
Most folks said, 'Mike that should have been you."
Three bullets to the head
My man was dead;
And no one to see his kids were fed...

Chapter 13

1992

Timmy was killed in a drug buy gone badly in February of 1992. He was only thirty-three years old. I've outlived him and Ronald. Timmy and I were dealing with Orange Juice, but Timmy met some new people that gave him a better deal, so he chose to jump ship. That ship-jumping cost him his life.

Timmy's body was found on Texas Avenue in South East Washington. His truck was found at a Bowling Alley in the Greenway Shopping Center. I'd missed death by only a few minutes. Usually when Timmy went to cop, I'd ride shot gun. I think that was his way of letting me get some air. I was usually trapped in the house, and I really looked forward to our excursions.

That particular day, I had purchased a car and was waiting for the mechanic to bring the car back to me. I tried to get Timmy to wait for me, but he was in a hurry. That afternoon, at T & T Carryout, was the last time I saw Timmy alive. He was on the phone with his murders. His sister later called my mother's house to give me the bad news.

I was highly upset about the incident. At 8:30 pm that night, the guy still hadn't brought my car back, so I accepted a ride to Timmy's mother's house in a stolen car with Greg, the same buddy I'd been with in the 1990 shoot-out. When we got to Timmy's mother's house, there were about one-hundred cars out front. Greg went in and got Timmy's sister Cee-Cee. She came out to the car and explained everything to me since I was unable to walk.

Cee-Cee told me Timmy had died at D.C. General Hospital. They were all in the house consoling his mother and making funeral plans. A few of our other friends were plotting on his murderers. I had all the heart in the world, but no legs. I still did what I had to do. I still actually believe the person that killed Timmy hung himself in his mother's basement.

Three days after Tim's death, I remember being in my mother's house in the bed. It was about 3:00 am in the morning, and everyone in my mother's house was asleep. That's when the doorbell started ringing over and over again. I yelled for my mother or father to get the front door, but no one moved. Tired of listening to the bell ring, I got into my wheelchair and rolled to the front door. When I opened the front door, to my surprise, Timmy was standing there. Me, like a fool opened the door. When he walked in, my heart skipped a few beats. He looked stronger, and wiser.

The first thing Tim said was for me to get out of that chair. I told him that I couldn't walk. He abruptly answered me, "Yes you can". Then he snatched me in my chest and pulled me out of the chair. To my surprise, I was really standing.

Tim told me he needed me to take a ride with him. I'll never forget the car he was driving, a brand new black 300zx. The car looked like a space-ship on the inside. We rode for about an hour, mostly talking about my life. Since my brother Ronald had died, Tim took up the role of my older brother. He tried to teach me everything he knew and protect me as much as possible. My crazy ass just wouldn't listen. He had been down the addiction road and tried to let me know that there was no future for an addict.

That's when the car stopped. We were in a project of some sort. On one side of the street it was so dark that you couldn't see your hands before your face. You could hear people laughing, women moaning. Everyone sounded high as hell. On the other side of the street, the street lights very bright. I saw children playing and mothers sitting close by, watching with joy in their eyes.

Tim told me to get out the car and walk to dark side of the street. He said that's the place I've always wanted to be; my heaven, my place of ecstasy. I told Tim, "I'm not going down there, I can't see a thing." He told me, "That's right, my brother, Stay to the light; stay away from the darkness." The last thing I remember him saying was that I would walk again.

I awoke the next morning, fully clothed, mud on my shoes, and my wheel chair still at the front door. The first thing my mother asked me when she woke up was, "Where did you go last night?" I still can't explain what happened. That was the realest dream I've ever had.

The funeral was held on Division Avenue at his family's church. They had the wake and the funeral the same day. I was determined to walk into the funeral home. I had a walker that I was given at the hospital, but I never went to therapy. I called my buddy Gator and asked him to pick me up for the funeral. When he arrived, he was astonished to see me attempting to walk. I did the best I could do with Gator's help, but before that day, I had never tried to walk. Tim, in a dream or another dimension, gave me the strength to rise to my feet.

That strength soon dissipated. I had no one to help me financially, with my drug habits, or with life itself. As a result, I took refuge in a wheelchair. The only motivation I had was my addiction. I had to figure out a way to stay high. I no longer had the luxury of mobility, so I had to come up with a gimmick to keep me high in that wheelchair.

That gimmick was panhandling. People naturally felt sorry for me because of my physical state. All I had to do now was to find a unique way to exploit it. I always had what they call "a gift of gab," so I used my creativity to come with slick rhymes to deepen people's feelings. This actual book was written from a poem I created in 1992 called "Ten Years of Disaster." Now, the ten years have turned into twenty-four years. I had an unlimited amount of time to think and write. I no longer had the luxury of a woman, or close friends. I was now a drug addicted hermit.

During this time, my personality changed from that of an extrovert to an introvert. I climbed into a shell within my mind. I created a new world. A world that only consisted of three things: juggling to get high, looking for the product, and actually getting high. I lived, existed, and thrived only to have the euphoric feelings of heroin and cocaine. The drugs were my legs, my world, and my existence.

I also came up with a way to sell the lottery numbers to customers at the liquor store on Kenilworth and Eastern Avenue. The name of the store was Franks Tavern. It was there that I posted up daily in my wheelchair rapping for change. I took panhandling to a new level. On a good day, I'd make between $200 and $300. Some people made it their business to give me something every time they came to the store.

I even had a man that went to the grocery store and purchased three full bags of groceries. I had told him I was hungry. My father and I both felt embarrassed when the man pulled up at our home with the food. Mind you, we lived in a baby mansion. Even though at the time, my parents were both senior citizens and receiving pensions and social security, we never went a day without food. In fact, because of my crack usage, I wouldn't eat if you paid me at the time

My favorite line during that time was:
Give a cripple man a dollar,
And I'll give you the number for tomorrow.
I'm giving it to you late,
But it's coming out straight.
I had a dream, like Martin Luther King,
I'll put you in the swing,
Even make you sing like Elaine Champagne King
See, I need it in the morning; I need it in the night,
any little change will do just right.
Please help me...
If they gave me the dollar, I'd quickly whisper in their ear:
Play 868,
play it early, don 't play it late;
Because it's coming out straight...

Can you believe that number actually came out several times, and I never put a dollar on it myself? I still remember a couple of old ladies coming up to me and handing me money the next day saying, I was their good luck charm.

Once I'd established myself as a money-maker, the other addicts would sit around and wait for me to finish, so they could push me to cop. The dealer would come by in the morning and give me something to try just to ruin my days, for if you took a hit of crack in the morning; your entire day was spent chasing a crack ghost. They figured since they had given me something, I'd spend all my money with them. All I cared about was who had the best stuff, and the only loyalty I had been to my pipe.

I spent many hours in that chair in front of either Franks Tavern or T & T Carryout. In fact, the owners of both establishments threatened to have me arrested. I had become a toll both in front of these people's stores.

I must have worried my parents to death, for I was in the streets in a wheelchair day and night, rain, sleet, or snow. My friend Bo used to call me "the ever-ready Energizer Bunny." It was nothing to see my seventy-something year old mother coming on the liquor store lot looking for me after I'd been missing for a few days. Once she showed up, someone would push me home to get some well-needed rest.

When I did come home, it was usually late at night, and I would awaken my mother from her sleep to open the door for me. My parents wouldn't give me a key in fear that someone might take it from me. My brothers and sisters wanted me out of my parent's home. They even went as far as to call the police to have me thrown out, but my father and mother would never concede to their wishes. I felt really bad when I was incarcerated in the state of New Jersey, and my brothers and sisters put my mother in a home. As much as she did for me, I could never have put her in the hands of strangers. I owed her that much: her dignity in her old age.

In '93, I just couldn't see
All the damage drugs did to me.
Almost got 15 years, Boy was I scared
For Judge Wynn made her intentions clear,
But thanks to a wheelchair and a criminal mind,
I got away again without doing some time...

CHAPTER 14

1993

In 1993 I had taken addiction to a new level. They even changed my name from Michael Moore to Wheelchair Willie. I never even attempted to walk. I did a lot of sliding on my behind. I got so good with my wheelchair that I could bounce down the front steps of my home without any help.

I had lost the will to live. I actually wanted to die, but was afraid to put a gun to my head and pull the trigger. I just continuously polluted my system with foreign substances; it was a slow death, but a sure one. Today, I have liver problems as a direct result of my over-indulgence in narcotics.

The court date for my robbery case came up in 1993. My case was heard before the Honorable Judge Wynn. She was a black judge. Up to that point in my life, I had always been lucky and drew an African-American Judge. They had more sympathy towards me because of my educational and family backgrounds. Judge Wynn made her intentions very clear to me from the very beginning. If I was found guilty of the charge of robbery, she would roll me and the wheelchair down to Lorton.

I think the only thing that saved me in that case was the testimony of my senior-citizen father. The fact that these two large white police officers had pushed my little mother down to enter our home weighed heavily in our favor. My father had retired from the federal government, and he was a navy veteran; he wasn't a hoodlum.

Another big factor that weighed heavily in my case was the fact that the Capital police officer that had chased me had also given her service weapon to the victim: to gain my whereabouts from Deadface. She put a pistol to Deadface's head and threatened to kill him if he didn't tell where I lived. That ploy alone made the two of them seem guilty of some crime within itself.

My attorney on the case was Atique Amead. Mr. Amead was a Muslim, and in the 1990s, he also represented some of the terror suspects in the first trade center bombing. I thank God for him, for he got me two years' probation for the robbery charge. I just knew I was going back to Lorton.

I put on an eloquent speech at my sentencing. Judge Wynn was very impressed. In addition to the probation, I had to complete two-hundred hours of community service. I did my community service at a home for mentally challenged children. I counseled them and help them with their homework.

Judge Kennedy, the judge that had given me a twenty-month sentence, with five years of probation to follow in 1988, wasn't as sympathetic as Judge Wynn. Judge Kennedy felt he had given me a break in 1988, and here I was back before him five years later with a robbery conviction. I know the two judges conferred on my case because Judge Kennedy cursed me out at the show cause hearing. He told me, "He wasn't going to make any decision for the next two years, and to get out of his court room before he rolled me and that wheelchair down to Lorton. My niece, Kimberly, took me to court that day. The judge's statement scared the both of us. Kim was supposed to take me to a disability doctor that same day, so she went to court with me also. That little excursion cost me a lot of money and a day of getting high. After I had spent almost all my money on parking and gas, she picked up her friend, and dropped me off at the subway station.

In 1993, Tarsha decided to leave the Washington Area. She had gone to see a palm reader, and the lady told her that she had a curse on her. The lady also told Tarsha to put an allotted amount of distance between herself and Washington, D.C. Tarsha decided to move to Pensacola, Florida to live with her aunt Pearl.

Pearl had retired from her position at the U.S. Capital and had moved to the sunny state of Florida a while back. Pearl and Tarsha lived in a trailer park near the beach in a small town. Tarsha eventually got her own trailer and settled down to some good old country living. Country living came easy to Tarsha, for her mother had married Big Britt when she was a baby, and he'd raised her as if she was his own daughter. Britt was from Alabama and was definitely country slick. Tarsha, Bootsey, and James had lived everywhere from Alabama to Washington.

Tarsha soon tired of living in the slow in Pensacola. That's when she decided to move to Atlanta, Georgia. She had a cousin, Fee-Fee, and Britt's brother Jim there, so the actual transition went smoothly. She was a single, non-attached woman with no children, simply a dream for a man that didn't know her past.

Tarsha got social security check and food stamps because of her cancer; so she did alright in A-Town. She moved, into the same apartment complex as Jim Britt and Fee-Fee in Union City, Georgia. Jim had a special relationship with Gina, the resident manager at Shannon Woods He actually got a discount on his rent for every new tenant he recommended into the complex.

Tarsha got a job babysitting for a wealthy, black couple in Atlanta to help support herself. She made enough money babysitting to completely furnish her apartment, she told me.

Tarsha was the last woman I had in my life in 1993. When she left town, I got a feeling of total loss. I had always looked upon her as someone that needed guidance, but now I missed the part she played in my life. Since I no longer had anyone in my life, I threw myself into my addiction wholeheartedly. I was the rolling dead. I think the only thing I existed for was my lust for euphoria.

In '94, I fell in love with a whore,
She was real cute, and my heart's still sore.
For two or three years, I lived life in a cup;
How'd a slick dude like me get the game fucked up?

Chapter 15

1994

Something very amazing happened to me in 1994. I regained the feeling in my legs. It's a strange story of how I actually stood up from my wheelchair; I'll just say crack made me walk.

It was about 1:30 am, and I was in the Frank's Tavern parking lot. A friend by the name of Man had given me some crack to sell. I had paid him, and I was down to my last two bags. I had plans of going home smoking those last two bags. Right before I left the liquor store lot, a station wagon pulled up. The driver asked me for something for $50. I showed him the last two bags I had, and he said he'd take them. Mind you, it was almost time for the store to close, and my friend Ghouls only had grams, that he was selling for $40.00. I only had $30 in my pocket, and Ghouls didn't take shorts. I figured with the extra $50 from the sale, I could buy two grams; so I attempted to make the sale.

I had the crack in my right hand, and the buyer attempted to hand me the $50 in my left hand. The transactions were supposed to happen at the same time, but after the buyer had received the crack, he attempted to snatch his money back. I guess the buyer felt, since I was in a wheelchair; I was in no position to put up any kind of fight. Boy, was he in for a surprise. At that moment, I forgot all about being in a wheelchair and not being able to move my legs. My minds only thought was to either get the crack back or the money.

The next thing I knew, I was out the wheelchair, on my feet, punching the potential buyer in the face. I snatched the gear selector into park, and commenced to beating the man as if my life depended on it. I took the $50 and the crack back. The potential buyer was so surprised by my actions; he jumped out of his vehicle and screamed, "Robbery."

I still remember my friend Keith yelling, "Mike, you're walking!" When I noticed I was actually standing, I immediately fell back into the wheelchair; but from that day on, I knew in my mind I was going to walk again. I put a great deal of work into my rehabilitation from that day on. I think my paralysis was more psychological than it was physical. My love for crack withstood any sense of logic. In fact, that drug had a serious mental hold on my mind. That little piece of hope gave me new found strength. I now had the hopes of a normal life again. That year, I was granted my SSI. They gave me a check that was retroactive from October 1991 to May 1994. Mind you, Social Services had given me a welfare check and food stamps, so that money was deducted from my check. I still got a decent amount.

When the check got to my parents' house, my mother was afraid to give it to me. She thought that with that amount of money in my hands, I'd kill myself. My brother Melvin had to convince her to give it to me.

My father took me to his bank, Bank of America on Kenilworth Avenue in Hyattsville. We cashed the check and went to Beltway Plaza so I could buy new clothing. I did get a few things I needed, but that money was burning a hole in my pocket. I wanted to get high. I gave my father the bulk of the money, and took the rest and disappeared for a few days.

My father was so upset with me; that he threatened to throw me out the house. That really surprised me, for I knew I was at the end of my rope. I had to figure out a way to get myself together. I came up with the bright idea to go to Atlanta with Tarsha. Tarsha and I had been corresponding, and since she had her own place, I felt I could go there and fit right in.

I had filed a lawsuit against the person that had hit me with the car. The case was coming up in court, so I guess Tarsha figured it would be to her advantage to have me in her corner. At the time, I just couldn't imagine that the only reason she wanted me was for the lawsuit money. I actually thought she still loved me. I packed up, went to the Greyhound Station, got a ticket to Atlanta, and was off to a new life, or so I thought.

When I arrived in Atlanta, Tarsha's cousin Fee-Fee brought her to pick me up from the Atlanta bus station. Fee-Fee was country as hell, but she had a nice shape. I actually thought she was cute. She had a very nice personality, I thought. But you know how the saying goes: "if it doesn't come out in the wash, it will come out in the rinse." I soon found out Fee-Fee's true colors.

Tarsha's uncle Jim was the slickest of them all. He had actually been a pimp, and he had control over Tarsha and Fee Fee. Little did I know Jim had orchestrated my coming to Atlanta in the first place. He played those two girls like a fine-tuned piano. The thing that messed up his entire plan was Jim got too greedy. He actually tried to cut Tarsha and Fee-Fee out the picture and get everything for himself.

Jim had a bullshit business of selling oils, lotions, and makeup. He actually had plans for me to buy him a booth in Shannon Mall. Boy was he in for a surprise! I was raised in the streets, and I could see a con a mile away. From the very beginning, I saw that Jim was a "Gopher", (someone that would go for anything as long as he saw some money in it) that's when I started to play him.

They gave me the best send-off when I went home to go to court for the suite. You would have thought I was a celebrity. Tarsha even invited her so call wealthy cousin, Keita over to play cards and meet me. I guess I was going to be Tarsha's new ticket to the "life" again. The problem was I was a college graduate, and I saw through all their niceness from the very beginning. I did think Tarsha really loved me. I guess once again I was a sucker for love.

When I went to court for the accident suite, Allstate insurance company had every drunk in Chapel Oaks there. Apparently, they had been paid to say, I walked in front of the car, not the real truth that the car had jumped the curb and hit me. The case went to trial, and I lost because of the many testimonies. I had endured years of pain for nothing. I was simply distraught over the verdict.

When I came home from court, not even my family believed I didn't get a dime. My sister Judy even accused me of lying. Once the truth came out, Tarsha's feeling towards me also changed. When Tarsha found out I didn't get any money from the lawsuit, she came up with the excuse, I was on drugs and would bring her down. She told me I couldn't stay with her any longer.

As I mentioned earlier, Tarsha and her greedy family were gophers, (they go for anything having to do with money). I knew my mom and dad needed a rest from me, so I needed to get back to Atlanta. I had a friend, Man, who hustled on a large scale. He was in need of a large amount of cocaine. Tarsha's father Britt thought he was mob-connected; if you listened to him long enough, he'd have you believing the same stories. When I told Britt and his brother Jim of Man's need, I could hear the cash registers ringing through the telephone. They just knew they had hit the jackpot. I got Britt and Man together on the telephone, and everything was in motion. Man and I left for Atlanta early one Sunday morning. He purchased two first-class, round-trip tickets.

We left from what is now Reagan National Airport. We arrived in Atlanta around noon after a layover in North Carolina. Man had a busy schedule, so he looked upon our trip as both business and a vacation. Man actually needed the rest.

I still remember him talking to this beautiful woman from Florida during our flight. She said she would be in Atlanta for a few days with her girlfriend, and maybe the three of us could get together. Man had been in the service, and was well- rounded as far as the world is concerned. He had no problem connecting with any woman of the opposite sex.

Once in Atlanta, we caught a cab to the Days Inn in Union City. We called Jim from the hotel. When Jim arrived, he was all teeth. He looked like a whore with a million-dollar trick. I'm sure he'd already been briefed on Man's resume, so his intent was to be the gracious host. Jim just knew he had a payday somewhere in the picture.

The first thing Man asked me about Jim was, "is he gay?" It was just the look Jim had in his eyes. He looked like he wanted to eat Man up. I still question Jim's sexual preference today, so I couldn't give him a definite answer. I don't know if it's just the fact that Jim thought he was a player / pimp, or he was on some kind of sensitive tip. That look made me and Man both uncomfortable.

Britt was still in Alabama at the time, so Man and I lived it up a little while we waited on Britt's arrival. Jim was our gracious host, so he took us to all the after-hours spots. We went to the Underground for our first night in town. There was a Jamaican club there; we drank Remy Martin, danced with college girls, and listened to Calypso music.

I had a wonderful time dancing with a WNBA star. I won't mention her name, but I do remember her giving me her hotel address and number. Sweetheart, if you are reading this book, please accept my apologies. I know it's a lame excuse, but I did lose your address. I still remember seeing you playing on television and me kicking myself for losing that number. I would have loved to have pursued anything with you...

We went to the Play Boy Palace next. It was on Garby Road in College Park, Georgia. I still remember the table dance I got that night from a woman I've seen several times since in music videos. She was smack-your-mama beautiful; I often reminisce about the week Man and I hung out together in Atlanta.

When Tarsha heard I was in town with Man, she just knew I had some money. I still think she believes I lied about the lawsuit. When we finally saw each other, she invited me over to her apartment. We made love, and discussed my staying in Atlanta. I told her that I wanted to change my life, and I felt, together, we could have the world.

I guess she went for my lies, because the next day I was back in the house. I had achieved my goal: I got back to Atlanta. I got back in Tarsha's house, and in her pants, heart, and mind. Man, if you are reading this, I'm sorry I had to use you to complete my goal. You have always been a good friend, and if I make something off this book, I'll return the favor with a vacation to Mexico. This time we can hang out with some Spanish Senoritas

When Britt finally arrived, he and Man drove off to Florida. They both said their goodbyes. Man even gave me some startup money.

(Money to get me on my feet) Man was more than thankful for my assistance.

When I got back to Atlanta, I actually tried to be responsible. I got a job at a detail shop buffing cars, came home every night, and paid bills. I thought I was at the beginning of a new life.

There were three things that continuously ruined our relationship: Tarsha's jealousy, the neighborhood lesbians, and the arrival of her cousin, Kee-Kee. Tarsha had very low self-esteem, so she felt I was always cheating on her. I guess she couldn't trust herself. The neighborhood lesbians didn't help matters, as they continuously kept something going. Now that I've had a chance to evaluate the entire situation, I now question Tarsha's sexual preference also. As the saying goes, "birds of a feather flock together."

Kee-Kee was the worst of my problems. She was also recovering from a drug addiction, but she brought her problems with her. Tarsha was very impressionable as far as drugs were concerned, so I didn't want anything or anyone throwing a monkey wrench into my program. Maybe I was too overly-protective of Tarsha, and that's what caused the constant disagreements between Kee-Kee and me. I still remember the big fight between Tarsha and myself. We had rented some videos from Block Buster that night. Kee Kee, her daughter Keisha, Tarsha, and I, all sat down to dinner and movies. Today, I realize I was wrong for putting my hands on a woman, but at the time I felt my manhood was being questioned. People still call me Ike Turner because the events that occurred that evening.

In the middle of one of the movies, Tarsha said, "That's it — it's time for bed." She didn't pull me to the side and say she wanted to have sex, and I do believe my testosterone was up because Kee-Kee was half naked. I was enjoying peeking at Kee-Kee's legs, so I didn't want the evening to be over. When I contested Tarsha's demands, she hit me, and I hit her back. That's when the all-out war started. Anyone that knows Tarsha knows she will jump on a bull. Kee-Kee was terrified of Tarsha, so she took her daughter and went into the next room. We wrestled for a while until I popped her; that's when you would have thought I'd killed her; she went hysterical. We made up, but I had embarrassed her in front of her cousin, and she didn't take to kindly to that. She actually wanted me out of her home, but I'd paid half the rent and my name was on the lease. I didn't have anywhere to go in Atlanta, so I just moved to another room.

The next evening, Tarsha, Kee-Kee, and Tarsha's cousin all went out to a club. They stayed out until about 4:00am. Tarsha was so drunk when she came back that she fell out and started throwing up. I noticed blood in her vomit, so I called the ambulance. They took her to the hospital, and I followed in my 1978 Riviera.

At the hospital, the doctor told me she had a bleeding ulcer, and he wanted to keep her for further observation. I was upset because I did love Tarsha, and I didn't want to see her in any pain.

When I returned to the hospital the next day, I was told I couldn't see Tarsha. Her family had gotten involved and had opened a domestic violence case. At that moment, I should have left town, but my dumb ass stayed around thinking everything would blow over.

The next evening, after I had gotten off of work; I stopped by KFC to get some chicken. I could feel that something was wrong, so I ate quickly and left out the house. While sitting in my car, I noticed Tarsha pulling up in Jim's car. About four police officers were with them. That's when I panicked and left the parking lot.

I was arrested on Shannon Parkway by the Union City Police Department. I was charged with simple battery. Simple battery is a charge that gives you a $110.00 fine. After a lot of thought, I figured, instead of sitting in jail, why not just pay the fine and get out; so I did. In essence, I was pleading guilty to the charge of Simple Battery.

Mind you, the Union City jail is structured like the Mayberry jail; everything was in one room. I actually think the judge, the chief of police, and the man that ran the impound lot were all the same person; they just changed hats.

While I was paying my fine, Tarsha, Jim, and Kee-Kee, was speaking to the judge. They were putting up a great deal of opposition to my release. They told the judge I was wanted in Washington for murder. The judge finally asked me step into his chambers. The judge looked like General Custer with all his white hair in a ponytail. He spoke with a heavy southern drawl. As I stood before him, mad about my arrest, he asked me, "Did you hit my woman?" I answered in a sarcastic tone, "Are you screwing her too?" That statement made the judge so mad he put me in jail, bound my case over to Fulton County, upgraded my charge to aggregated assault, and gave me a $75,000 bond.

I called my friend, Tom Short, and asked him to get my car out of the impound lot. I also told him he could keep the car until I got out. Short was a good friend, for he took good care of the car and brought me cigarettes to the jail. Can you believe, Tarsha was upset because I didn't leave the car for her. She actually told Short I was selfish for leaving the car with him.

Jim Britt was upset with me for not helping him with his business and the deal with Man also fell through, and he took one hell of a loss. He coached Tarsha and Kee-Kee like a little league coach. He had their stories and lines rehearsed, and had it set up to send me away forever. I just know he doesn't think I've forgotten all he did. Jim even tried to steal my lease to the apartment Tarsha and I shared, out of the trunk of my car.

Mind you, I had already pled guilty to simple battery, so the prosecution thought they had an air-tight case. After a brief court appearance, where Tarsha and Kee-Kee both testified, I sat in the Fulton County Jail for about three months.

I was finally given a public defender. He was the most incompetent, badly-dressed fool I've ever met in my life. The first thing he said to me was, "When we get into the court room, just say 'Yes, sir' to everything I say, and you will get out today." I couldn't believe it, but I went along with the program. This man was dressed in a lime-green suit and white shoes. He really looked like a clown.

When they finally called my case, my public defender said, "Your honor, this man is a hardworking man, and he knows he's done wrong. I recommend a twenty year suspended sentence with ten years of probation." The judge asked me if I agreed with my attorney's recommendation, and I quickly said, "No, sir". The judge and the attorney look at me like I was crazy. The lawyer bent over and said, "I said to say 'Yes, sir,' not 'No, sir.'"

I asked if he was crazy. I was not about to accept a deal like that. I couldn't stay out of trouble for a year; I knew ten years was out the question. The judge postponed my case for two weeks so I could think about the deal.

When I got back to the jail, I quickly called my momma. I told her what had gone on in the court room, and asked her to please get Daddy to come down here and get me out of this mess. Mind you, I was momma's baby, so if my father didn't come to Atlanta, it would have been hell living in that house. My dad was on the next flight out.

When my dad reached Atlanta, Tommie Short picked him up from the airport. My dad got a hotel room in Union City, and had a sit-down with Tarsha. He told her he would help her out with a few bills, she could have my car, and he would get me out of town if she got me out of jail.

Tarsha went along with the deal, and Short knew a man that worked in the prosecutor's office. Short called the fellow, and he gave Tarsha and my father an appointment. The man asked Tarsha why she wanted to drop the charges. She immediately said, "Because I love him." I was out of jail that evening.

I had been in jail for three months, so I was horny as hell. Me and Tarsha made up, and made passionate love that night. The next morning, neither one of us wanted me to leave. We went to see my father that afternoon and gave him the crazy news. My father looked at me like I had fallen out of the coo-coo's nest. He said I had to come home so my mother could see I was all right. He promised to buy me a round trip ticket, but he warned me he wasn't coming back to Atlanta again to get me out of jail.

I went home for a few days but grew homesick for Tarsha like a fool, and I went back to Atlanta again. We moved to a new apartment on Garby Road. The apartment was in the mist of crack heaven. You can only guess what happened when two addicted fool moved around coke from Miami; we lost our minds again..

Soon after I got back to Atlanta, Tarsha and I were at odds again. We both had drug problems, but Tarsha took getting high to a new level. She wanted everything for herself. During that time in my life, I never liked getting high with women. First of all, crack kills the sexual drive in 90 percent of the male users, and also, women never get enough crack. I had to have some heroin in my system in order to endure any female presence while smoking crack. I had a rhyme I used to sing: about how I liked to get high:

I used to sit up all night hitting the pipe;
I smoked so much coke I couldn't sleep at night.
My hair was nappy; I didn't have a comb,
And when I smoked my coke, I smoked it alone.

Tarsha jumped on me again outside our new apartment. This time, the resident manager witnessed us and called the College Park Police Department. When the officer arrived, Tarsha was running out our front door with another knife. I had already taken one knife from her after she cut the front tire on my car because I'd attempted to leave.

The officer calmed down the situation, and asked for some identification. When the officer said he wanted to see my ID, my heart hit my stomach. I was on probation in Washington, D.C., and I hadn't reported my arrest in Atlanta to my probation officer, and I just knew I had a warrant somewhere.

Like a fool, I gave the officer a fake name. The name came back bad, so Tarsha gave the officer my wallet. When the officer realized I had given him a fake name, he immediately put me in handcuffs, and I was rolled off to the College Park Jail.

I only needed $100 to get out, but I didn't have the money. I called everybody. Finally, the owner of the barbershop in Union City paid my fine. I never even paid him back. I owe so many people that I'm going to have to write another book just to make some money.

Mike's brother came to get me out after the shop closed. He dropped me off in front of the apartment Tarsha and I shared. He gave me $10.

I never went in the house. I had my car keys in my pocket, so I jumped in the car and made a beeline to the gas station. Once the car was gassed up, I headed for Simpson Road. Tommie Short was staying there with a friend name Toot Wilson on Simpson Road. Toot's mother had died, and Toot and Tommie stayed in her house. This house was a mess. There was no heat, no hot water, and the roof had a hole in it the size of a basketball.

Toot came from a good family, but he also had a drug and gambling problem. The thing that kept him afloat was the fact that he was a blackjack dealer for both the Silver Fox on Bankhead and Little Sampson's on Martin Luther King. Both these establishments had illegal gambling. I learned a lot about carrying the Slick from Tommie and Toot.

The Silver Fox was owned by Q-Ball, better known as Mr. Bankhead. Q-Ball was a suave dude. I respected him to the utter most. During that time, my hustle was cleaning cars. Everyone in Atlanta liked to keep their rides shining, so I made a lot of money. I just smoked up all my profits. I had contracts all over Atlanta. I could have really done well if I didn't have a gorilla on my back.

When I was completely broke, I did one of two things: I either gave people rides in my car, or I played blackjack. Atlanta is the only place in the world where you can sell your hand in blackjack for $20.

When you approach the blackjack game, in order to play, you have to announce yourself as the "new man." There might actually be $500 in the pot, and in order for someone to stop the pot, they have to bet on your hand. Thus, they purchase your hand for up to $100 in some instances. All the average addict had to do was to sit there until the bet fell on their hand, and sell the hand. You could make a lot of money if you were patient; but what crack head is patient? Thus you saw addicts running in and out all day and night.

I met a lot of people with money in Atlanta. The men from Tennessee came in Little Sampson's with briefcases full of money because they played Georgia Skin. That was one crazy game; I've seen people lose

$50,000 in twenty minutes, playing Skin. I never had enough money to get in a Skin game.

Eventually, after wearing out my welcome at Toot's, I begged my mother for enough money to get back to Washington. You know she sent for her baby; Momma even had my brother Donald meet me at BWI Airport when I returned.

I had fun in Atlanta, but most of the people I met were jealous-hearted. I did meet a few good ones, but I think they've also left Atlanta. The dream of being in a so called "Black Mecca" was truly over-exaggerated. There are poor people in Atlanta the same as everywhere else in America. When you are around people that are hungry, there's always going to be trouble in the mist...

In '95, I stopped getting high;
I gave drug treatment a final try.
Started 13th-stepping, thinking I was slick.
C. English-EL put me out the program real quick. .

CHAPTER 16

1995

1995 was a strange year for me. I made a considerable amount of changes in my life that year. Once I got home from Atlanta, I still had a gorilla on my back, so I started hustling with an old friend; I'll just call him Scrooge. My mom and dad were tired of my drug usage, so I actually moved in with Scrooge.

Scrooge had a profitable cocaine operation going. He had been at his business for quite some time without arrest or conviction. Scrooge had never seen the inside of a prison wall. That fact within itself was remarkable, because 70 percent of the youth in Washington D.C. under the age of twenty-five have either an arrest or conviction, if not both.

If you just look at arrest statistics, you can see that the District of Columbia is profiting from the arrest of African-American youths; we make up 90 percent of the arrests. In 1987, when I was first arrested in the District, my prison number was 227407. In 2006, the prison numbers are up to 400,000, and climbing. That means that over nine thousand new people go through that city jail each year, not including the repeat offenders and parole violators. The federal government pays over $25,000 per year for the housing of inmates. Thus the prison industry is no longer in the business of crime and justice, but in all actualities, it's in the warehouse business. I hope you can now see why there is a problem with over crowdedness. Inmates are now on the stock market. We are a considered a commodity. People are actually profiting from our demise. So, you ask yourself, do they really want to stop crime?

I won't state Scrooge and his brother Splib's true names for legal purposes. I have to say that this family has had a definite effect on my life. Some people look for material riches. I too, have been chasing that elusive pie in the sky for the last twenty years. Even though, I've never actually gotten rich I've gained an unimaginable amount of wealth in knowledge.

Scrooge was one of the smartest business men I've ever met. Believe me I've met a few people that can make $1.00 out of 15 cents, Negro economics. Scrooge never used drugs or alcohol. He wore the same old clothes daily and drove the same old car. He never showed any visible sign that he had money. He also never let too many people into his fold. I was one of his chosen few. Scrooge had started hustling in the '70s, and the last I checked, he still conducts his business the exact same way. He let me in because I was a smart minded, college boy. He took in some of my ideas, but he continued with his original routine.

Scrooge got his routine from Y.C.Y.C. is an older and more knowledgeable hustler. His famous saying is, "You can find something in any man you can use." I learned what I could from Y.C., but my phobia of being used has kept me from learning his complete routine. His routine has kept him safe for more than thirty years.

People believe what they see. If you show them a bum, they believe you are a bum. They use the same concept in television commercials; it's called "subliminal seduction. That knowledge has continuously kept Scrooge out of the clutches of "Officer Friendly." I'd rather be a rich bum than a locked-up fool any day.

Scrooge's brother Splib, like me, was a drug user. People lose respect for drug users. Even though, Splib devoted his entire adult life to the "cash money corporation," but he was only used as a pawn. Those types of things hurt, especially when your little brother is the C.E.O. Can you believe Splib worked over twenty years with the same organization, and he never even got a company car?

Addicts get high to things like that. *My brother, no sense in crying over spilled milk. Do like me, use your skills, and make you a different kind of milk.* Hustling has been around for centuries. People have been selling something or another since the beginning of time. As long as there is a market for something, people are going to sell it. There are a few mistakes I've seen people make in my life time, and I'd like to discuss them with the readers of this book.

A mistake most Hustlers make is that they tell someone what they are doing. I guess we like to look big in the sight of our peers. The problem is that the only people that can get you are people close to you. Never let your right hand know everything your left hand is doing.

The biggest mistake I've seen over the years is that once most hustlers get to a certain level, they forget that their way of living is against the law. We don't work for Microsoft; we sell drugs. That is against the law!! Most people are jealous hearted, petty, and vindictive. If they see you making .10 cents over lunch money, they will turn your ass in. People like Rayful Edmonds, Wayne Perry, Toney Lewis, and Kevin Gray, all forgot hustling is illegal. The list goes on; please don't you be added to it

Scrooge and I had a good business relationship. We both benefited from the organization. I even got a company car for my birthday, because of the catchy slogan I came up with that raised sales considerably. I came up with the idea of selling tickets. This way the person that is actually dealing the drugs never has any marked money on their person. A potential buyer would purchase a ticket from a spotter, and tickets were created differently every day on a computer system. A buyer takes that ticket to the dealer, and the dealer would dispose of the ticket directly after the sale. In order the sell these tickets, I came up with the slogan: "Get your $10 tickets to dizzy world; once in the park, all rides are free!"

There's an old saying, "right when life is at its best, the devil steps in and screws up the rest." That's exactly what happened; the lust for money is what ruined my relationship with Scrooge.

Scrooge had a customer that spent a considerable amount of money with him each month. This man had been Scrooge's main customer for some time, and he didn't want to lose his business.

Well, I first met this man on a Sunday Morning. He came to me to purchase a ticket. I had a rule that I never sold something to anyone that I did not know. So I told this individual, I didn't know what he was talking about. In order to make his identity known to me, the man told me a story that made my head burn with rage.

This man told me his name was Jim West. He said that he had killed a man in the 80s, and had left town until everything had blown over. When I heard the name, I almost lost it. See, a man by the name of Jim West killed my brother Ronald in 1985. He wouldn't know anything concerning me, because I was in college at the time of the event. I was drinking an orange Juice at the time when he told me his name; It took everything I had in me not to split his head with that bottle. If this man was in fact the man that killed my brother, I didn't want to hurt him; I wanted to kill him. If I had hit him with that bottle, I took the chance of not seeing him again. So, I just smiled perversely and welcomed him back to the neighborhood. I actually gave him two tickets.

After the sale, I ran back to Scrooge's house. His older brother and he were engulfed in conversation. I disrupted the conversation to tell them my newly found information. I felt in my heart they were my family, and he would give me the proper advice on handling the situation.

Scrooge's older brother gave me a 9mm pistol. He told me to trick the man into the woods on the premise of me wanting to secretly get high; that seemed like the perfect plan.

Since I had been dealing with Scrooge's organization, I stopped using completely. I had a car, a new woman, and was in the process of renting my own apartment. The actual thought of using again was the farthest from my mind.

Mind you, this particular man, the man that killed my brother was one of Scrooge's best customers. He in no way wanted to lose that source of income. Thus, Scrooge told this man of my plans to kill him. The next day, the man moved from our neighborhood. I've never seen him since.

Scrooge's brother Splib told me about Scrooge warning the man. I had very mixed emotions about Scrooge's betrayal. I didn't know whether he wanted to keep me out of trouble, or protect his investment, but as a result of what happened, I reverted back to my old self. I sought refuge in drugs once again.

When I went back to using drugs, Scrooge banished me to a security position in a crack house. I guess he figured I couldn't mess up any money doing security.

Soon after I started at that position, Scrooge's cousin came home from prison. To protect his identity, I'll just call him Fool. Fool was the perfect name for this individual because once he started using drugs, he might do anything. One night while I was doing my security, Fool came up to the house. Since Fool was Scrooge's cousin, I felt safe letting him in. He had some cocaine and was looking for a safe place to get high.

Once I saw the amount of drugs Fool had, I thought a party was about to be in session. I just knew I was going to get twisted. Fool simply gave me two 20s, and he asked me to get back to my job.

After about thirty minutes of them getting high, a lookout came to the house and told us that the narcotics squad was in the neighborhood. To avoid felony arrests, we hid the majority of the drugs and the pistols in an abandoned apartment. I took refuge in another apartment in the building myself.

I had a bed, a television and a VCR in the apartment, so I was actually quite comfortable. After about one hour into the movie *Jurassic Park*, I heard about five gun shots. Since I had hidden my weapon, I quickly hid in the bathroom tub. I cut off the lights, pulled back the shower curtain, and played possum.

When all the commotion was over, I got out the tub and ventured into the next apartment. When I opened the door I saw both the two workers on the floor bleeding. I quickly ran to the phone and called 911.

The two workers were actually a couple, and they also had their children in the apartment. I ran to the back room to check on the kids; I found them hiding in a closet under some dirty clothing. I quickly assured them that everything was going to be ok. I told them that their parents were going to be ok, and that I'd already called the ambulance.

The older of the two children was a girl. I told her that the police would soon be here, and we needed to clean up any drug paraphernalia that was lying around on the floors. We didn't want the police to consider this event as drug-related.

I also told her to say that she knew nothing about what her parents did in this house. She was to say that when she gets out of school, her little brother and she play outside until dark, and then they retire to the back room. There was a bathroom in the back room, so there was no reason for them to have come out. They eat their meals in that back room. This was exactly the way these children lived, but they did know their parents were addicts.

When the police and ambulance arrived, I quickly ran down stairs to let them in. When I got to the door the officers had their guns drawn and made me get on the ground. I had to explain with a gun in my face that I was the one that called them.

Once the officer figured out I wasn't the shooter, they simply walked away from me. I should have walked away at that moment, but I thought about the children. I followed the police back into the house and went in the room to keep the children company until their aunt came to get them.

Later that evening, I found out the true story of the events that occurred in that house. Apparently Fool and the two people had smoked up everything that Fool had. While Fool was still in the house, another dealer dropped off some more cocaine for the people to sell. When Fool saw the large amount of cocaine they had received, he asked for some to try and make some of his money back; the man of the house quickly said no. This couple then proceeded to smoke right in front of Fool, and not give him anything.

Little did I know, but the man of the house had a twenty-five automatic in his possession. When he had me hide my weapon, he actually kept his. While this guy was smoking, he took the twenty-five automatic from his waist and set it on the stove. Once he was smoking, Fool grabbed the gun and asked for all the drugs. When the woman saw him with the gun, she charged him with a knife. Fool shot her four times. He shot the man twice. I assume he left the home while I was still in the tub. I didn't see him when I went into the other apartment.

After the police and everyone else had gone, I called Scrooge and told him what had happened. He was furious. He actually blamed me for letting Fool in, and not attempting to stop him. If I had shot Fool, then I still would have been in the wrong, because they were family. I was definitely in a lose/lose situation.

The events of that evening totally ruined Scrooge and my relationship. No matter how much I tried to explain, he didn't want to talk to me. Fool even told him I wasn't involved, but not even Fool's confession eased Scrooge's rage.

I eventually went back to my parent's home. Because of my drug usage, I spent more time in the car than in the house. As result, I blew up the engine. I was once again broke and on foot.

I remember the night I decided never to use again. I drove a U-Haul truck to help some friends move. When we were done moving, they fed me and gave me $75. That money was burning a hole in my pocket. It a funny thing about crack, I never wanted any when I was broke. A dime rock was only a tease to me. I had to have at least $50 to enjoy myself.

On my way home, I notice my buddy, Bo-Bo, in front of T & T Carryout. He claimed he had some crack that came from New York. He said the stuff was out of this world. He saw the money I had, thus figured if he gave me a tester, he could eventually get everything I had.

He gave me two $20 rocks for $30. They were a nice size, so I could not complain. He told me he would only be in the area until 1:00 am, so if I needed anything else, I better hurry back.

I took the stones and went directly to my mother's house. It was 11:00 pm when I reached the house. My mother told me she was tired and warned if I left out the house tonight; she was not getting up to unlock the screen door. I kissed her, gave her $20, and went directly to my room.

Once in the room, I couldn't wait to try out the new stuff. I waved at my dad as I passed his room and went directly to my crack pipe I had hidden in the room. I locked my door, opened my window to blow out the smoke, and proceeded to take a hit. I fired up my lighter and pull hard on the stem. Once I exhaled, it sounded like I was in a bell tower. My body felt numb; this was the best hit I'd had in years.

I still had at least $30 worth of crack left, but I just had to have more. I needed to catch Bo before he left, but my mother had told me not to leave out again that night. I just had to sneak out.

I slipped pass my dad's room and down the stairs. We had a split foyer, so the front door was directly at the bottom of the stairs. I eased the door opened very quietly, slipped out, and left it ajar so 1 could easily return.

Once outside, I couldn't just walk around the corner because I ran the risk of my mother seeing me, so I jumped over the front porch railing, ran across street, and attempted to run through the yard of an abandoned house. That house had been abandoned for some time, and the grass was extremely high. I figured I could run through the yard, go through someone else's yard, and get to the next street where T & T was.

While I was on my journey through the abandoned property, I fell in a hole of some sort. The problem was the hole seemed like a bottomless pit. I fell, and fell, and fell, until I was in what looked like an elevator. Once in the elevator, I seemed to go down, and down, and down. Finally, the door opened and a man was standing there with a clip board in his hand. He told me to follow him.

This man carried me into what looked like an auditorium. Once there, he walked behind a podium. That's when he started to list all my bad deeds I'd done. He went all the way back to the '70s. He told me

I had tried my entire life to get there, and now I was in Hell and there was no return.

I quickly asked him, "Can we make a deal?" The man looked at me strangely, and asked what kind of deal I wanted to make.

I said that if he was to give me a kilo of cocaine, I would put momma, daddies, and babies, whoever on it. He asked, "You would do that for me?"

I said, "I'd do that for anybody." The man just smiled.

The next morning, I awoke with mud on the bottoms of my shoes, and a pile of uncut cocaine on my dresser top. I still had my money in my pocket and the crack had purchase from Bo. The question that lingered in my mind was, had I sold my soul!!!

I was raised in a religious family, and the thought of having sold my soul scared me to death. I quickly sought help from ministers and checked myself into drug treatment. I no longer wanted anything to do with drugs. I met with Ministers, Priest, and Rabbis Drug addiction was the hardest job I've ever had. I definitely needed a break.

During that year, I successfully completed my probation. Both Judge Kennedy and Judge Wynn released me from my commitments to the Office of Probation. I had already promised God and my mother that if I ever walked again, I'd leave drugs alone. My task now was to seek treatment. Since had health insurance because of my disability, I wanted to get the best treatment possible. I figured the state ofVirginia would be my best avenue.

My old friend Ty Thomas, the same guy who introduced me to Lemuel and Leprechaun in 1984, he had gotten saved and was now working as a substance abuse counselor. He was employed by the Fairfax Social Detox on Walney Road in Fairfax, Virginia. Ty had been there for some time and had a little pull.

I always had a great deal of respect for Tyrone. After my brother Ronald died, it was he and Bo that stepped in as my surrogate big brothers. After Timmy died, it was he that came and got me from time to time. I still remember the two of us going to see *The Last Boy Scout* with Damon Wayans. Just seeing Tyrone with his life together gave me the courage to try to fix mine.

I didn't want to go to treatment alone, so I tricked my old buddy Tony into coming along with me. I actually had to sell my car to get us some drugs, cigarettes, cosmetics, spending change, and car fare to get to Virginia. The engine on the car had locked up, so I didn't mind getting what I could for it. My old friend Mr. Perry brought my car just to assist me in going into treatment. Mr. Perry knew I was intelligent, and he believed that if I got off of those drugs, I could achieve greatness in life. I wanted so much not to let him down. I'd been high for the last ten years. My entire life depended on a substance in order for me to function, and I wanted control of my life again. I wanted to be a part of my children's lives. I had neglected my relationships with them long enough.

Tony and I took the subway to Virginia. On the way, we stopped at Potomac Gardens to get a couple of bags of dope (Harlem Nights) before going on the rest of our journey. We ducked under an underpass so we could get high before leaving. I've always been a snorter of heroin, Tony, like so many of my brother Ronald's friends used it intravenously.

Once we were through with our so-called "last hurrah," we got back on the subway and headed for Fairfax Virginia. The subway didn't actually go that far, so once we got to the end of the line in Vienna, we called the program to come and get us. They came and got us in a brand new van. The driver was also a counselor at the program, and he assured us we were going to a nice place.

I was immediately in awe of Fairfax Social Detox. This was one of Virginia's best-kept secrets. The place was recently built, and it had the finest of furnishings. Attached to the detox was a 90-day treatment program called New Beginnings. The clients from the New Beginnings Program ran the kitchen at the detox. Once inside, we were guided to a day room to wait until we were processed into the detox. They had a big screen Television, and stereos, a Ping-Pong table, and a kitchen full of food. We were each told to fix ourselves a sandwich, and promised that they would be with us momentarily.

Inside the icebox was every type of cold cut imaginable; they had all the fixings and about five different types of fruit Orange Juice. Since we both had recently gotten high and weren't sick yet, we dug into that refrigerator like two homeless men. During my first fourteen-day stay there, I gained twenty-five pounds.

Once we were finally processed, we were placed on a 24-hour watch for the first 72 hours. The only thing I hated about the program was they didn't give us any methadone to combat the withdrawal of heroin. We had to fight the pains cold turkey.

After we were feeling better, we had to attend groups for nine hours a day. They had every kind of group imaginable: community meeting, morning group, goals group, feelings group, evening group, and Narcotics Anonymous. In between each group, we were allowed a smoke break.

The counselors there were quite knowledgeable, and I was actually serious about my recovery, so I paid close attention to all their suggestions. I took up reading the so called, 'big book" and tried to practice the twelve steps. It suggested that I keep all the pain of my addiction in my face like a mirror. Most addicts had selective amnesia; they forget all the pain they have endured once they have been clean for some time, and they eventually go back to using. In order to remember all the horrors I experienced during addiction, I used my creative mind to come up with a poem to help me remember.

One more Time:

I first left Lorton in 89,
Looking good and feeling fine.
Hustling every day, saving every dime,
selling dope and coke was my crime.
I was hooked on money; that aint no joke;
Creeping on a come-up was my only hope;
Buying nice things, taking care of my folks;
Thinking all the time I was stronger than dope.
Then one-day crack messed with my mind;
The devil told me, "you can beat it this time;
Just take you a hit, one more time.
That one more time made me lose my mind;
That one more time should have been a crime;
That one more time sure put me behind.
All after that, I was looking for a bump,
Looking real crazy and acting like a punk;
Picking up rocks and looking under stumps;
How 'd I let myself become such a chump?
It's funny how coke stole my self-esteem;
All my thoughts and killed my dreams;
Busy running around involved in every scheme;
All that was on my mind was a beam.
Even had a nice woman that was very fine;
My addiction got in the way, and I lost her with time;
And all this came from that one more time...

Once my two weeks was up, instead of referring Tony and myself to further treatment, we were asked to leave. I guess the people from the program didn't feel we were treatable. They did try to get Tony and me into The Salvation Army; but after the reception committee at The Salvation Army found out about our criminal records, they quickly refused us. Ty Thomas told me to stay out the neighborhood and hang out in a drug free environment until he talked to his superiors. Ty Thomas assured me he would get me into treatment.

I didn't go home when I left the detox. I went to stay in Cheverly Maryland with my old friend Darryl Dickey. Darryl worked for D.C. General Hospital, and he had a bachelor pad in the Cheverly Terrance Apartment Complex. Darryl was happy to hear I had been in treatment, and he generously allowed me to stay.

The only problem was that Darryl was an orderly by day and a cocaine dealer by night. Since I had been clean for a while, I felt I could handle being around the drug. Boy, did I fool myself. That coke drove me nuts. I was using again only two days after my release from detox.

Darryl was a true friend, and he trusted me with everything. When he went on vacation to California to spend time with his old friends Shawn (Nipsey), and Martin Lawrence, he left me his car, his apartment, and a considerable amount of cocaine. Two days after he had left, I had messed up most of the drugs. I took what money I had made, gave his car keys to his older brother, and made a beeline back to treatment.

When I showed back up at the detox, I looked so bad that they took me back in. Tyrone had spoken in my behalf, so they did their very best to assist me in getting treatment. I still remember sitting in that detox watching the Million Man March. I wanted badly to be there because that event was a part of history; but I knew I needed treatment in order to have any type of future. I still remember Chris Rock's statement about Marion Barry: "in our most defining moment, we had a crack head on the stage.

I sat in the detox for another three weeks. During that time, I was elected president of the program. My responsibilities were to voice the complaints of the other clients and to run the community meetings. I met quite a few fine women in treatment; they had ruined their lives with drugs and alcohols, but so had I. I learned the hard way that two addicts can't live together and have a productive relationship.

Eventually I was sent to the Phoenix House Drug Treatment Program in Arlington, Virginia. My counselor, Betty, dropped me off. The place was an old apartment building in the poor section of Arlington, near the Boston Commons Shopping Mall. I felt very discouraged when I first saw the outside of the buildings. I had been in the luxurious Fairfax detox for over a month, and they had spoiled me. Now, I was in Arlington, back to reality.

The last thing I remembered from the meetings at the detox was to accept treatment where ever you could get it. They had a saying: "Go to treatment even if it is in a barn; it could save your life." Betty laughed when I said, "Hell, I'm going to treatment in the projects." The Phoenix House was an old building, but it had saved a few lives.

There were forty-five people in the program, and statistics predicted that only two would actually stay clean. I came in with the attitude that I was one of the two that was going to make it. I was placed in a room with two of the guys I had spent considerable amount of time with at the detox, David and Yaz. We had already lived together for quite some time, so we knew each other's habits, good and bad. Just like the detox, the program was co-ed. The only problem was that there weren't enough women to go 'round. If you were seen spending too much time with a woman, they charged you with fraternizing. The thing that got me was that it was the other people in the program that mainly enforced that rule. They would say things like, "Seeing you with that woman is affecting my recovery." Since I'd spent time in prison, I felt they were being hot. The program claimed that telling was a form of helping you; I thought it was policing you.

I had a beautiful black counselor from Harlem New York. She actually left New York with her husband and son to try and give her child a better life in a safe environment. Her name was Kim, and she rubbed me the wrong way from the door. She could see I was from the streets and didn't feel I had much of a drug problem. I still had nice clothing, a loving family, and money in my pocket. She felt you had to hit rock bottom before you would be willing to accept all the different tools that were involved in treatment.

She was right, because I saw right through that bullshit. The first thing they said was, "Your best thinking got you here." Being educated, and able to exhibit critical thinking, I soon rationalized, "how could it have been my best thinking, if I was high?" The total concept of treatment is itself uncomfortable. Most addicts get high when they are uncomfortable, so the programs premise was to make you as uncomfortable as possible to show how easy it was to deal with your problems without getting high.

I've always had a problem with authority. I certainly wasn't about to turn my mind and my will over to another human being. I got the feeling they were attempting to brain wash me. I realize I did need to change my ways of thinking, but to give another human being control over my mind was beyond my comprehension.

Instead of concentrating on my recovery, once I saw all the bullshit that was going on inside that place; my only concern was to stay there until my Section 8 Apartment came through. I knew it would be coming around the first of 1996.

I did everything I could to antagonize the staff. One time, while I was in a group discussion, Kim asked, "Why did you come to treatment?" I thought I would get a big laugh by being sarcastic, but the response I got created uproar amongst the staff. I told them the only reason I was in treatment was to clean up, so I could sell my drugs successfully. I said, "Hustling was my life, and if I used up my entire product, I'd starve."

The next day Kim invited Mr. C. English-El to join our group. Kim and Mr. C were both from New York, so whenever she had a problem with one of us, she called for C's assistance. Once the group started, Kim began with the exact same question from the day before, "Why did you come to treatment?" Fate had it that the question was directed at me. I gave the same answered as I did the day before; C went through the roof. He said never to make that statement again as long as I was in his program. You know my smart ass answered, "I thought this was a program of honesty; I was just being honest." C told me to keep my honesty to myself. Right there, I knew the entire premise of the program was a scam. They were profiting from our demise. They knew that only a few people would be susceptible to treatment, and they were receiving tax dollars to treat people that they knew 95 percent of them would fail. When they took the common-sense part out of addiction and made it a disease; they created a job for thousands of "substance abuse counselors."

Many of these counselors were not drug users, so how could they relate to the actual problems of a user? The ones that were ex-users were so happy to have well-paying jobs and an honest life that they simply went along with the program. What ever happened to "being sick and tired of being sick and tired?" What ever happened to simple common sense? No, we now have a disease that cannot be cured, but can be arrested at some point, and then recovery is then there possible. These people simply created a new service, one with millions of hopeful clients.

After reading several psychology books, I am now a firm believer in aversions. People have food aversions, sleep aversions, so why not cocaine and heroin aversions? Why not simply give the addict enough of the substance with an additive to make the addict dreadfully sick? After that, whenever the addict comes in contact with the substance, he or she would not use it again. The trick to the experiment would be not to tell the addict what was actually going on. I know this method is unethical, but this might clear up 60 percent of the drug problems today. If Ivan Pavlov could classically condition animals, why can't we use classical conditioning to keep human beings away from drugs? I guess we would be stepping on a lot of toes; Messing with people's lively hoods.

The next problem I had was hormones. Once I'd been clean for a period of time, my testosterone with through the roof. The women there had eaten a few meals, and their shapes had come back. They were clean, so their complexions were clear, and they felt the same way I did. I started practicing the 13th step with a girl from Seat Pleasant, Maryland. We were homies, and I thought I could trust her.

Once the other people in the program found out Alicia and I were an item, we were the center of everyone's attention. On one Sunday morning, everyone was in group. We had planned to both be sick that morning. Once the group was well in action, I snuck down stairs, went through the offices over to the female side, and into Alicia's room. We made love in her bed. Everything would have worked out perfectly if we had kept our mouths closed. I told my so-called boy, Timmy, and she told her so-called girl, Rhonda. Before we knew it, we were suspended from the program.

They only gave us a 24-hour suspension. The man that ran the reentry program, Sidney, got us back in. The thing that got me was they waited until we put on the graduation program and they got donations from the audience before they put us out. I put together a junk yard band and preformed my poem/song "One More Time." We got a standing ovation. That very next day, we were out.

In '96,
My mind's still sick,
Hanging out again with my man Slick.
Went to New York to cop some coke;
The New Brunswick Jail was no joke.

Chapter 17

1996

I spent New Year's Eve in Seat Pleasant, Maryland. Since Alicia and I were given a 24-hour suspension from the program, we decided to spend the time together. My older brother, Melvin picked us up from the program. He took Alicia home and took me to my brother Donald's house to borrow his car.

Donald lives in Laurel, Maryland with his wife Sharon. They have a beautiful home and three cars, so I didn't think I would be putting them out by borrowing it. Mind you, Laurel is about twenty-five miles outside of Washington, and we called Donald before we came, and he told us it was alright to pick up the car.

When we arrived at his house, all the air had been let out of the front tires. Donald claimed that he tried to call us to tell us the bad news before we left, but it seemed we were already on our way. I know Donald let the air out of those tires, and I wasn't about to be defeated by a little air. I sometimes think people think I'm stupid because of my drug use. What they fail to realize is that it take a great deal of intelligence to be a successful addict. When I say successful, I mean an addict that stays continuously high, and has no visible source of income. I had about $50 in my pocket, so I told Melvin to take me to Auto Zone. Once there, I simply brought two cans of Fix-a-flat. Once back at Donald's, I pumped up the tires and was on my way. I know Donald called me a lot of nasty names after I left.

Once back in Washington, I made a beeline for Alicia's mother's house. They had a beautiful brick home right off of Addison Road in Seat Pleasant, Maryland. Alicia's mother had to be in her 60s, but she still was a looker. She was as slick as goose grease. She showed me their home and invited me to stay for a while, but not overnight. I definitely had to get my thing off quickly. Alicia and I were infatuated with each other from the moment we met in treatment. I guess the long wait only made the sex better.

Alicia also had a son, Billy. Billy had been raised in Seat Pleasant, so he had heard all the old stories about Slick Stand, Mango, and me. I actually think he found it fascinating to have an old gangster with his mom, He knew I got money in the streets, and he more than likely felt I could be beneficial to the both of them. I really liked Billy; I actually looked forward to hanging out with him.

After our wonderful night together, we had to meet with the staff at Phoenix House the day after New Year's. They chewed the two of us out. Even though we went into the office with Mr. C. separately, I know he gave us the same brow beating. I know the staff at the Phoenix House just knew Alicia and I would not come back on time, so they would have reason to put us out, but we were back at the program early; ready, willing, and waiting for whatever punishment they threw at us.

The first punishment we got was we were not to speak, look, or write to each other for the remaining time we had in the program. Phoenix House was only a ninety-day program, and we had already been there over sixty days. I could stand on my head for thirty days, so I decided to tough it out.

Once you have completed sixty days of the inpatient phase of the program, you are allowed to seek employment. I was still drawing disability money, so I wasn't allowed to look for a job. I had to sit around, looking stupid.

When Alicia went on her first interview, the program sent an escort with her. The rules were that you were to go directly to your destination and come straight back to the program. On the way back to the program form her interview, Alicia and her escort stopped at a CVS to get cigarettes. As soon as they got back to the program, Alicia's escorted reported her deviation. That deviation was all that the counselors at the program needed to put Alicia out. They came up with a lame excuse that they were tired of her shit. They said she was also still conversing with me.

Alicia was at the program because of legal problems. I was there on my own free will. I simply told the staff that I would leave if they allowed Alicia to stay. They tried everything possible to get me to stay, but I refused. The last thing I remember Mr. C saying was, "You will be in Lewisburg within the month." Once again, I put someone else ahead of my own needs. I needed to be at the program just as much as Alicia, but instead of putting myself first, I once again played hero. I left the program on January 7, 1996.

Once out of the program, I went directly to see Slick Stand. He was staying with his mother at the time in Nalley Apartments and was doing quite well. He and Super Poo had rented a home in Waldorf, Maryland, and the two of them had Ebony Inn locked down. I apologized to Slick Stand for messing up his money before I entered the program. I told him that I valued our friendship, and I didn't want money to come between us. I promised to pay him back if he allowed me back into the fold.

As soon as I hooked up with Slick and his gang; they tricked me into renting them a car. I felt obligated because I owed them so much money. Since I still got SSI, the rental company used the SSI as an income. All we needed was the cash to rent the car. We paid Sonny's Rent-a-Car for two weeks of use. Everything was in my name, so I kept the car in my possession. Sonny and his wife were nice people. They had a small business, and I knew something about cars, so after the two weeks, I pretty much worked for them.

At that time, Slick was messing with Bonnie, this young, cute, and slick-as-hell young lady by the name of Bonnie. Bonnie is Super Poo's daughter, so they were all one big happy family. Even though Bonnie was almost half Slick's age, he couldn't touch her mentally with a twenty-foot pole. Slick's nose was so far open; you could drive a truck into it.

Bonnie also had a buddy named Janice. She had cute features, a nice shape, and was street-smart. Best of all, she knew how to keep her mouth shut. I fell for Janice. She was only eighteen years old, but you could see the pain and stress in her face. She wanted so much to be in a relationship, but she was afraid her past would come back to haunt her. She told me several times, "if you knew all about my past, you wouldn't want me."

I've always had the Sir Lancelot Syndrome; I think of other people before I think of myself. I really wanted to help her; plus, she had the best coochie in the world. She was my second chance, a chance to relive my youth, a chance to correct some of my mistakes.

Since Alicia was still in the program, I did what I could to help her out financially. I was still crazy and definitely didn't know who I wanted in my life, Janice or Alicia. I was at the point where I was weighing options.

Alicia was a few years older than I, and she had some unachievable goals, as far as I was concerned. She was close to forty and still wanted another child. She had had her tubes tied, so having a kid would require a surgery that neither one of us had money for. Besides, she couldn't take care of the one she had, and to bring another child into that situation would have only been an injustice to both children.

I wasn't taking care of the children I already had, and I was looking forward to enjoying life for a change. I wanted to travel and see the world. I'd been on drugs for years; my world had consisted of a three-mile radius. I hustled to get high, looked for the product, and only a small period of the time was spent getting high. Then the entire process started all over again;Total madness. I was finally through with probation, so there were no limits in my mind to what I could achieve.

Alicia and I talked on the phone and made our plans, but deep in my mind, I knew they were out of the question. She knew that I was in the process of getting housing because of my disability, so if she was with me, she had a place to live upon her release from treatment.

I also saw my old friend Darryl, the same guy who let me stay in his home while I was awaiting a bed space in the program. The same guy whose money I'd messed up before going to the program. When Darryl saw I had a car at my disposal, he asked me for a favor that would clear my debt to him. He asked me to drive him to New York to help a friend move back to Maryland.

Mind you, I've seen more money than any of the people I came in contact with. I've seen more money than most of the people that work on Wall Street. I am a hustler; I could sell George Bush Canada, and he would think he got a good deal. But somewhere down the line I got "stuck on stupid." I guess the drugs turned off the smart button in my brain. Why I continuously allowed these morons to use me still baffles me today.

First and foremost, I made these fools a considerable amount of money. Any debts I might have created should have been overlooked; we were making grand theft money. Besides, the knowledge they gained from me was indispensable. Most of the morons I was in constant contact with never read a book, and especially not a Business and Finance book. I set up organizations, business plans, and financial statements simply trying to give my peers the benefits of my education. Most uneducated people take niceness for weakness; they simply can't see the forest for the trees. I was a blessing in disguise; but a blessing with a drug problem. Therefore, I was never given my just due.

Darryl had a friend name Charlie who went to college in North Carolina. While in college, Charlie met a young lady from Long Island, New York. They eventually got Maried, and made their home in Maryland. Charlie's wife had a little brother named Mike. Mike and his buddy Keevie came down to visit Charlie and his wife and simply fell in love with the area. Mike also wanted to move back to Maryland.

This particular weekend, Mike was going home to get his girlfriend and their belongings. Darryl being the lazy type didn't want to catch a train, so he asked me to drive them. This was the beginning of a journey that would keep me in captivity for the next eleven months.

We left for New York on Saturday, January 27, 1996 at 7:00 a.m. It was raining that morning, and I really had a bad feeling about going. I had spoken to both Alicia and Slick about the trip, and the two of them both told me not to go. My hard-headed ass went anyway. Darryl and I had known each other for years, and the least I could do was to drive him to New York, especially since he was paying for everything.

It was a long ride up 95 North. Once we got to Delaware, we decided to go across the Delaware Memorial Bridge to the New Jersey Turnpike. I though once we got on the turnpike the trip was half way over, so I let Mike drive. I'd been up most of the night, and I was tired as hell.

I always thought of New Jersey as a city. I should have known from its nickname the Garden State, that the place was full of vast farmlands. After an hour or so of driving through small towns, I finally noticed a city I had heard of, Trenton Exit 7. We continued on up the turnpike until we got to Perth Amboy. That's when I went to sleep. When I woke up, we were going across the Verrazano Bridge in Brookland New York. Apparently, they sold some good weed in Brookland, so Mike and Keevie just had to get a bag.

I was in awe as we drove through New York. Everything there is so much faster than in Washington. Even the children are mature way past their ages. The people drive like maniacs; everybody is in a tremendous hurry going no place. The women are the same in New York as they are in Georgia: gullible, looking for something for nothing.

While in Brookland, I had a chance to actually talk to some of the kids there. They were actually reciting poetry, and poetry had been my thing since the late '80s, so I stopped to listen. They were no more than ten or eleven, but they knew their culture well. They were well-informed of the African-American quest to freedom, and were rapping about our history. Here I was from the south, where most of the marching took place, and I wasn't as informed as eleven year olds in New York.

Next, we went to Long Island where Keevie and Mike's girl lived. They already had a U-Haul truck in front of the house. We only had to move her bedroom set and a few other personal items. The only problem was that we had to wait until her parents got home from work at 6:00 pm. Her mother was supposed to give her some money for the trip, and they couldn't leave without the funds. While we were waiting, Mike took us on a tour of the city. First, we went to a mall in Nassau County. The place looked the same as a mall in Maryland. The only difference was the prices; they were considerably higher.

Next, Mike took us to Harlem. I got the chance to see the Cotton Club and the Apollo theater. Broadway Avenue reminded me of Adams Morgan in North-West Washington: Latino town. They were clocking at the same magnitude as a 7th and T Street, or Division Avenue in Washington.

The Latinos in Harlem were very organized. They actually had the drug trade down; everything was business with them. They had dealers, look-outs, and even kids that guided you to whatever product you wanted. Harlem was actually a shopping mall for narcotics.

I got a kick out of the women there. I simply loved their accents: half New York and half Spanish. Mike and Darryl left, supposedly to get some more weed and Keevie and I sat in the car and talked to two Spanish girls. The ladies kept our company until Darryl and Mike returned.

Once back in the car, Darryl told me he was contemplating getting some cocaine, but the prices were only a fraction of a difference in cost from the prices in Washington; it wouldn't worth the risk to buy in New York.

From there, we went to the McDonald's near the tunnel. Mike's girl was supposed to meet us there. We had dinner and waited for about an hour. When she still hadn't shown up after an hour, Darryl got impatient and wanted to go home. He claimed he had something to do. I also was supposed to meet Janice at midnight. So Mike jumped out of the car and said he'd wait in McDonald's until his girl got there. As soon as we pulled out of the parking lot, she pulled up in the U-Haul.

When we got to the tunnel, Keevie lit up his weed. Mind you, I've heard a great deal about the New Jersey Turnpike. They have been locking up African-Americans on the turnpike for years. I didn't want to give them any reason to pull us over.

We traveled along smoothly until we got to exit 12. That's when I spotted a trooper in the rear-view mirror. He followed us to exit 9 before pulling us over. The trooper walked up to the driver's side window with his gun drawn. He asked me for my license and registration; I quickly obliged. He came back to our car claiming we had a malfunctioning tail light. He asked me to step out from the vehicle and asked where we were coming from in New York. He also claimed he had reason to believe that we had guns and drugs in the car. I asked him how he based that assumption. He told me it was from years of experience. We had a choice: allow him to search the car, or sit on the side of the highway until the "dope dogs" came. There wasn't supposed to be anything in the car, so we allowed him to search the vehicle.

Even though New Jersey is in the north, I got the eerie feeling I was in Alabama.

I was driving a brand new Nissan Altima, which I had gotten from a rental agency. Rental agencies do what is called a "bumper-to-bumper" inspection on all their vehicles before they leave the lot, so there couldn't have been anything wrong with the car.

The next crooked thing they did was that they claimed each of us gave conflicting statements. The officer asked me where I was coming from, and I told him New York. He then asked me to put my hands on the car while he asked the other two passengers, Darryl and, where they were coming from, and each of us said exactly the same thing. I always thought this kind of stuff occurred in the south, not a northern state like New Jersey.

They have a phrase for what happened to the three of us that day: racial profiling. That when the cops stop a particular group because of their ethnic background. In my addiction / drug stupor, I'd failed to read the newspaper or look at the news, for they have been racial profiling on the New Jersey Turnpike for decades. They even have a term for African-Americans being arrested on that turnpike: "DWB" or Driving While Black. I got caught up in the center of racial injustice.

We were each searched, and all three of us were made to sit on the side of the turnpike while the trooper searched the car. He had called for backup, and the other officer watched the three of us while the initial trooper did his search. Mind you, it was January 27th, and it was snowing; thus we were made to sit in the snow while they searched. The officer started his search on the driver's side of the vehicle. He went under the dashboard, under the seat, and checked the ashtray. Next, he went to the passenger's side. He searched the same three areas as he did on the driver's side. Both sections came up clean. I had been driving, Darryl had been in the passenger seat, and Keevie had sat in the back seat. The officer then ventured to the back seat. He checked the seats, the floors, and then I noticed he was carrying Mike's coat. In his rush to meet his girl, he left his coat in the back seat.

The officer asked me whose coat that was. It was especially odd since the three of us were already wearing coats. I quickly told him, "We had another friend, Mike, that road back with his girlfriend, and the coat belonged to him." After only a few seconds of searching the coat, the officer came out with a jewelry box. He proceeded to open the box, and inside there was approximately eighty grams of cocaine. I know the exact amount from my charging documents, and chemistry reports.

We were then thrown to the ground, handcuffed, and taken to the trooper barracks. Fate had hit me in the head again. I was in the backseat of that police cruiser hearing my counselor's voice all over again. Mr. C told me, "If I left the program, I'd be in Lewisburg in 30 days." I wasn't in Lewisburg, but I was certainly going to jail again; and in less than thirty days; twenty to be exact.

When we arrived at the trooper barracks, they put each one of us in separate cells. The officers figured they could get a confession from one of us. Since we really didn't know where the drugs came from, we all told the same story. That made the arresting officer angry. He actually told me he'd fix it so I couldn't get a bond.

We were then transported to the Middlesex County Jail in New Brunswick, New Jersey. The jail was actually new, and it was quite clean if I say so myself. The three of us were charged with possession of CDS, possession with intent to distribute, and conspiracy. Darryl had a quill in the watch pocket, so he was also charged with possession of drug paraphernalia. They fingerprinted us again to make sure we didn't have any outstanding warrants.

We were taken to the medical unit so they could check our blood and see if we had any other illnesses. They also tested us for TB. Then we were given orange jump suites and placed in the intake unit, N-unit. As soon as I got on the unit, I called my sister Judy. She had a touch-tone phone; you had to press (1) in order for me to make a connection. My parents had a rotary phone in their home, so they couldn't accept my call; they were old and set in their ways, just simply would give up that rotary phone.

Judy seemed heart-broken when I told her about my predicament. She had come to visit me at the Phoenix House and really thought I had gotten my life in order. I guess my family thought I was naturally evil because I had rebelled against any kind of help. In their eyes, I was destined to be nothing. N-unit was full with black, white, Puerto Rican, and even Korean men. This was the first time in my life ever seeing-an Asian man in prison.

New Jersey definitely didn't have any problem locking men up. They had become a prison state, with more prisons than factories. The first person I met on the unit was Melvin. Melvin was from North Carolina, and he was also in jail for getting caught on the turnpike. The first thing he said when I met him was "Did you get locked up on the turnpike?"

When I answered yes, he handed me a lawyer's card. Melvin said this was the best lawyer in New Jersey. He went on to tell me about him being caught on the Turnpike with a kilo and only getting three years. When I finished listening to Melvin, I ran to Darryl and Keevie's perspective cells. I showed them the card and told them exactly what Melvin had said.

It just so happens that Darryl's cellmate was Melvin's co-defendant. He was on the top bunk while we were talking, playing possum. When he heard me mention Melvin's name, he jumped right up. He said, "Melvin didn't have no kilo; me and Melvin came all the way from North Carolina to get some cocaine, but we smoked it all up in New York." He said, all they got caught with was two $20 rocks, and Melvin's old car got them stopped. Melvin's co-defendant went on to tell us that Melvin had a '69 Chevy with a bad tailpipe. He said when the trooper pulled Melvin over; Melvin had a stem in his hand. He was wearing a Mexican sombrero and had a case of Bamboo rolling paper tied to the roof of the car. Melvin had claimed they could sell the papers in North

Carolina and make some of their money back. This guy also said, that "Melvin told the trooper that each one of them had a $20 rock and that he was holding them so I wouldn't smoke mine up before we got home."

Most of the black men from New Jersey had Divine names like Knowledge Born, Quasan Koran, and Kendu; a great deal of them was 5 percenter's. I had never heard of the 5% Nation until being arrested in New Jersey. They actually believed they were Gods. They also had their own clothing line at one time, but they sold it out to the Koreans.

Then there were the Puerto Ricans, Columbians, and Cubans. They made up about 30% of the prison population in New Jersey. Since the cost of living was so high in New York, many of them had come to New Brunswick for affordable housing and a better life for their children. For protection purposes, they started their own gangs: Latin Kings and Neatta's. They had a great deal of power within the New Jersey Prison system. The white men had the Aryan Brotherhood and the different biker gangs.

After we were classified general population, they separated Darryl and me. He was sent to K-pod, and Keevie and I were sent to I-pod. This was the first time I had ever seen anything that even resembled a pod. The pods were in the form of a dormitory, and they each held over 150 men. They had three floors, and a different group controlled each floor. I noticed right off that the New Brunswick projects ran the jail. That's where the majority of the men were from, both black and Puerto Rican. The majority of them had some kind of drug problem. It seemed like New Brunswick had been hit hard by the cocaine and heroin bug.

The majority of the top tier was from out of state. They had men from everywhere from Texas to Boston; all were arrested on the New Jersey Turnpike. They called themselves the Turnpike Crew. I had been in and out of jail for a lot of years, so I fit in with all the groups quite easily. I learned different things from each of the cultures.

The thing I see in prisoners from Georgia all the way to Boston is that they are afraid to fight their cases. They all simply cop out, give up, and take a plea bargain. If just half the inmates in America would take their case to trial, that would bankrupt the entire criminal justice system. We will fight and kill each other, but we are afraid of the white man in a black dress. I would rather fight my case. Why lie down and let them throw the book at you? I'd rather stand up, and at least that way, I can possibly duck the book. No one in the world is perfect; simply we all make mistakes. If you can find that mistake in the case law, you can find a way out. The law is simply logical deduction. Most of the prison population was simply afraid to fight. Indians say, "white man speaks with forked tongue", simply, for every wrong they cause, they have a way out. A smart man seeks that way. A very smart man doesn't fall victim in the first place.

When I was finally taken to court for my bail hearing, I was given a $35,000 bond. The court figured since I was from Washington, D.C., if I wasn't given a stiff bond where I was going to need someone to put up property or something, I wasn't going to come back to court. I even had the pretrial people call the Phoenix House to confirm I had just left. My urine was clean at the time of my arrest, and a favorable recommendation from my counselor, Kim, could possibly get my bail lowered. I signed a release of information so Kim could respond. When the pretrial people called Kim, she told them that I had left the program with all aspirations of selling drugs. She even mentioned that I had stated my intentions not once, but twice in a group setting. She stated, "Michael is heartless and needs to be in prison." Can you believe I signed a release of information, so she could tell my only hope for freedom; I needed to be locked up?

Darryl was given a $15,000 bond, and Keevie a $20,000 bond. My bond was higher because I was the driver of the car. Since no one took ownership of the narcotics, in the eyes of the court, the drugs were mine, and Keevie and Darryl were just conspirators.

I called everyone for money to get out. For the first time in my life, I was really innocent. I hadn't bought any drugs; I was just caught up in someone else's bullshit. I knew my parents were not going to put up $35,000 to get me out, so I asked them to send me my SSI checks. I also wrote to the administrator of the jail and asked for a daily pass to the law library. I had to figure a way out of this mess, and the first thing I had to do was to get that bail lowered. I dove head-on into the law; I read everything I could that pertained to my case. I eventually got the Judge to lower the bond to $20,000, so now all I needed was $2,000 to get out.

The person that hurt me the most during that time was Alicia. She got out of the program and got a good job. I just knew I could count on her to sign my bond so I could get out. Besides, I'd left the program so she could stay. If I had never left, I wouldn't be locked up. When I called Alicia on a three-way phone call through the Bondsman's Agency, ABC Bonding, Alicia said she had to think about getting me out. She told the man to give her his number and she would call him in an hour, to let him know her decision. She then told me to call her back. Once I called Alicia back, she went on to tell me she and Billy were moving in with a man she had met before me when she was in Alexandria Detox. She said that they loved each other, and she was moving on with her life. Once again, I'd screwed myself for a woman. Mind you, I made the decision to take Darryl to New York, not Alicia; but I did think we had a stronger bond. She just threw me away like yesterday's trash.

I was actually given six different attorneys, and each of them said the exact same thing, "How much time are you willing to do, and am I willing to testify for the state?" All accept one, Ms. Linda Smith. Linda actually listened to me, and looked at my educational background. She knew of all the wrong-doings that occurred on the New Jersey Turnpike, and when she saw I wasn't afraid to fight, she threw herself fully into the case.

In six months' time, I had raised over $4,000 towards my bail, but I couldn't get anyone to sign the bond. My father and my sister wouldn't even consider the thought of getting me out. Darryl's brother Winston bailed him out, so I just knew, once in the streets, Darryl would get me out. I guess I was simply wishing on a star, for Darryl never came through. I actually sat in that jail for eleven months, and all Darryl sent me was $20 to get some commissary.

It wasn't until November that I was finally released on bond. A guy by the name of Homicide, from Elizabeth, New Jersey knew a Bails Bondsman named Bonny. When he heard about the amount of money I had in my inmate account, he called Bonny. Bonny, in turn, called the finance office at the jail to confirm the amount herself, and then she called me at the jail.

I had all but given up on the thought of getting out on bond. The other guys in the unit gave me hell because I was continuously calling someone in hopes of freedom. Most of them had been arrested on the turnpike themselves, and were unable to make bond. Men like Clarence Crue, Billy Moore, Scotty, Big Gene, Carolina, Bob Carter, Tommie Mack, Robert Simmons, and my main man, Fifty Grand. Each of these men was in jail because of someone else's stupidity. I guess in the life, there is always the fall guy and I-pod is where the Court system in Middlesex County dropped off its fall guys.

Bonny worked for B&B Bonding in Elizabeth New Jersey. She first tried to get me to give her $4,000 to get out on a $20,000 bond. That was actually $2,000 more than the actual cost, but I wouldn't need a co-signer if I took her deal. I had been in that hole in the wall for so long, I told her I'd rather just hold on to the money and use it for commissary in prison.

Bonny then asked for some of my relative's phone numbers. I gave her Melvin and Donald's phone numbers. We hung up, and she went about making her calls. About 20 minutes later, I was called to the officer's desk, and I was asked to call B&B Bonding. When I finally got through to Bonny, she told me that my brother Melvin had promised to sign the bond. He had given her the information she needed, and he was on his way to retrieve the faxed papers for his signature from Kinko.

I couldn't believe it. I was finally going to get out of jail. The thing the weighed on my mind was what ever did she tell Melvin. Melvin is tighter than Scrooge in the story *A Christmas Carol*. He wouldn't give sand to a desert, but he was a sucker for a pretty face. At the time, I wondered if she promised him some pussy for getting me out. It turned out the actual truth was my mother was sick, and she wanted to see her baby before she died. Once again, mom got me out.

Bonny didn't come to the jail until 2:00 am. I guess she waited until she got a few more people to bond out before she came to get me. The problem was that I'm from Washington, and I had no way of getting out of New Jersey other than the bus or train. Both stations were closed.

The jail gave me a check for $6,300. Bonny took my picture and did her very best to give me change. She gave me cash and money orders. Then she called me a cab to take me to the New Brunswick Train Station.

Before the cab arrived, I hid my money everywhere. I had money in my shoes, money in my underwear and only a small amount in my pockets. I said good-bye to Bonny, and I waited for the cab.

When the cab arrived, it was almost 3:00 am. The driver took the long way to the train station. He had a meter in the cab, and the longer the ride, the bigger the fair. Once at the train station, I took my belongings and sat on the bench out in front.

I sat there for about thirty minutes. Then I saw the Rutgers Campus Police making their rounds. When the officer rode by, he looked directly in my face. About thirty minutes later, the officer rode by again. This time, he called me over to his car. The officer asked me why I was sitting on that bench. I told him I had just recently been released from the jail, and I was from Washington, D.C. I said I was simply waiting for the train station to open at 5:00 am. The officer looked me right in the face and said, "Let's put it this way, if you are still sitting on that bench when I come around again, you are going back where you just came from." When he left, I waved at him and proceeded to get away from that bench.

Mind you, I had $4,300 in my possession. It was November and cold, so all I had to do was rent a hotel room for a few hours until the station opened. But that's not crazy Michael. I notice three people walking from the Rutgers campus, so I asked them in what direction I would find the New Brunswick project. All three of the people looked at me like I was crazy. One even said, "You want to go to the project this time of night?" I said yes, so they told me to follow them.

Tommie Black, BC, Kendu, and Quasan were all from the projects, and we had become friends in my stay at their jail. I figured I'd see one of their crazy asses and hang out with them until the train station opened in the morning. The people I was following walked straight up George's Road and pointed in the direction of the projects. The girl actually said for me to be careful.

As soon as I entered the projects, two men in black hooded sweatshirts accosted me with a knife. Fortunately, I knew both of them: Kendu and

Quasan. I still remember Kendu saying, "hey man, this is D.C.; D.C they finally let your crazy ass out; whatever are you doing in the projects this time of night?" I quickly replied, looking for you.

Kendu went on to tell me how he was dope-sick, and could I get them some dope? I didn't let them know how much money I had, but I did say I'd get all of us a bag. We walked to my friend Bruce's house over by his father's barber shop to get some bags.

When Bruce saw me, he was ecstatic. Bruce and I would sit for hours in the jail, telling lie after lie. We also were quite close. Bruce told me he had six bags left, and he needed $80 to go to Newark New Jersey to get some more bricks. A brick of dope was the equivalent of five ten packs. Hustlers in New Brunswick would go to Newark, buy the dope for maybe $5 a bag, and bring it back to New Brunswick and sell each bag for $20.00 a bag. I had a few dollars, so I was happy to help Bruce out. The last thing Bruce told me was to get away from those two derelicts.

I didn't let Kendu or Quasan know how many bags I had. I simply gave them a bag a piece. The dope in Jersey was three times as good as the dope in Washington. It was raw dope cut with morphine, so just a snort or two would take you where you wanted to be. We snorted the bags, and we were twisted. Kendu took me to their sister's house in the projects to wait on the train.

Mind you, it was now almost 4:30 am, and when we entered Kendu's sister's house, children were playing everywhere. I asked them why the kids were up this time of morning, and was told that children never sleep in the projects.

I still remember Kendu having to slap his nephew when we turned off the cartoon network to watch videos. At that next moment, a woman in men's boxer shorts and timberlands entered the room, carrying a bat.

She said to Kendu, "I told you about having these junkies in my house around my kids."

Kendu quickly replied, no Sweetie, this is D.C., he's a big-time drug dealer from Washington. He's just waiting here until the train station opens in the morning. I think he's rich. She kindly relied, "D.C., are you hungry?"

Sweetie went back in the bedroom and got dressed. When she came back, I handed her a bag of dope. She took the bag but said she'd rather have some cocaine. She asked me whether I knew Seal. Seal was a Puerto Rican hustler I'd met in the jail. I had actually helped him with some legal work, so he owed me a favor. I told Sweetie yes, and she quickly went to Seal's girl's house to get him.

When Seal heard it was me in the building he awakened quickly. He actually came out into the hallway in his underwear. Seal told me he had two ounces of cocaine left, and he needed $500 to go to New York in the morning. He said if I gave him $500, he would give me both ounces of powder cocaine. I told Seal I had a $500 blank money order. He looked at it, and quickly handed me the cocaine. I just knew I had been beat, so I stashed the bulk of it and got Sweetie to walk with me so we could cook some of it up to test its purity. There were just too many kids in that house to get high.

The first place we went was to Tommie Mac's house. Tommie lived with his mom in the senior citizens building. On our way there we ran into Nate and Carol. They were looking to but some coke, so Sweetie told them to come with us.

Carol was maybe in her early 40's, but she had the body of a 25 year old. She didn't have a blemish on her face. You could tell she took excellent care of herself. Nate on the other hand had smoked some PCP back in the day, and now thought he was Bruce Lee re-incarnated. He had a good job, so Carol stuck by him. Well, Carol shot coke (used it intravenously), and Nate smoked coke, so Carol gave me $20 and I broke her a nice piece off the package. She gave Nate half, and went into the bathroom with Tommie. Can you believe, Nate had bacon soda, and spoon, and water in his pocket. I just sat there and watched him cook it up in a matter of seconds. He gave Sweetie a piece and put him a piece on his stem. He lit the stem and sucked real hard for about 45 seconds then passed the stem to Sweetie, and went immediately into a hand-stand and knocked all the pictures off the wall. That act awakened Tommie's mother. Tommie ran out of the bathroom to calm his mother, and I noticed Carol was butt naked sitting on the side of the tub. Sweetie explained every time Carol gets a good hit she takes her dam clothes off. We eventually had to leave Tommie's, so we walked up the street to Big Bobs house.

Big Bob had worked on his job 30 years and after he retired he took up smoking coke as a hobby. Rather than throw him out in the street, his wife banished him to the basement. I gave Bob about a 1/16 to cook up. He cooked it in a spoon, and was trying to hide coke in his finger nails. I just wanted to try the coke to make sure I didn't get beat. I should have used Carol and Nate's performance as an example, but my hard headed ass had to try it for myself. I simply put a nice piece on the stem for myself. Everybody in the house warned me not to hit such big a piece, but my crazy ass thought I was a professional crack smoker. Sweetie begged me to take some of the coke off the stem. She knew I'd been in jail for the last 11 months, and she figured my heart couldn't handle such a large blast.

I simply paid them no attention, and proceeded to light the stem. Once I had the crack completely melted, I sucked the smoke with the intensity of a Hoover vacuum cleaner. When I finally exhaled the smoke, the room started to move in circles; then my ears started to ring as if I was in a bell tower; then paranoia hit, and I just knew everyone in the house was trying to rob me.

I immediately grabbed the trash bag I had that contained all my possessions from the jail; and commenced to run out of the house. Everyone in the house jumped up in attempt to stop me. In my paranoia, I just knew they were going to rob me, so I ran as fast as I could to the New Brunswick Train Station. Behind me, I heard Sweetie screaming for me to stop. She actually had discussed the possibility of her coming back with me to D.C. She had about four kids and a crack habit, and I have problems taking care of myself, so I wasn't about to add five more mouths to feed.

I ran into the train station, purchased a ticket, and ran to the upper platform to await a train. I still remember seeing, Sweetie, BC, and Nate watching me board the train; they had lost their meal ticket.

Once on the train, I was still skied up. Sweat was running down my face, and I was nervous as hell. The car I was in was full of dudes going down south to sell heroin. When one of them saw the condition I was in, he quickly ushered me the restroom and filled my nose with raw heroin. He then took me to the dining car and paid the patron extra for a double Remy and coke. I drank the drink down straight and then found a seat. After being seated for five minutes, I was knocked out. Then next thing I remember, I was at New Carrolton Station, and ten minutes from home.

Instead of going home, I went to Darryl's house. I never let on the amount of money I had in my possession, and I asked him for some money. I think he gave me $50. All I got was $50 for being locked up for 11 months.

The next thing I did was call Alicia. She had written to me about two weeks before I made bond to tell me that she and her new friend had broken up. She claimed he had been taking some type of psych medicine that prevented him from performing sexually. She also claimed that they eventually got on each other's nerves, so he just left the apartment. Alicia was living on Martin Luther King Highway in Seat Pleasant. Janice's last address was directly around the corner from Alicia. I looked forward to seeing them both.

I caught a cab from Darryl's house to Pleasant Homes in Seat Pleasant Maryland. Janice was staying with Super Poo's sister at the time of my arrest in the Pleasant Homes Apartments. Once at their door, I was informed by a neighbor that the apartment was empty. I felt distraught. I had looked forward to holding Janice in my arms; I guess I had to settle for Alicia.

I walked around the corner to Alicia's house. She was living in the Glen Willow apartment complex. When I arrived, Billy answered the door. I think Alicia kind of felt bad about how things had turned out with us. I just wanted to show her that I still looked good; I had three pockets full of money and almost two ounces of cocaine in my possession. When she saw the cocaine, the first thing she said was, "You have balls of steel." Here I had been in jail eleven months, supposedly for trying to smuggle eighty grams of cocaine back to D. C., and after my release, I still brought some drugs home. I thought of it as retribution; I'd been locked up 11 months for nothing, so at least this way, I got something for all the time I'd spent in the jail.

I left Alicia's house and wished her luck in life. From there, I went to the Ebony Inn. Colby was finally out of jail; he and Little Carl were sitting at the bar when I walked in. They both seemed very happy to see me. I asked Colby about Janice's whereabouts, and he gave me the entire low-down. It seems that after my arrest, Janice started messing with Slick. Slick really didn't want her; he just wanted to make Bonnie mad. In the process, Janice got pregnant, and Slick didn't want to claim the child. Slick knew how I felt about Janice, but he didn't care about my feelings; all he cared about was his own self. That was a major setback in my life; as a result I went to the closest crack house to relieve my tension.

I got released from Middlesex County Jail, November 30, 1996. Before New Year's, I was broke again, and I was a full-fledged addict.

In '97, I lost my trial;
It would be (3) more years before I would smile.
Got pulled over for a bad taillight
In a brand-new car; now that ain't right.
Judge Munkasci gave me a 9 with a 3,
But I came home with a college degree.

Chapter 18

1997

I don't know why I didn't just stay in jail. I could have saved a lot of money. I had a problem with feeling sorry for myself. When things went wrong in my life, I'd simply got high in attempt to escape the reality of the problem. All drugs did was make the problem worse.

I'd sat in jail for eight months without a court date, but now that I was out it seemed like I must go to court every other month. They had played the game of "Bull Pen Therapy" with me for the first six months of my incarceration. That's what people call it when you're taken to the court building but made to sit in the Bull Pen all day without seeing anyone. That alone has a big effect on the human psyche. I think the system felt as long as they had one of us in custody, there was a big chance that that person would eventually plead guilty, but now that all three of us were out, they were in a hurry to close the case.

I pretty much existed for the first five months. In February, we had a status hearing, and in April, we had our suppression hearing. The suppression hearing is when we had a chance to finally interrogate the state trooper that had arrested us. At the hearing, they had several police detectives and even a crime psychologist. They were there to make a case that we were big-time drug dealers and that the court should overlook anything that the trooper might have done wrong. Judge Munkcasi, being an ex-prosecutor, went right along with the state.

They tried to make a case that the state troopers are good officers and their integrity should not be questioned. I guess they didn't take into consideration all the wrong-doings they had been doing on that turnpike for decades.

We had an affidavit from the owners of the rental car that stated nothing was wrong with the car when I took it, and nothing was wrong with the car when they picked it up from the impound lot. Judge Munkcasi said the letter wasn't good enough, and she wanted the owner there, in person, after lunch, if we planned to use their testimony in the hearing. Mind you, we were in New Jersey, and the owners were in Maryland; it was simply impossible to get those people to the courtroom after lunch. I blame the people not being there in the first place on my drug addiction. If I was on my job, like I was supposed to be, the entire personnel from Sonny's Rent-a-car would have been in New Jersey with me. I was too busy getting high to think about my freedom.

We eventually loss the suppression hearing, so our next step was trial. The trial was set for September of 1997, so I had five more months to play. I got a part-time job at a Modular Furniture company, SMEAD. The warehouse was directly behind my mother's house, so I could walk to work. They paid me $10 per hour, but I sometimes worked 100 hours in a two-week period. With overtime, I made a pretty good wage.

The only problem with the job was my fellow employees. They were retired service-men, and truly unable to think outside the box. I always had a problem with people that claim to be holier–than-thou but steal and lie like sailors. They actually thought they were better than me because they were salaried employees. What they failed to realize was that with overtime, I made more than them. Besides, they had homes and families, and all I had to do was to hit mom and dad off and the remainder was mine. I also did what I could for my children, but the majority of my money went towards my drug habit. I got paid on Fridays, give mom and dad some money and smoke until work started that Monday. Then, the whole process started all over again. I really felt like a damn fool.

Believe it or not, my sister Judy's love stopped me from getting high. At the time, I had about $1,400 and wanted a car. She took me and my father to Tyson's Auto Auction in Tyson's Corner Virginia. Most of the nice cars went for prices considerably higher than the money I had, so I really looked distraught. She asked me what kind of car I wanted, and I told her a Coup De Ville, and she told me to bid on it. I got the car for $2,100. She loaned me the extra money I needed and took me back to Virginia to pick up the car. I was so happy that someone in my family had faith in me. I wanted to do my best to prove to her I was deserving of the car, so I stopped getting high. I even stopped hanging around people that got high.

Around the same time, I met this young lady name Bernice. I had grown up with her cousins and was introduced to her at a family party. She seemed like a nice woman; but she had problems beyond my comprehension. Bernice lived with her parents in Forestville. They were very nice people that loved their daughter. They even let me stay with her. The entire situation was simply too good to be true. I know somewhere down the line there was a cake baking for me. Bernice and I stayed together all the way until it was time for me to go to trial. I guess God once again saved me from some unknown danger.

I started trial on September 8, 1997. The trial lasted a week. Munkcasi took Linda Smith off my case because she was too thorough. She gave me a nut by the name of Tony Smith. I still think today that Tony Smith was in the judge's hip pocket.

The trial lasted all week. Each one of us had a different attorney, and we each presented our cases separately. When my attorney, Tony Smith, finally put on my defense, I could tell he was ill-prepared and was speaking from the top of his head. He did make one statement that I thought would keep me from being convicted. He said, "If Mr. Moore knew there were drugs in the car, why would he allow the troopers to search it?" That seemed like a sensible question, and a logical human being would put some thought into it.

When it was the prosecutors turn to rebut our defense, she jumped right on that question. She said, "He allowed them to search the car because he is dumb. Drug dealers are dumb; that's why they don't have jobs like me and you." I looked directly into my attorney's face, and asked him to clear that up, but he didn't. I was advised not to speak on my own behalf, so the prosecutor's statement went unchallenged.

I had attended major universities and was working as an International Technician for SMEAD, but I was advised not to speak in my behalf because the prosecution would bring up my past criminal history. It never occurred to me that the jury would not have anything from me, per se. As a logically-thinking individual, if I was on a jury, I would at least want to hear "I didn't do it" from the defendant. If only I had thought about that at my trial. I guess wisdom comes with age, for they can never get me that way again.

Now, later on in life, I realize the state's Attorney's Office, the courts, and the Public Defender's Office are separate entities, but they all work for the same organization, Middlesex County. How can you beat them if they are all on the same team?

On September 12, 1997, we were all found guilty of all three counts: possession, possession with intent to distribute, and conspiracy. The prosecutor told the judge that she was going to seek an extended term against Darryl and me, so she asked that our bails be revoked. An extended term would mean we were facing as much as twenty years.

Judge Munkacsi didn't revoke our bails, but she did raise them to $40,000, so it was back to Middlesex County Jail for the two of us. At the time, I didn't have another $2,000 to get out again. Keevie didn't have any past convictions, so he was released on his same bail. When we left the court that day, Keevie told me he wasn't coming back, and I haven't heard anything from him since.

I had driven my car to court that day because Darryl and I had had a falling-out the night before. My car was in the parking garage in New Brunswick, so I gave my car keys to my attorney, Tony Smith. I told him that someone would be contacting him when they came to pick up the car.

I called my father, my brother Melvin, and my sister Judy to come get my car. None of them would come, so I was forced to confide in both Bernice and Slick Stand. Slick Stand eventually came to get my car; him and his lady, Patsy. Patsy fell in love with the car and attempted to buy it, but once the car was back in Washington, my family refused to sell it.

Once back at the jail, I was placed in I-pod again. This time, Darryl was also put in I-pod with me. I really don't think Darryl realized we were the only two men in that unit that was from Washington, for he started a store. He was selling commissary items to people from New

Brunswick, but he wasn't from New Brunswick. I've been locked up all over the country, and there is a level of respect necessary, especially when you are in another town. I know if we were in Washington and someone from New Jersey came to our jail trying to open a store, we'd hit his head. I just couldn't get that message through Darryl's thick head. Most of the guys from New Brunswick had a great deal of respect for me, and that's the only reason they didn't hit Darryl's head.

In the meantime, while I waited for my December 8, 1997, sentencing date, I worked out hard. I simply lived on the pull-up bar. I also had my sister Judy hire Linda Smith to represent me at sentencing. She only charged me $500 since she didn't like Judge Munkacsi.

The court was trying to extend my sentence because the prosecutor stated to the judge that I had two prior convictions for drug distribution. The truth was I only had one prior conviction. With one prior conviction, I wasn't facing the extended term. I tried continuously to get Linda to bring this to the courts attention, but she never would. I guess she figured if she got me out, I wouldn't come back to court. She kept giving me this sob story about how it's going to be harder to turn myself in, knowing I was going to prison. The reason I wanted out was to put some money together for appeal purposes.

Linda had done some background work on my family, and had found out they were more than financially stable. I guess she thought she could drain them. I knew if I didn't have my own money, I was going to sit in prison until I was released by either the parole board, or the institution.

During the time I was awaiting sentencing, Bernice hung by my side. She even tried to put my car in storage. After weighing the scales, I concluded that I had only known Bernice a few months, and deep down inside, she was in love with this killer by the name of Richie Rich. I didn't want to take the chance of him getting out and her feelings towards me changing. If that was to happen, I would have had hell getting my car back.

With Linda Smith handling my case, I felt I had a slim chance of getting a smaller sentence. My sentencing guidelines were between five and ten years. I was hoping for the lower on the scale.

I was sentenced December 8, 1997; I even fell out in the court room in hopes of leniency. I told the judge I had a seizure condition and wasn't in the best of health. I even cried in the court room. Darryl started to snicker, and I actually hit him to make him stop. Judge Munkacsi didn't want to hear anything I said. She didn't give me the maximum sentence, but very close. She sentenced me to nine years with a 3-year parole stipulation. I think that was a good sentence compared to the ones they give out in Maryland and Washington, D.C.

The Pre-sentence investigator tried to get me ten years; for he wrote: that I was a risk to commit another offense; the extent of my criminal record was a factor; and I needed to be deterred from violating the law. He also wrote: Defendant is a thirty-three-year-old drug addict who has engaged in lawless acts since 1985; this resulting in ten arrests. He is a resident of the state of Maryland, who transported drugs through our state for distribution in the state of Maryland. I actually had no mitigating factors.

I already had three-hundred and seventy-two days' time credit, so I was considered minimum custody as soon as I reached the Central Reception Assessment Facility (CRAF). Darryl and I were sent to CRAF on December 30, 1997. From there we were sent to our perspective prisons. Since Darryl had three prior drug convictions, so he was given twelve years. After a short stay at CRAF, I was sent to Mid-State Correctional Facility, and Darryl was sent to Northern State Prison.

In '98, a fresh nine years was hard to see,
but a man named Walter taught me how to make time work for me.
He said, use your mind and start to thinking;
Before this shit gets worst and really starts stinking.

Chapter 19

1998

Mid-State was a small prison in Burlington, New Jersey. The prison was actually on the Fort Dix Army Base. The only reason I was sent there was because of my legs. The prison only had two floors, and the majority of the prisoners were old. Also, they had a hard time getting thirty guys from the population for minimum custody. The prison had a contract with the army base to have thirty workers at all times. After I arrived there, I found out that most of the prisoners had "tree jumping" charges. They couldn't go anywhere else in the system and exist safely.

When I first arrived, I was made a Teacher's Aide. I work for a nice black lady named Ms. Baptist. She was very well-educated, and she taught me a great deal about public speaking. She ran many of the organizations, but her baby was the Toast Master program. I only worked for Ms. Baptist for a few weeks. I was classified full minimum when I came into the jail, so once I showed the administration that I wasn't an asshole, they moved me directly to the Minimum Unit.

The general population at Mid-State was in dormitories. When you got to the Minimum Unit, they gave you a single cell. You were then allowed to order a color television and a fan. I got my sister Judy to send me a Television, and from that day on I found a new form of solitude.

There are two levels of Minimum Custody at Mid-State: Full Minimum One and Full Minimum Two. When you first get on the unit, you are classified as Full Minimum Two. Full minimum Two cleans the exterior of the prison, washes buses, and cuts grass around the outside perimeter.

One day while picking up cigarette butts, I noticed the sign above the front entrance of the prison. The sign stated, "Let's keep this place clean for your kids." Now, to a small-thinking individual, they might think the prison was talking about keeping the place clean for visiting purposes. I knew exactly what they were saying: they wanted to keep the place clean for when our kids became prisoners themselves.

The detail officer for Full Minimum Two was a nice guy. Once he saw that you weren't an asshole, he pretty much left you alone. If he saw you were an asshole, he got rid of you quick. After only two weeks at the Full Minimum Two stage, I was made Full Minimum One.

Full Minimum One was a whole new adventure. They had a Sgt. Billips that was really an asshole. They paid us $3.50 a day, and Sgt. Billips wanted his money's worth. He had us in holes, in creeks, and cutting down the forest. I didn't like Sgt. Billips at the time, but he actually saved my life. After about three months with him, I was determined to get a better trade and to stay out of prison. I actually think I went back to college because of Sgt. Billips. Today, I hear he's a lieutenant. I thank you, sir, for being the asshole you were.

My detail officer was named Smokey. Smokey was a good dude. He made sure we got the work done, but he didn't work us like slaves. When Smokey went on vacation for a week, Sgt. Billips honestly had me thinking I was a field nigger.

I still remember that week today. There had been a tornado in New Jersey, and it knocked down an entire city-block-worth of trees on the Fort Dix Army Base. Sgt. Billips volunteered our crew to do clean-up. I'd never seen that many fallen trees in my life. The good sergeant gave our crew approximately one week to clean up the area. If we didn't complete the task within that week's period, we lost all of our weekend privileges.

If we had modern equipment, the job wouldn't have been that hard; but we were only given hand saws and a chipper to spread the wood. I still remember four of us carrying full trees to the chipper. We actually completed the job on time, but I was in so much pain after we finished that I couldn't move for the entire weekend.

The people we worked for were quite pleased with our work, and they actually offered us employment after our perspective releases. They also tried to buy us some extra food, but Sgt. Billips wouldn't let us have it.

Smokey and I were buddies from the moment I started with his crew. I kept him laughing the entire time we worked together. Smokey was in his 60's and on the verge of retirement, and my antics simply made his days to retirement move faster.

I once told him a story about an ax-murderer chasing me. That story kept me from having to work, many a day. The story went something like this:

When I first got classified for camp, I was sent to Marlboro Camp in Marlboro, New Jersey. In Marlboro, they had a crazy house, and the prisoners in the camp work for the crazy house.

On my first day there, the sergeant gave us a big speech on what we could and could not do while working there. The sergeant said, "There are two things you don't do here: screw any of these crazy girls, and mess with the ax-murderer out back." He said that the ax-murderer killed his entire family and was crazy as hell, but he hadn't killed anyone lately, so the state says they had to give him recreation. He warned us a second time to stay away from this nut.

My job was to clean up the picnic area, so I grabbed a rake and commenced to working. That's when I noticed this gigantic man walking across the yard. This man had to be seven feet tall and over 400 pounds. He had his hair in a long ponytail, and his entire body consisted of noting but tattoos. When I first saw the man, just the sight of him scared me to death. I figured, hell, he was on the other side of the yard, so I had nothing to worry about. So I went about raking my area.

My father always told me to keep my head up, but as usual, I didn't listen. I kept raking until I heard a noise behind me. When I turned around suddenly, I noticed this so called ax-murderer was directly behind me, and I'd accidentally hit him with the rake. When I attempted to apologize, he roared at me with the magnitude of a grizzly bear.

That's when I dropped the rake and ran. I ran up the hill, around the ball field, and through the dugout. Can you believe this man chased me the entire way with his arms extended, trying to grab me. I then ran to the picnic area and put the picnic bench between the two of us. The guards were scared to death of this man, especially when he was angry, so they all ran to the building and screamed for me to run in that direction.

By that time, I was out of breath. I felt like my heart was about to burst. Instead of me searching within my inner self for the strength to continue, I said the word that has kept me in trouble since I was a little kid. I said "Fuck it."

I then came from behind the table with my hands in the boxer's stance. I told that crazy fool that he wasn't running me to death and to come on and fight. Mind you, I did mention this man was seven feet tall and over 400 pounds. I even scared the guards. I still remember one of them saying, "Look, D.C.'s going to fight that monster!" I looked that behemoth in the eyes, and told him to come on and fight. The next thing that monster did, made me feel like David when he slued Goliath. He walked over to me, touched me on the shoulder, and said, "You're it," and skipped off. Can you believe that? I felt like David when he slew Goliath. This nut was actually playing tag, and I was the only one he ever caught! I was so mad, I threw the rake and a trash can at that monster.

Whenever another officer came around, Smokey would tell me to tell that officer about the man chasing me. I got out of a lot of work with that story. I still remember the creek over flowing, and all of our crew was waist-deep in mud, everyone but me. When they asked Smokey why I didn't have to get dirty like the rest of them, he told them to shut up before he had him put in the hole. Then he asked me to tell the story about the man chasing me again.

I actually think Smokey retired after I was sent to the Talbot Hall. Talbot Hall was a new assessment center. They were supposed to assess convicts that were eligible for community release and send them to the house that would best fit their needs. Talbot Hall was owned by a man named Clancy. He had started a corporation called Community Correction Corporation (CC&C). This was the first privatized jail in the state of New Jersey. I was one of the first five-hundred people sent to Talbot Hall, and I was really upset I had been sent there. I and the other four hundred ninety-nine other people sent there thought we were going to the Halfway House.

Talbot Hall was tighter than the Minimum Units we had all left. We were making $3.00 and $4.00 a day in prison, and we didn't get a dime of state pay at Talbot Hall. We went to meetings all day long, and half of the evenings. The only upside was the food. We could eat as much as we wanted. They also had an Olympic weight room and a large recreation area.

Most of the Counselors there had either been incarcerated, were ex-correctional officers, or ex-drug addicts, and only a very few were psychology and substance Abuse students. I still remember Miss B. She ran the unit I was on, Serenity. My primary counselor was Mr. Salverese. He was from Coney Island, New York, and his Nephew was the boxer Lou Salverese. Mr. Salverese was a brilliant man. I learned a great deal from him, especially about keeping my business to myself. I had told the Department of Corrections, that I had a drug problem, in hopes of being sent to an outside drug treatment program. Instead, I had to sit in this nursery school / Talbot Hall until I was assessed.

I was sent to the Talbot Hall in May of 1998, and stayed there until August of 1998. From there, I was assessed to the Bo Robinson Center in Trenton New Jersey. Talbot Hall wasn't all bad, for I got a chance to meet some very interesting people. I also got to perform every morning in our Community Meetings. It was at the Talbot Hall that I learned I had a knack for comedy.

The Bo Robinson Center was simply another warehouse owned by Mr. Clancy. Talbot Hall is in Kearney, New Jersey, and Bo Robinson is in Trenton, but both programs operate on the same premise. The actual program phase of the program was excellent. They had some educated black men and women that really wanted to help you. They took pride in their work, and they taught with empathy.

The program consisted of three phases: (1) the orientation phase, which lasted about ninety days; (2), the program phase, which lasted about ninety days; and (3), the re-entry phase, which had you actually go out and work. The final phase lasted until you were released. Since I had already spent ninety days at the Talbot Hall, once at Bo Robinson, I was placed directly into phase two.

The program consisted of groups and meetings five days a week; we had the weekends off. I gained tremendous amounts of information which I still use within my daily life. I was told to keep a journal of my daily feelings; I was taught to keep a daily planner; and I was instructed on the seven Habits of Highly Effective Individual.

My primary counselor's name was Ms. Dixon. Ms. Dixon was an ex-addict, and she tried her very best to mentally and graphically, to show us all the negatives of drug use. I could see in her eyes the fact that she cared for all of us and wanted each member of her group to move on to a better, drug-free life.

I was given a job as a teacher's aide for a very nice woman by the name of Mrs. Wade. Mrs. Wade was a retired public school teacher, and she really wanted the guys to get a better grasp on education. My job was to tutor the Spanish-speaking inmates in reading and writing. Then I was to go to the computer lab and assist Mrs. Slick with her Microsoft Windows class. Mrs. Wade and Mrs. Slick were both members of the same church. Mrs. Wade had actually got Mrs. Slick her job.

Mrs. Slick had come to Trenton from Denver, Colorado. I do believe her husband was in the service, and they had traveled extensively. She really knew her computers, but she also had an aide from New York that was a computer wizard. Once I found out exactly how smart Walter was, I attached myself to him with the intensity of vice grip pliers. I wanted to know everything Walter knew. I wasn't a slouch in the education department either, and it wasn't until I scored one hundred out of a possible one hundred ten on the Adult Education Test that Walter opened up to me. I guess he found it hard to find someone to have an intelligent conversation within the confines of a prison setting. I really looked forward to and my conversations.

When Mrs. Slick saw I was stealing Walter's loyalty from her, she started talking about me behind my back. I once over heard her telling Mrs. Wade that she thought I had cheated on the Adult Education Test. Mrs. Wade was down to earth, and early one morning she let me know what I was up against. That's when I started to push for phase three. I figured, with what Walter had taught me about computers, I only needed a little more formal instruction and I could get certified through Microsoft. With a Microsoft Certification, my chances of excellent employment were much better.

To reach the phase three portion of the program, you had to show the addictions counselor exactly how much you learned while in the group phase. You had to recite in front of the counselor; the twelve steps, the seven habits, the ABC's of Addiction, Attitudes, and Choices. Once you had successfully completed this task and you had completed more than ninety days of phase two, you were allowed into phase three.

I made phase three in December of 1998. The Assistant Administrator at the Bo Robinson Center, Ms. Judy, told me about a program they had in Trenton called the JTPA. She said with the help of JTPA, I could gain computer training through the local college; Mercer Community College. Ms. Judy was a stickler for education. She wanted guys to further their educations while we still had use of the Federal Loans and Grants. I knew that going back to school would be advantage towards my future. The good thing was, not too many of the men at the Bo

Robinson Center were willing to take on the challenge. They wanted jobs so they could save up enough money to get a good-size package once back in society.

When it was time for the interview at JTPA, I talked Walter into going too. I figured with Walter at my side in the computer classes, I was guaranteed a passing grade.

When we first started school at the Mercer County Community College, we were transported every day in vans by the transportation staff. There were eight of us, and we did so well in school that eventually we were allowed to catch the bus to school on our own. That also cut down the fuel cost for Bo Robinson because we had to spend our own transportation money.

My classes were held at the West Windsor Campus of Mercer County Community College. The name of my course was Microsoft Office. This was a complete course of all the software packages within the Microsoft Office suite: Word, Excel, Access, and PowerPoint. We were given textbooks that contained floppy disks that allowed us to do hands-on work within the book. This was a twelve week course which cost over $2,000, and JTPA paid for everything. I was given a counselor that kept track of my attendance, and he made sure my transition back into society went smoothly.

My instructor's name was Jim Carlota. Jim was an excellent instructor that knew the software packages like the back of his hand. He had once taught at the Satone Institute, and there he had made great strides with autistic children. From there, Jim went on the open his own firm: Software Training and Business Solutions. Jim went to various companies and schools, teaching different software packages. At that time there was a great demand for software trainers, and Jim and his partner capitalized on the industry.

Since I had been working for Mrs. Slick in the Computer Room at the Bo Robinson Center, I was way ahead of the rest of the students in my class at Mercer. Jim immediately saw how advanced I was, and he asked me if I would consider being his aide. This was the perfect situation; I was being paid for assisting in the class I was attending. I quickly said yes before Jim had a chance to change his mind.

I was honest with Jim from the very start. I told him I was in a halfway house situation, and I also told him some of the intricacies of my case. Being a liberal, Jim automatically had empathy for my situation. Racial profiling had been going on in the state of New Jersey for decades, and Jim felt, training in computers was a chance for me to benefit from the entire situation. The computer industry was a booming field, and with the proper training, there were no limitations to what I could achieve.

The only problem I had was getting the Bo Robinson Center to allow me to work. I had been assigned to school, not work, and the Center took 1/3 of the pay from people that worked. My counselor, Ms. Dixon, went to my defense. She knew I honestly wanted to change my life, and since we were now responsible for our own transportation money, to get to and from school, the work-study would only help me financially. After a grueling meeting with the administrators, Ms. Dixon not only got them to allow me to work, but they also agreed I could also keep all of my pay for transportation.

The faith Ms. Dixon and Jim put in me, only made me want to work harder to prove I was worth all their efforts. When I had started using drugs, I had lost the drive to achieve. Now, with people willing to put their necks out for me, I simply had to be responsible.

In '99', lost one of a kind,
Getting through this took a long time;
I'll never see my mother any longer,
But like Nietzche says, it made me stronger. .

Chapter 20

1999

Everything in my life was going great. I had saved over $1,500, I was learning a great deal about computers, and I was networking with some very influential people. I was at the top of my game. That's when disaster struck once again.

My mother had been placed in a nursing home in Southern Maryland because of a diabetic stoke. My mother had always been everything to me. She had come to my defense more than once. I felt bad that I couldn't visit her. I had a dream that my mother had died. During this dream, she told me to be strong because my brothers and sisters all resented me because of all the attention I'd always received from her. In a sense, she told me I was now alone in the world.

The next afternoon, once I returned from school, I was called into my counselor's office. Ms. Dixon allowed me to use her phone to call my family. She told me there was an emergency in my family. When I called, Judy told me that Mama had died in her sleep. The entire family was grieving and making funeral plans.

Since I was in New Jersey, it was simply impossible for me to get an escort home, so I thought. The Department of Correction told my family the trip would cost $1,000, but no one informed me that I could pay to come home to pay my last respects to my mother.

I really wanted to see my mother before they put her in the ground, so I wrote everyone. Finally, in the eleventh hour, I was granted permission to go to the funeral. But apparently someone from the Department of Corrections called my family again before they brought me, because the night before I was supposed to leave, the administrator called me into his office and told me my family didn't want me at the funeral. Someone in my family, I still don't know who, told the administrator at Bo Robinson that my appearance at the funeral would only be an embarrassment to the family, and they didn't want me there. Thus, I was denied the chance to see my mother before they put her to rest. My family never even sent me pictures from the funeral.

At that time, I was a "forgive and forget" type; today, I hold grudges forever. I know I've done a lot of wrong in my life, but to deny me the chance to see my mother was the straw that broke the camel's back, after this happened, I became completely heartless.

The students in the class at Mercer treated me like family. They knew what I was going through, and tried to ease my pain. I got more gifts and food that week than at any other time in my life. I never knew people could be so friendly.

Also during that time, my friends Trinny and Charles introduced me to the people that worked for the Educational Opportunity Fund (EOF). This is an African-American organization that assists underprivileged students with their tuitions. These people really tried to teach the kids the value of a good education. I got to meet Kalata, Niel, and Neicey, who all worked for the EOF. There was also Spanish Counselor, whose name I can't remember to save my life.

I continued with my Microsoft classes until they ended in February of 1999. After the completion of the Microsoft class, students had an option to take a test in typing, Word, and Excel; if you passed these tests, you were given nine college credits. They call this Credit for Life Experience.

I passed this test with flying colors. I had already applied for Federal Student Aid before I started the Microsoft class, so I could simply switch to taking regular college courses afterward. I decided to take a graphics course. Walter was the graphics man, and I wanted to get a taste of what he was into. The class was actually easy, so I completed it with my usual "A."

Once I completed the graphics course, my counselor told me that with the credits I already had, if I took three more courses, I could get another certificate in Microcomputer Applications. This meant I had to endure the grueling schedules of summer school. During summer school, I took Western Civilization, another Access Course, and a networking course. Everything seemed to going perfect, until the New Jersey Department of Corrections decided that Bo Robinson was better suited as an Assessment Center.

When this happened, the Administration stopped all inmate movement. What this meant was we were now no longer allowed to attend college. Mind you, the eight of us that were attending school were all doing wonderfully. People within the school and the community, wanted us to stay in school, so they wrote letters and called the Department of Corrections on our behalves. As a result of the numerous amounts of calls they received, the DOC amended their regulations and allowed us to continue our education.

During the time of this drastic change in the Bo Robinson Program, I was assisting another Microsoft Instructor named Susan Zimbalist. Susan was like a big sister to me. She gave me a lot of advice and introduced me to foods from different cultures. I still remember the first time I tasted a cannoli.

I had worked for Jim for three months, so when I started working for Susan, I knew the textbooks inside and out. Since I had been a basketball player, I also knew to concept of being a team player. My main concern was that the classes ran smoothly and that Susan didn't have to stop several times a day for a student to get up to speed. I made sure they were caught up, even if I had to take their mouse and bring them up to speed myself.

The Assistant Administrator at the Bo Robinson Center, Ms. Judy, made arrangements with a halfway house in Trenton, Clinton House, to accept the people that attended Mercer College. Every one of us except Walter transferred to the house. Walter's girlfriend was from New York, and he wanted to be transferred further north. When I left the Bo Robinson Center, I never saw Walter again. He taught me a great deal. I simply combined what he had taught me with what I already knew, and thus became a "computer genius" myself. I believe God puts us in certain situations so we can grow in life. Walter certainly was a blessing, and I will never forget him.

In June of 1999, I arrived at the Clinton House. At that time, they had a new administrator, Maurine. Ms. Maurine was a very intelligent black woman. She had a shrewd demeanor, but she was actually a nice person. I had been in and around criminals for so long that I had a problem understanding honest, law-abiding black citizens. These people wanted to get ahead in life. They worked hard for everything they got, and they definitely didn't like people that took short-cuts. At the time,

I considered this group as "sellouts", but today I understand that there is a bigger world than just the projects and poverty. Most poor people can't see past the life they live, so they never move any further, and they hate people that do move ahead. I guess that's just the crab syndrome" in black people. Mind you, a great deal of children and adults don't have certain advantages, but to never try to rise above a bad situation or to create a worse situation through crime and drugs is only adding to the genocide of my race.

It took a bit of time, but I finally convinced the staff at the Clinton House that I was serious about my education. I even volunteered to teach some of the other men in the Halfway house how to use a computer. I submitted a proposal to Sal, the Assistant Administrator, and was allowed to teach my class.

In July of 1999, I saw the parole board. They were determined to give me an eighteen-month setoff, but once I submitted some of the letters that the Deans and other college officials had written to keep me in school, they changed their minds. I still remember the hearing officer state, "You need to thank God you came to jail." I was given a parole date for December of 1999.

The Clinton House required me to do community service. I did my community service for the Educational Opportunity Fund. Neicey was the secretary, and she simply filled out the proper paper work, and two days a week, I volunteered for them.

While working for EOF, I met this pretty young lady named Patty. Patty was from Trenton, and she thought of me as country. Patty had a son and a place of her own. I figured if I got Patty's heart, I'd have a place to go on the weekends. Neicey had literally adopted Patty, and I gave her some of my best D.C. lines, but nothing seemed to work. I guess I just wasn't her type.

I got a Certificate of Proficiency in Microcomputer Applications in August of 1999. Once I had completed the certificate, I decided to go for an Associate's Degree in Business. That required me to take on a full 15 credit hours in the fall semester. I took Office Accounting II, Business Letter and Report Writing, Principles of Management, International Business, and Principles of Marketing.

Since I was always in the Technical/Computer section of the college, I was given a job with Technology Services. This was a great group of people, and it was a good opportunity for me to gain valuable technical experience.

My responsibilities included upgrading computer hardware, installing software and hardware, troubleshooting and repairing PCs and software. It seemed like everyone was my boss: Doug, Michelle, Bob, Sue, and Tanya; Mr. Albert Magson was the Dean for Technology services. They also knew of my legal problems, but they still gave me an office and the run of the college.

Whenever I had some free time, I chatted in the Washington, D.C. chat room. My login name was lockedup69. I met a lot of lonely women with my opening line: "Locked up in New Jersey and looking to meet a nice female friend." I met women in these chat rooms from all over the world. A few of them even came to visit me at the school.

The first was Fannie Black. She was from Fairbanks, Alaska. Fannie was half black and half Eskimo. She was attending the University of Portland at the time, and we really hit it off. We sent each other cards, gifts, and pictures. Fannie was a very beautiful girl. I couldn't for the life of me figure out why she would be chatting on the internet. I guess most men don't bother to get to know the total person. Our main concern is getting into their pants, and once we have achieved that goal, nine times out of ten we lose our interest. Fannie was my pen pal, and she helped me through some very lonely times. Fannie, if you are reading this, please know you will always have a special place in my heart.

Women are very sensitive individuals, and if you show concern and attention to what they have to say you will definitely make it to first base. An old pimp by the name of Shaky once told me, "If you screw the mind, the body will soon follow." The older I get; the more truth I see in that statement.

The next woman I met was Barbie. Barbie was from Maryland and worked for the lawyers at the EPA. She was a wonderful woman. I still owe her a great deal. I didn't realize what I had until she didn't want anything else to do with me.

Barbie actually drove all the way to Trenton to meet me. I gave her the address to the Clinton House, and she used the Yahoo map for direction. She was my first visit in over two years.

Barbie was in her early 40's, but she carried herself like a much older woman. I was so use to being around hood rats; I couldn't see the good thing standing in front of me. All Barbie wanted was to be loved and respected. We had a few rendezvous, where we had dinner and spent the entire days together. Since I had never been in any trouble at the Clinton House, and I never deviated on my passes; I was given twelve hour passes to go to school and to the shopping mall every weekend. Barbie and I simply met at the college one Saturday morning, and spent the entire day together. The two of us also sent each other cards, letters and pictures.

One Saturday while in the college library, I met this beautiful Light Skinned girl. She was half black and half Latino, with the shape of a dancer. She had long beautiful hair and a wonderful personality. Her name was Liza. Liza had been through the mill with her last boyfriend, and she was attempting to advance herself through education. This was her first college semester, and she was having some trouble with an English paper. I noticed her looking distraught, so I offered my assistance. That act of kindness led to a beautiful friendship.

For our first date, Liza met me at the college, and gave me the scenic tour of Princeton, New Jersey. She even took me to the historic home of the Menendez brothers, two brothers who had killed their parents. The house was on a lake, and on that particular day, someone had rented the home for a wedding. We walked and talked around the lake as if we were part of the wedding party.

We were like kids. We kissed and held hands in school, and I even carried her books to class. I did my very best to make her happy while we were together. Liza worked for a testing company, and when we weren't in class or at work, she would come to the Clinton House and visit me. We made all sorts of plans, but they didn't seem realistic to me because I was going back to Washington once I was released from prison. Liza did everything in her power to get me to stay in New Jersey.

What my crazy ass failed to realize was the financial potential I possessed. Here I was, still in prison, teaching and working at a college. Liza knew that with the proper grooming, I could be the one to buy her first home. I had no idea what was going on. When men meet a woman, they look at her ass and face. Women might do the same thing, but they also ask three questions: Where do you work? Where do you live? What type of car do you drive?

I eventually passed all five of my classes and graduated with honors from Mercer. When I was released on parole, Liza picked me up in a brand new Dodge Durango she had rented. We packed everything I had into the truck, went to the bank and withdrew all my money, and we went to her parents' home for a graduation party. Mind you, I had never met these people, but they accepted me as one of their own from the very start. Liza's father had retired from the government and started his own business. Mr. Burk knew I intended to go back to Washington, so he offered me the use of his company name as a job reference. They were a wonderful bunch of people. I really wish I had stayed in New Jersey.

When Liza took me back to Washington after the party, I showed her all my old hang-outs, my family's home, and the Ebony Inn. After our tour of all the places that added to my demise, I took her to my sister's house in Clinton, Maryland. Since my mother's death, my father had been staying with my sister, Judy in Clinton. Judy and my nephew Brian waited on him hand and foot, so he had no intentions of going back to our house on North Addison Road. Since Judy would never allow Liza to stay the night, I got us a room at the Motel 6.

When we spent our first night together, neither one of us got any rest. Mind you, we had wonderful sex together, but when it was time to rest, my snoring was simply too much for her. She simply could not sleep with me. I snored like a grizzly bear during hibernation. I had gained a considerable amount of weight while in prison, and I guess the excess weight caused me to snore.

After I met with my parole officer the next day, I drove Liza and the truck back to New Jersey. We spent another night together, and I caught the Amtrak back to Washington. Liza and I kissed at the train station, and that was the last time I ever saw her.

When I reached New Carrolton Train Station, I called Barbie to pick me up. Barbie had a new green Toyota Camry. She was all smiles when she pulled up in front of the train station. She believed she was the first person I called when I reached the city, and that made her feel special.

Barbie lived on Brooks Drive in District Heights, Maryland. She had a nice efficiency on the 5th floor of the Oakcrest Towers Apartment complex. We eventually made love, and she drove me back to my sister Judy's home in Clinton.

I spent Christmas with my family. I had the chance to spend some time with my two children, and the Cadillac I had before being incarcerated was still in my sister's driveway. I worked on that car until the New Year came in. I gave my sister Judy all the money I had in the Bank of America in Maryland as a Christmas present. I was relieved to finally be out of prison. I had new skills, and I just knew my future was boundless.

In 2000, I fell in love with Nita Buy.
After three long years, I went back to getting high.
At T&T Carry Out, I got shot in the leg.
The bullet broke me up, and even made me beg.
My baby nursed me back to health from day to day;
I pray every night that she's in a better place. . .

Chapter 21

2000

There was a general scare among Americans; everyone thought the world was coming to an end at midnight; (End of Days) Everything in America is run by computers, and at midnight of the year 2000, they were supposed to stop. There were some great parties that night, and my father and my sister, Judy, both insisted that my nephew Brian and I stay in the house. I did my very best to convince them that nothing was going to happen. You would have thought we were living in medieval times. People were actually frightened. Judy brought tremendous amount of food, water, and other necessities. She even filled all the sinks and the tub with water.

I still remember sitting in the kitchen watching the Dick Clark special. The New Year came in, and the only noticeable thing I saw happen was the clock on my computer went back to 1987. At 1:00 am, I sarcastically asked Judy, "Can I please let the water out of the sinks now?" We got a big kick out of it the next day.

I started out the New Year with a temporary computer job for a firm on Vermont Avenue in North West Washington. Since I had knowledge of all the Microsoft software packages, I had no problem finding a job.

When I finally went for my interview, the supervisor at Career Blazers, Mickey, seemed quite impressed. I was hired that day and given a $32,000 yearly salary. There was a probationary period, but after that time was completed, I was given full benefits. Thank God for the Clinton administration. Never in the wildest of my dreams would I believe I could get a teaching position on the most prestigious street in Washington, Connecticut Avenue. Bill Clinton did wonders for the United States economy.

This was the best job I'd ever had. I was definitely climbing Maslow's hierarchy of needs. The majority of the students were women in the Welfare to Work Program. Bill Clinton no longer allowed women to sit on their asses and make babies and get benefits without working. They now had 5 years to get training and find a job, or their benefits were cut off. I saw women that knew me in my addiction, and just my presence in the school gave them a sense of hope. I think most of them figured, "Hell, if Mike can turn his life around, I know I can." It gave me a sense of pride to know I was doing something to help my peers. I actually felt a sense of redemption in teaching. I've always had the gift of gab, so I fit right into the teaching profession.

I guess I got bored with my success, because I ventured back to the old neighborhood. I know that if my addictive mind gets too much time to think, it tells me to do something crazy. When you have spent as much time as I have getting high, once you decide to stop, you have to have something that fills those gaps. I recommend daily planners. I find that when I plan my days and don't leave time to screw off, I do better.

I started hanging out with my old buddy, Fat Daddy. He was well established in his profession, and I thought I could make a few extra dollars following his lead.

I think I started off with a 1/8th ounce of crack cocaine. I sold the product so quickly, and my hustling addiction simply turned on once again. It felt good to be around the drug and not crave using it. I got the feeling that I'd overcome a major obstacle in my life. I also felt good having people look up to me once again. I was now Mike-Mike again.

I had my heart and my mind set on buying either a Mark VIII, or a Cadillac Eldorado, preferentially 1998. I had spoken to Barbie several times about my dream, but she simply brushed it off. I think Barbie had been taken for a ride by a past boyfriend, so she was extremely over-protective with her assets.

I was still staying with Judy in Clinton from time to time, but I usually stayed with Barbie during the week so I could easily get back and forth to work downtown. The 1988 Coup de Ville I was driving couldn't continue to make the haul form Clinton to Northwest Washington Daily. My dad's home on North Addison Road was empty, so I asked him could I stay there to get back and forth to work. Boy, why did I ask that question, because my father just about shouted my head off. I then asked about the bed I used to sleep on in the house, and he went at me again. I simply packed a bag and left the house.

When I got back to Barbie's home that evening, she said I had a message from my sister on her answering machine. Judy, in clear and understanding terminology, told me she didn't like the way I had left her home, she also emphasized all the things she had done for me, and she explicitly told me to come get my things from her house. I used my Brother Melvin's truck to move my things. The bulk of my things, I left at Melvin's home; everything else, I took to Barbie's home on Brooks Drive. Barbie was a nice woman, but she wasn't someone I wanted to settle down with at the time. I didn't want to hurt her feelings, so I kept up appearances.

During my travels back and forth through the Chapel Oaks area, I ran across an old friend, Nita Buy. Nita used to mess with my friend Jit, but Jit had committed suicide years before. I always had a crush on Nita, and she had a reputation for being able to sell large amounts of narcotics. I figured with Nita's clientele, she could move three times as much cocaine while I was at work. Somewhere down the line, the two of us had sex and we both liked it. Mind you, Nita wasn't a looker, but the pussy was better than court-order release. That's when you have been incarcerated for a month or two, and the judge calls you back to court and releases you; well her sex was better than the feeling of going home.

During the same time, I also hooked back up with two of my old acquaintances, Slick Stand and Scrooge. I knew neither one of these men meant me no good, but they had connections I needed these connections to further my business ventures. Both of these men could not accept the fact that I had moved on with my life, both mentally and financially. They wanted the old Mike back. The Mike they could use. When they found out they could no longer use me, that brought tension to our relationships.

Barbie happened to see me with a young lady named Twin. Twin used to hustle for me, and I was just giving her a package when Barbie saw us together. Barbie made a big deal out seeing me with another woman. I guess she also had a fear of being used.

I think the straw that broke the camels back in Barbra's and my relationship was when she searched through my coat pockets and found two condoms. I had a young lady in my Computer Classes that had a crush on me. She came to me one afternoon and put two condoms in the top pocket of my leather jacket. She said, "When you are ready for me, you have protection." After I got off work that day, I forgot all about the condoms. The next day I wore another coat to work, and when I got home, all my things were packed by the door. I asked Barbie what was going on, and she showed me the two condoms. I tried to explain how they got there, but Barbie wouldn't listen to anything I said. She even had the maintenance man there changing the locks on the front door.

I never told Barbie I was selling drugs, so she didn't know about the money I had stashed in her closet. When she saw the enormous amount I had stashed, she wanted to talk, but truthfully, I was glad she put me out. I was trying to figure out how to get out of her house without hurting her. She simply saved me some unnecessary stress. I took my clothing to the Motel 6 in Capital Heights. The only problem was I had $10,000 in my pocket. I couldn't leave that much money in a room.

I was forced to contact another snake, Alicia. Nita had a drug problem, and I wasn't about to leave my money and another $20,000 in clothing in her possession. The only other person I could think of was Alicia. Alicia had a condominium in Largo, so I made a deal with her to pay her what I paid the motel. I stayed in her home about 3 days before her larceny came out. Once she saw the amount of money I had, she needed to borrow some. I had already given her $300, and I hadn't been there but three days. I made my mistake when I had sex with her.

Not long after that, Women think their bodies are made of gold; they don't take in consideration ware and tare and depreciation. I made up my mind, after my relationship with Carol, if I was going to buy a woman; it was going to be Holly Berry. I found an apartment on Quarrels Street in North East Washington. Scrooge had lived in the complex years before and his father was a personal friend of the owner. He put in a good word for me.

When I went to view the apartment, the place was in shambles. You could tell that it had been used as a crack house. There were still crack bags on the floor in the kitchen, the windows were broken, and the place was filthy. But the owner only wanted $380 a month, so my cheap ass jumped right on the place. I figure with all the crack heads I knew that did home improvement, a little crack would have the place looking like a home in no time.

I was now in the mist of crack heaven in the same area that I used to get high in. The place was still the same — all the same faces, all the same names. The only person that had changed was me. I now had goals and aspirations. I wanted to rise above the situation, but I simply wouldn't leave the area. I wouldn't leave my comfort zone. My father once told me that he had worked all his life to make sure I didn't have to struggle like he had. He told me that he had raised my educational and economic levels in life high; and if I continued to hang around people that were not on my level, they would never reach my levels, but eventually I would go down to theirs. Boy was he right. . .

I paid Nita and her friends to clean the apartment, and I had a friend named Alfred paint and do cosmetic work. Within a few weeks, the place started to come around. In all, I think I put about another $5,000 into fixing that place up. I had the hardwood floor sanded and painted with polyurethane. I changed all the lighting fixtures, added chair rail to the neatly painted walls, and even brought a refrigerator with an ice maker on the outside door. I added carpeting and a ceiling fan to the bedroom and a washer and dryer to the kitchen. I brought air conditioners for the entire apartment. I tried to make the place look like home. Once I had completed all my home improvements, the apartment looked as if it didn't belong in that area. I've had people come to my home, and once they step inside, they look astonished

I really liked my position at Career Blazers. I looked forward to putting on a different suit and tie daily and going to work. When I first came home from prison, Barbie had taken me shopping and gave me a good start as far as dress clothing was concerned. I simply continued what she had begun.

The majority of my students were women, and most of them really wanted to get ahead in life. I met a lot of interesting women. I had a crush on two in particular: Shania, and Kenya. Both these young ladies were at least ten years younger than I, but my arrogance told me I could make at least one of them mine. I spent countless hours taking them home and picking them up from their perspective jobs, to no avail.

There was another young lady from my old neighborhood I've always had a crush on, Wanda. Wanda could have been a model, but I don't think she really knew how good she looked. When I was younger and in my addiction, she wouldn't give me the time of day, but since I was now a computer instructor, she all a sudden looked at me differently. Mind you, I've been in the presence of some of the best womanizers in the country, (pimps) so I knew she only had dollar signs in her eyes. She even spoke to my sister several times about my money.

One Sunday afternoon, I gave Sis Brown a ride to the Safeway to get milk for her new baby, on the way there, my Cadillac was struck from behind by a lady arguing with her children in the backseat of her truck. The accident resulted in the total loss of my vehicle. Since I now had no formal mode of transportation, I walked to sell my product instead of riding.

I still remember my old friend Bo giving me a warning. He told me people were talking about the amount of money I was making, and he told me to stop walking around after dark. Mind you, I've lived in that neighborhood my entire life, so I didn't feel any fear. Every evening after work, I would go to T & T Carryout on Olive Street in Capitol Heights Maryland and eat king crab legs or simply eat dinner. This particular evening, when I was leaving the restaurant, a man in a suit came from around a parked car with his gun drawn. When I attempted to run, he shot me in my right calf. The bullet severed the right tibia, so once again, I was incapacitated.

I still remember the man standing over me, gun in hand, and his serious demeanor. He looked me in my eyes and said, "Give me your money or I'll blow your brains out." My cheap ass held on to my pockets tighter. At that moment, an old friend, Rick, saw me lying on the pavement and ran to my aid. Rick knocked the man out of the way and asked me what had happened. The predator that shot me, was so startled by Rick's abruptness that he simply ran off only snatching the medallion off my Cuban link chain before he fled.

The street was full of people that were supposed to be my friends, and no one made a move but Rick. I was so appreciative of Rick's bravery that I gave him the $500 worth of crack I had in my pocket. Today, I wish I had simply given the robber the money. I only had $1,300 in my possession. I could have made the money back in a day's time. Instead, I lost the use of my right leg for maybe 6 months.

I sat on that pavement for maybe 40 minutes before someone called the ambulance. If it hadn't been for a lady tying my leg off, I would have bled to death. When the ambulance finally got there, they assumed the incident was some type of drug deal gone badly; especially since I had $1,300.00 in my pocket. I was taken to Prince George's Hospital Center in Cheverly, Maryland.

Tarsha came to town from Atlanta that same night to see me. When she arrived at T & T Carryout to meet me, she was told I had just been shot, but she claimed no one would bring her to the hospital because she was hysterical.

I gave the people at the hospital my family information, but no one showed up that night. My friend Bo sat in the hospital all night. He picked up my clothing, but they wouldn't release my money to him.

Nita was really upset, because I had called her to come and get me before I had left the house that evening. The next day, she and her friend Kim sat in my hospital room all day.

My sister, Jean and Scrooge both showed up the next day to see me. I gave Scrooge my identification and a note to pick up my money from the security unit in the hospital. When I did that, Jean had a fit. She insisted on picking up the money herself. Against my better judgment, I finally conceded to let Jean pick up the money. Scrooge and I were close enough for me to trust him with $1,300; besides, Scrooge already owed me $2,000. He knew where my stash was, and he had the keys to my home.

When it came time for me to leave the hospital, Nita was on her job. She borrowed her father's truck and took me to my apartment. Nita had a boyfriend, Jerry, but she still stayed at my home every day until I was able to take care of myself. Nita got high, and I had an unlimited supply of cocaine. I simply couldn't fathom that she was only there for the drugs. I was the perfect situation for her: incapacitated, nice home, and all the crack she could smoke.

When Nita didn't involve Jerry into her smoking sessions with Kim and Dee-Dee, he talked to her mother, Miss Jessie. Miss Jessie was a piece of work; the nicest woman in the world until she had a drink of rum. That's when the demon came out of her. This lady was the nosiest person in the world. From the first time I met her, she involved herself in my business. I guess she thought I was slow or something, because right away she got into my financial affairs. She even attempted to have me give up my apartment and move to her home, but I wouldn't concede. She also told me Scrooge was using me, and that was from only one meeting.

Nita and I had a special kind of relationship. She was there when I started hustling, she was there when I had big money, she was there when I started using drugs, and she was there when I lost my brother and a few others that meant the world to me. I loved her unconditionally; it didn't matter to me what she had done in the past, for she had always been straight with me.

Nita really didn't care anything about Jerry. He had a job that kept them high every two weeks when he got paid. She had a big heart and always accepted the good with the bad. I don't think she had the heart to tell him we were having sex. Eventually, I guess she just better dealed him, for me. Jerry, if you are reading this book, "no hard feelings my brother, and always remember there's nothing colder than a whore's heart."

I was off work for about 1 month. Through physical therapy, I was able to walk with crutches. Barbie even fixed my work pants so they would fit on my leg around the external fixation. That way, I looked presentable at work.

The staff and students at Career Blazers were extremely happy to see me back at work. I even brought another Cadillac, a Sedan de Ville, to get back and forth to work. When I went to see my sister Jean to get my money back, she brought up my old debts to her, and stated, "Broke people don't buy Cadillac's. They buy used Hyundai's. I had hell getting that money back."

I had some money stashed at my brother Melvin's house, and when I asked him to bring me $1,000 to pay up my rent for a few months, he got angry and told me, "Look, I don't work for you. I have things to do, and you are interrupting my schedule." Once my mother died, I knew I was on my own in life, so I simply thanked him and went on about my regular routine.

Through all the bullshit I experience with my family, Nita was sympathetic. She told me she had been through a lot with her family also, and she seemed to understand my problems with empathy. Our long talks simply made me feel closer to her than anyone else.

My neighbor Wanda worked in the same section of town as I, so I asked her to drive us to work every day in my car. The situation worked out for the two of us, as she got free transportation back and forth to work, and I had a driver. After several months of us riding together, I think we both started to have feelings for each other. I had been warned by several people never to cross her because she has had more than one man put in prison; the fury of Hell has nothing on a woman scorn. My hard-headed ass led her on anyway.

I got the rods removed from my leg in October of 2000. Nita took me to Prince George's Hospital for the surgery. She stayed there with me, drove me home, and tucked me in afterwards. After about six months, I trusted Nita more than I trusted my own family. She even had a key to my home.

Wanda rented me a car to go back to New Jersey for Thanksgiving. I told her I was going back to handle some business, but I was actually going back there to see Patty and Neicey. I took Scrooge with me, and after only one hour in Trenton, he was ready to come home. Patty had put herself in a bind, and I wanted to look out for her, but I had to leave so Scrooge could pick up his friend from work before Patty had a chance to get to Neicey's.

Meanwhile, I still had a thing for Shania. She was a Security Guard for the Housing Authority, and was stationed at the Fort Lincoln Retirement Home on Bladensburg Road and at another Retirement home on M Street in South West Washington. This particular night, she called me to pick her up some dinner from KFC, and for some strange reason I felt depressed. It finally donned on me that I was fighting a losing battle by trying to be with Shania. I felt so distraught that I went home and smoked crack for the first time in over 3 years. That was a beginning to another end...

I can't put my relapse on Shania. She was simply an excuse to get high. I had actually relapsed months before I put the stem to my lips. It felt strange that the craving was so strong; I hadn't been high in years. I wanted to get high so badly that I brought a stem at a gas station and bought a bag of crack on the corner. I had an unlimited supply of cocaine at home, but my cravings wouldn't allow me to wait until I got home. I simply pulled over in a parking lot and took my first hit in over three years.

Once I got back to my apartment, I barricaded myself in, took my phone off the hook, and refused to answer the door. I got high all Friday night, all day and night Saturday, and all day Sunday. Sunday night, I was tired of getting high by myself, so I invited my neighbor Evelyn in. Evelyn was so petty, after only1 hour of us getting high, I stopped completely. I had the cocaine set out in a buffet style, but she did more stealing than smoking.

Wanda called and knocked on my apartment door for the entire weekend. Nita also got on my nerves. They just knew I had some estranged woman in my home, and they wanted to catch me with my pants down. They simply had no clue I was getting high, and I didn't want them to know. Women are strange, if they sense any form of weakness in a man, they exploit it, even in the ones that claim to be head-over-heels in love with you.

After that one weekend in November, I gained my composure and stopped using before the problem got worse. The problem was that I had gotten a taste of the forbidden fruit. I had felt the rush and the numbness of the mouth. My heart and my mind told me to leave this madness alone, but my soul wouldn't let go that easily.

I took my vacation from Career Blazers in December. They had a "Use it or Lose it" policy, so I had to take a vacation or lose the time. I spent some quality time with my children. I had stopped spending a lot of time with Nita, and I started spending more time with Wanda. She had been laid off for Christmas, and I was just trying to be a friend.

It wasn't Nita that was complaining she knew the extent of our relationship; it was her mother. Miss Jessie had been a supervisor on her job for years, and she loved to be in control of everyone. I had a problem with authority, so I wasn't very compliant. Besides, she wasn't my mother, and I had no obligation to her or her family.

Nita's mother asked me to take her to Baltimore to visit her family, but my son, Michael was acting up at home and in school; so Carol sent him to my house. I didn't want to leave him alone in my home his first night there, so I called Nita's mother to cancel our trip. Mind you, Miss Jessie had a car and a truck and several family members, including Nita, that could have driven her to Baltimore, but she blames the trip being canceled on me.

Miss Jessie was so upset that she called my house and left me a nasty message. She accused me of having used Nita to take care of me. Now that my legs were better, I was throwing her away like trash. She also told me to bring Nita's things back to her home. Nita had left her nephew's, Mike's Christmas toys at my home, so when I brought her things; I also brought the Christmas toys. They now blamed me for ruining little Mike's Christmas.

Nita's Cousin Darryl was in town from Philadelphia and witnessed the entire fiasco. Darryl and I had become friends, and it was he who told me that Nita wasn't even home when her mother made those calls. I should have left the entire situation alone that Christmas, but my sadistic ass continued to pursue a friendship with Nita. Nita was 4 years older than I, but her mother still had total control of all her affairs.

I lost my dad in 2001,
He left 1/4th his money to his baby son.
His death had a big effect on my mind,
Because my family still hates me for that will he signed
A bunch of brothers and sisters who claimed to love Mama so,
But for six mothers days they never put her picture in the Metro...

Chapter 22

2001

I spent New Year's with Nita. We promised each other that we would try to make a change in our lives for the New Year. I made a decision not to sell anymore drugs. I figured I had tested fate long enough, and if I continued, I was destined to spend the rest of my life in prison. This decision made Scrooge furious. He had plans for my business skills, and if I was out of the game, he would lose a valued asset. We even stopped speaking, and he also returned my house keys.

I was still caught between Wanda and Nita. I simply couldn't make up my mind. This made Wanda extra mad; she somewhat had her life together, and here I was having a hard time deciding whether to be with her or Nita. Nita had a good heart, and we were equally yoked in the drug world. Wanda wanted a lot out of life, and I knew with her I would be in constant debt. Wanda thought of Nita as nothing but a drug addict. I truly think the decision-making process made Wanda furious.

Around the end of January 2001, I went on another smoking binge. Wanda was acting like she was pregnant, and that scared me to death. When I get scared, I always resort back to my old friend, the stem. This time, I simply went to Nita's house to smoke. The last time I attempted to get high, Wanda called and beat on my door for 2 days. I figured at Nita's I'd have a little privacy. Boy was I in for a surprise.

I called my job and told them that my son had been hit by a car, and I was at his side in the hospital. I had sick leave, annual leave, as well as and vacation time for 2001, so my supervisor didn't make too much of a fuss.

Nita got a kick out of seeing me getting high. She invited the entire neighborhood into her mother's basement to see me geeking. The smokers got a kick out of seeing the so-called big-time hustler with a stem in his mouth. Nita thought she was actually doing something slick by exploiting my drug usage, but in fact, the hustlers in the neighborhood looked down on her. I was a school teacher, had my own place, a nice car, and a bright future; technically, I was an asset. They couldn't figure out, to save their lives, why she would even allow me to get high in the first place. I was not only Nita's meal ticket, but several other people. Nita had a way of irritating people, and with the right irritation, I would have stopped right off.

When Wanda found out I was at Nita's, she called my sister Judy, and Carol. She told them that Nita was holding me hostage in her home. She also told them that I had a large amount of money in my house, and she feared Nita was stealing the money.

That was the beginning of a new mess. I had moved to the Northeast to keep my family out of my business, and my stupid ass allowed

Wanda to meet Carol. She used to drop off and pick up my son, and in the meantime they became friends. I truly believe Carol feared my relationships with both Nita and Wanda because she loved to keep me hanging by a string. She once told Wanda I only loved her and no other woman, and to give up on having a lasting relationship with me. You know how the story goes: she didn't want me, and she didn't want anyone else to have me. To make a long story short, the two of them involved my sister Judy and my father into my escapade.

One evening, while Nita and I had gone out, Wanda, Carol, and Judy, showed up at Nita's home. Nita's mother let them all in. They walked through the house looking for me, and when they couldn't find me, my sister simply left her number and told Nita's mother to have me call her when I got back to their home. Wanda was furious. She wanted to wait until Nita and I returned, but Carol and my sister both told her I was grown and did what I wanted to do.

This made Wanda so mad, she called my job and told everyone that would listen that my son wasn't hurt and I was simply in a crack house getting high for that entire week. I had taken Wanda to the Christmas party, so most of my coworkers knew her, and they took her story as the truth.

That's what I thought had happened for the longest time. It wasn't until later that I found out that Carol was the one who made the call. I regret leaving Wanda. She really would have been good for my life.

When I arrived back at work the next Monday, I was called into the General Mangers Office. She said she knew where I had been, and if I didn't resign, she would fire me. Now, I was furious. I simply couldn't believe after all the great work I'd done for the school, they would simply throw me away like some old newspapers. I asked her where she had gotten this crazy information from, but she wouldn't tell me. It was one of my fellow instructors that gave me the low-down. I was so furious at the general manager that I left her office in shambles. I turned over her computer and knocked everything off her desk. One of my fellow instructors, Will, escorted me from the building. I guess they did a background check on my criminal history after I left, because they hired an armed guard to secure their offices. They also left instructions with the concierge not to let me back in the building.

I had climbed Maslow's Hierarchy of Needs, and I'd gone from simply securing my basic needs to gaining prestige. Now, I knew I would have to start all over again. At least I still had my apartment and my car. From that day on, I was on a road to madness. Nita moved into my home, and I had no more dealings with Wanda.

My criminal case in New Jersey had been reversed and remanded because of racial profiling allegations, so I stopped seeing my parole officer. I didn't have to worry about getting a dirty urine, so I smoked like there was no tomorrow. All I had to do was sell more drugs than I used; and I would survive so I thought.

The only problem I had was Nita. She threw a monkey-wrench into every successful endeavor I tried to make. As I mentioned earlier, she had an irritating way getting on your nerves. If you tried to put her on "pay you no mind" time, her irritation only intensified. I screwed up more drugs because she was getting on my nerves. Later on, I found out she was doing that on purpose.

Even under all these adverse circumstances, I still was able to keep my bills in order. My friend Tony and I did the math on our drug usage, and we came up with a figure of over $50,000 a year. We spent more money on drugs than the average human being made working in a year; and still were able to function normally.

My father had a stroke in April of 2001. I still remember not wanting to see him in that condition. My brothers and sisters didn't know what I was going through mentally, so they claimed I was being selfish by not making an appearance.

Nita and I went to see my father on a Sunday night. When he saw me, his eyes brightened. He held my hand for the entire visit. I talked to him for maybe 30 minutes or so and tried to raise his spirits. Today, I think he actually held on until he saw me, because he died that night.

When he died, my sisters Jean and Lenora put up a big fuss about the funeral arrangements. I didn't even want to be around them. Deep down inside, I knew they hated my father, and to be putting on airs after his death was simply hypocritical.

The funeral and the wake were held at my sister Judy's church in Temple Hills. My son and I went to my Brother Melvin's house and rode to the funeral with him. When we arrived, I noticed my daughter and her mother pulling in. When I attempted to say something to them, them both rolled up their windows and turned their heads.

My daughter wanted to go to private school. I paid for the first two semesters, but I got fired from my job during the third semester. When I tried to explain to my daughter that I didn't have the money for her school, she got indignant. I know I haven't done much for the girl, and I felt bad telling her I didn't have the money, but her response made me angry. She asked me how I was paying my rent. I replied, "You want me to stop paying my rent so I can pay for your school?" She kindly answered, "Yes". That was the last time I have spoken to my daughter; April 2001.

The funeral was nice. The entire family was there. My father's cousin Ruth even came down from Detroit. All the family bundled up in the first two rows of the church. I sat in the back with Melvin's niece. The thing that got to me was when the minister asked, "Did anyone want to view the body before he closed the casket. No one moved but Judy and my nephew Brian. I knew I had disappointed my father. He had big dreams for me, and here I was at his funeral dope sick. After the funeral was over, I brought two bags of dope and cried for the rest of the evening.

When we got to the graveyard, my cousins Erma and Towanda asked me how I was doing. When I told them I was teaching school, but I'd been laid off, they both laughed as if I was lying. Later that day, they both pulled my brother Melvin to the side and asked him. When he confirmed what I said was true, they both looked shocked.

My father was buried at Harmony Cemetery. When the workers were putting my father's casket in the ground, there was a tree root in the way, so the casket was only 4 feet from the surface. My sister Judy had them pull the casket up, get a backhoe; re-dig the hole, then put the casket back in the ground. We were at the graveyard for over an hour.

After the funeral, we went back to the church for repast. I ate a quick plate, and Melvin was ready to leave. My car was parked at his house, so Little Mike and I followed suit. Little Mike and I both kissed Judy goodbye.

As soon as I dropped Little Mike off, I made a beeline to the dope man in Lincoln Heights. I brought two bags of Platinum and $20 worth of crack. I sat in my car crying and getting high for hours.

It was a week or so before we got a copy of the will. We had to have it published for a certain amount of time before it could be executed. When my brothers and sister found out that my dad only left money to my sister Judy, my nephew Brian, my brother Donald, and me, they were furious.

Jean talked for hours about how selfish my father was, and me not deserving anything. At that time, I was close to my brother Melvin, and would have gladly split my money with him, but he sided with the others. This feud went on for the rest of the year and most of the next.

Nita and her mother had plans for my share of the money. They wanted to break me down to nothing. That way, I would be totally dependent on them. They tried every trick in the book to separate me and Judy. When all else failed, they tried to sabotage my drug business.

Nita died in 2002,
I lost my other half; what was I to do?
I put a lot of emphasis on my health;
Spent over $30,000 medicating myself..

Chapter 23

2002

As DMX might say, "2002 was a rough ride." My parole finally caught up with me. Apparently, New Jersey wasn't ready to have me released from custody.

My parole officer pulled the biggest trick in the book. He told me he had my release papers, and he needed me to come to his office to sign them. When I arrived, he had me arrested and taken to the D.C. Jail.

I called Nita's mother and told her that I was going to be expedited back to New Jersey, and Nita could have everything. I told her not to make any moves, as far as my apartment was concerned, until my 72-hour hold was up. The 72 hours came and past, and I was released from custody.

When I got home, all my things had been moved to Nita's mother's house. I no longer had a place to live. I called all my brothers and sisters, but no one would let me stay at their home; thus I forced to stay at Nita's mothers or go to a shelter. I should have gone to a shelter.

From the very beginning, they let me know I was an outsider, and they were doing me a favor. I got Unemployment, so I gave half my checks to Nita's mother every two weeks. I did odd jobs around their home, and basically kept things in working order. Many nights, I sat in the bed feeling like an indentured servant.

With the education I have, I should have had some sort employment and gotten out of their home; but I was too caught up in my inheritance to even think about a job. I had big plans, and my plans didn't involve working for someone else. I simply knew I could finally be my own boss.

I honestly tried several times to stop getting high. I would sit in Nita's basement for days, trying to sweat the heroin and cocaine from my system. Every time I thought I had the drugs licked, Nita would come into the house with an entourage of addicts. I simply didn't have the willpower to continue quitting "cold turkey" in the mist of crack smoke.

I actually started snorting heroin to alter the effects of the crack. I would mess up entirely too much money smoking crack alone. It got to the point, after constant use of the heroin, I couldn't even smoke crack unless I had a bag of heroin in my system. If I smoked crack without heroin, I got extremely sick.

Eventually, the heroin started tarring up the membranes in my nose. When I woke up in the mornings, my nose was extremely clogged with mucus. The only way I could clear my nose was to smoke a rock. The crack would make my nose run, and I was able to blow my nose and snort the dope.

Nita started to get frustrated because she couldn't control me. My transmission had gone out in my car, and I was at the point of total dismay, but I refused to be controlled by Nita or her mother. Nita had a way of pretending to hurt herself to get the things she wanted. She has put empty guns to her head; she has faked like she was going to cut her wrist. This time, one of her stunts went extremely wrong.

Nita and I were in her mother's basement early one morning. She and Dee-Dee had been out all night, and she came in intoxicated. I had some crack and some heroin, but I refused to give her some. I told her, "You should have gotten some from whoever you were with all night." She grabbed a bottle of rubbing alcohol from the bar. She took the alcohol and poured it over her head. She then grabbed the cigarette lighter and threatened to set herself on fire. I had gone through her stunts for the last three years, so I was really fed up. I told her to do what she had to do.

Nita took her lighter and struck it above her head, but she had alcohol on her hands and it ignited. She turned into a human torch. I attempted to snatch her shirt off, but it burned my hands. I then grabbed a bucket of water from the sink and dowsed her with it. The fire went out, but she was severely burned on her neck and arms.

She screamed so loudly that she awakened the entire house. When her cousin Darryl first came down stairs, I know he thought I had done something to Nita, but she told him she had done it to herself. He knew she was crazy, so he believed her. She then walked through the entire house screaming, "I did it to myself."

Nita's Mother and I took her to Washington Hospital Center in Northeast Washington. She was admitted into the burn unit. Nita walked into the hospital, so I didn't think she was hurt that badly. I still believe today, if we had taken her to Prince George's Hospital, she would still be alive. They were, in all actualities, experimenting on Nita.

They had her tied to a bed and heavily sedated. The bed rotated so she wouldn't get fluid in her lungs. The problem was that she had been placed on a respirator.The respirator did all her breathing, and she simply stopped breathing on her own.

I spent countless days by her side. I didn't want her life to end that way. I found myself, blaming myself for not acting sooner. I developed extreme mental problems because of her accident. I actually started having reoccurring nightmares. Each night, I was transported to the point when she set herself on fire, and each time, I was unable to change the event.

In August of 2002, I was awarded $10,000 from my father's estate. At the time, I was still staying with Nita's family, so I gave her mother $1,000 for allowing me to stay there. Mind you, I was already giving her $200 a month from my unemployment checks, so I felt another $1,000.00 should have been sufficient. I had only been there three months. I guess I though wrong.

A week after I got the money from my father, Nita died. She never got the chance to spend any of my father's money. All her conniving was for nothing.

When Nita died, I was in the street getting high. One of her close friends told me what had happened. Nita's mother was holding $2,000 of my money, so I went to the family's house and retrieved my money. I gave her mother another $500 for the funeral. I simply packed a bag and moved to the Motel 6, off of Central Avenue in Capital Heights, Maryland.

Little did I know that Nita's mother had an insurance policy on her death. If her death was considered suicide, the policy would not pay off. Those crooks tried to have me implicated for murder in order to get some money.They tried to get her cousin Darryl to go along with the plan, and when he wouldn't, he was forced to move to Nita's niece's house, Bee.They even involved Nita's ex-husband, Pete.

When the funeral programs and the article in the Metro came out about her death, they never even mentioned my name anywhere. I thought I should have been considered a close friend; we'd been together for three years. Then her uncle Cleon went about the neighborhood telling people I had killed Nita. I got into a lot of close calls because of those lies. Nita's God Brother, Manny, even pulled a pistol on me. Mind you, now that I have had a chance to think about all the mess I went through with those people, if I were not a Christian, they definitely would be in some trouble.

Nita's funeral was held at the First Baptist Church on Delaware Avenue in South West Washington. The church was filled with Nita's family, so I just attended the wake. I didn't want to take the chance of getting jumped after the funeral. Besides, at the time, there were a lot more of them than me.

When I came to Nita's mothers to retrieve my belongings, I brought seven dudes with me. I could see they had planned on beating my ass, but once they saw I had help, they simply backed off. Mind you, I have no qualms with any of Nita's nieces or cousins — the culprits know who they are. I stayed in the Motel 6 until I had depleted the $10,000. In September of 2002, I was awarded another $19,000. Judy took me to the Branch Avenue Auto Auction to get a car. I purchased a 1993 Cadillac STS. The car was money green and rode like a spaceship. I paid the auction $5,000.00 cash for the car. I didn't have tags or insurance, so I put the tags from my Sedan de Ville on the car. The car needed some work, but otherwise I thought I'd gotten a good deal.

Judy gave me hug, and $500, and she told me to be careful. The last time she helped me get a nice car, I had turned my life around. I guess she thought the same thing would happen this time; but this time I needed psychological help.

Nita's death was simply the straw that broke the camel's back. I had experienced a great deal of trauma in my life. When Nita died, it was like a button clicked off in my brain. I felt alone, and I also wanted to die. I guess I was just too afraid to pull the trigger. Even though, shooting myself would have been a more humane way to die.

Three days after I brought my car, I was carjacked by a so-called friend. I still think he was going to hold the car for a ransom, but Wanda saw the entire incident and called my sister and told her to call the police.

When the police arrived, I didn't want to say anything to them. One of the detectives was a beautiful woman, and she got me to open up. The so-called carjacker's family lived down the street, so the officers went to their home, and his brother in law gave them all the information he had on the guy.

I went to a friend and purchased two pistols. I had plans of putting one in his ass, and the other in his mouth, and firing them simultaneously. I simply never got the chance. When the culprit found out he was under scrutiny with the law, he returned the vehicle. Before I could retrieve it, the police seized it.

I called Judy and Melvin the next day, to see if they could get the car for me. The officers at the 6th District would not allow that. I had to pick up the car myself. From the very beginning, Judy smelled a rat. She told me not to go to the station, but my hard headed-ass went anyway. Judy though it had something to do with Nita. I knew I hadn't done anything to her, so I went to the station. When I got to the police station, they had a fugitive warrant for my arrest. They had been looking for me since March for my parole violation in New Jersey. No one ever contacted me, so I never knew I had a warrant.

I was taken back to the D.C. Jail, and my car was placed in impound. I had my sister Judy get my car out of jail, but there was no hope for me. New Jersey came to get me on the third day. I was on my way back to the Central Reception Assessment Facility.

I only had 11 months left on my sentence, so I was sent to Southern State Correctional Facility. I was in custody for four months and never saw a representative from the parole board. My case was political, and no one wanted to deal with it.

From the very beginning, I told all the prison officials that my case had been remanded back to Superior Court, but no one seemed to listen to me. I wrote maybe 20 letters a week, and finally I was contacted by the public defender's office. They told me that my case was before the Attorney General, and he would be making a decision soon. They locked me up in September 2002, and it wouldn't be until January until I got some relief.

In 2003 my New Jersey Case was dismissed,
Learning that I was dying put me in great distress;
And the psychological pain left me homeless;
Ended up living on skid row;
Never thought my life could get that low;
But thanks to Moon being Moon and Rick being Rick;
They kept my ass out a lot of shit. . .

Chapter 24

2003

In January of 2003, the doctors at Southern State Correctional Facility in Delmar, New Jersey told me I was dying of a liver-related disease. I have been experiencing seizures since my accident in 1991, so I was taking Dilantan. The doctors at Southern State continuously tested the Dilantan level in my blood system. This particular month, they did an hemoglobin, and detected the abnormalities in my liver levels. After several test, I was diagnosed with liver cancer.

I never saw a psychologist or anyone that might help me handle this news. I was simply told my condition and told to go back to the unit. The doctor gave me three to four years to live, and that was if I didn't do anything to abuse my liver.

Three days after I received this diagnosis, my criminal case was vacated by the Honorable Judge Lorraine Pullen. She found the state troopers at fault for racial profiling and false imprisonment. I was released from prison on January 14, 2003.

The prison officials took me to the New Jersey Transit Station and gave me enough money to get to Washington, D.C. This was the first time I was ever put out of a prison. When I was arrested, I was homeless, so I was in the same situation when I returned to Washington.

I didn't know it at the time, but I set legal precedent. My racial profiling case was used to release several other men from prison. Darryl and I hired an attorney who had been involved in the Civil Rights Movement to handle our lawsuit against the turnpike authority and the state troopers. This same attorney represented Keevie in our trial, and we had a great deal of respect for him.

I had done a lot of reading while incarcerated. I read about the life of Assata Shakur. She was an advocate of the black revolution in America and was convicted of murdering a New Jersey state trooper in 1973. In fact, this had happened in the same county, Middlesex, where I had been arrested. In 1979, Shakur escaped from the Correctional Facility for Women in Clinton, New Jersey and fled to Cuba. In the dedication section of her book, this particular attorney wrote a caption. I simply knew I needed to have a man that was going to fight for my civil rights and get me paid.

When I arrived back in Washington, I was distraught over my recent diagnosis. I was already suffering from the mental effects of Nita killing herself; with the combination of the two, I simply lost my mind. I had no one that I could truly sit down and talk to about my feelings. I couldn't show any signs of weakness because I was living in the streets; people in the streets exploit weaknesses. At the time, it never donned on me to seek professional help. To accept the fact that I was losing my mind was also a sign of weakness. I was raised under the Iron Jim concept.

Normal people, at this point in their lives, would begin to start planning for their death; especially since I had children. I should have put money away for their futures, but my selfish ass tried to spend everything I had before I died. Both of my children wanted nothing to do with me, and I had burned all my bridges as far as my siblings were concerned. Instead of being a man, I resorted back to drugs, praying that I'd die in a euphoric state.

I ended up living in my car on R Street in Beaver Heights Maryland. I functioned normally until the car broke down. My serpentine belt broke, a pulley fell off, the compressor went bad, and the heating blower malfunctioned all at once. Instead of taking my car to a reputable mechanic, I sort help from two "shade tree mechanics," Billy and Larry,

Both these men knew I had received an inheritance from my father, so they had plans on milking me dry. Mind you, this was during the month of January and I was homeless. I actually caught pneumonia sleeping in the car while they were making repairs. I also got arrested for sleeping in an abandoned car, which I did simply because the car had heat in it. The car had been stolen in Montgomery County before I had been released from prison in New Jersey.

My car was on the side of my neighbor, Tony's, house. Tony's mother had received a complaint from the county about junk cars being on her property, and they threatened to fine her. She insisted that Billy and Larry complete the work that needed to be done on my car as soon as possible, which they did. Little did I know, but both Billy and Larry hated me. Billy didn't feel I should have a Cadillac STS, and Larry had been Nita's boyfriend at one time. He was mad she was with me when he had gotten out of prison. I was simply too high to see their motives. I was hurt over all from the recent dilemmas in my life, and since I was feeding them drugs and had known the two of them most of my adult life, I didn't think they would sabotage my car.

To this day, I don't know which one of them did it, but someone drained all the oil from my car. Once they had completed their so-called 'repairs," I drove the car to the Motel 6 to get some well-needed rest. The next morning while I drove back to the Northeast, my engine shut down. Since there was no oil in the block, the engine locked. They had completed the work the night before. I didn't think I needed to check all my fluid levels; especially since I had paid them to change them.

The car broke down on Central Avenue. I called Tony to pick me up from the Glendale Baptist Church. We pushed the car into the parking lot. Later that day, I had Billy tow the vehicle back to R Street.

Seeing the position, I was now faced with, Tony's mother allowed me to stay in her basement. Miss Thelma was a very sweet woman. My mother and she had been friends for years. She told me she simply couldn't leave me in the streets, and she instructed me to get myself together and find a place to live as soon as possible.

Tony, like me, was a drug user. He had been my Brother Ronald's friend and I respected him a great deal. I finally had someone with which I could converse, and we got twisted in the process. Tony and his sister Patty were the best of host as long as I had narcotics. We watched movies, Patty cooked dinner, and we were one big happy family.

When the drugs ran low, and my sister stopped footing my drug habit, Miss Patty caused a lot of dissention between their mother, Tony, and me. She told her mom I had received a large settlement and was attempting to leave their home without giving her anything.

I still remember Tony's mother telling me to get my things out of their home. Tony and I both looked astonished because we had no idea what was going on. Only later did I find out who the culprit was.

Patty was also Billy's wife, and Billy was the one that had ruined my engine. Only out of respect for Tony's mother was I able to restrain myself from hitting Billy's head. I pray I can keep that same restraint once back in society. I have found in life, when people do me wrong to simply give it to God. About 3 years in 2014, Billy's body was found in an abandoned house on Eastern Ave. He had overdosed on heroin and froze to death. Larry, on the other hand, ate a pack of 8 pork chops and had a stroke. He is now permanently wheelchair bound.

Now that I was once again homeless and living in the streets; I came in contact with another of my brother's friends, Ray. Ray was a professional thief. He taught me how to creep in stores and how to shoplift. At that time, the only crime I was remotely good at was selling drugs. The fact that I was homeless and had a drug habit increased my learning capacity for theft. We had a profitable relationship until I started stealing more expensive items than he; that's when the larceny came into the game. Ray would pick arguments, and he claimed he needed money for providing the transportation.

Once, after making a big sting, we stopped at Frank's Tavern and got cigarettes and dope. Then Ray headed to 55th Street to buy enough crack to flip so he could keep money in our pockets and get high at the same time. But if you break the first rule of hustling, getting high on your own supply, you were fighting a losing battle.

On the way to 55th Street, in Northeast Washington, I fell asleep. While I was asleep, Ray preceded to buy the crack. On his way back to the car, he was accosted by police officers. When a chase pursued, he threw the drugs in the car. I woke up hearing all the commotion to see $100 worth of crack on my lap. Before I could get my faculties in order, I was snatched through the passenger-side window by one of the officers and beaten profusely. I tried to explain the fact that I was asleep and didn't know what was going on, but that was all in vain. I was once again on my way to the Central Cell Block.

From the very beginning, the attorney I had tried his best to convince me to plead guilty to possession, and take probation. This is one of the reasons I feel that the legal system is fixed. This man didn't even attempt to present a case or even ask me about the particulars in the case; his first thought was to clear up the case at my expense. How many other defendants has this man thrown to the criminal justice system?

Since I was just recently released from prison in New Jersey, I didn't want to be on any type of supervision. At that point in my life, I needed help with my drug problem, but I wasn't ready to stop getting high, and I definitely didn't want to be under the scrutiny of the Office of Probation. I knew if I accepted probation, my getting high days were over, and if I violated the probation, I was going back up the river. Besides, I didn't feel as though I had done anything wrong. The officers saw Ray throw the drugs, but I didn't put in any money with Ray, nor did I know what he brought. How could they charge me with possession? I was determined to fight this case.

Since my car was practically dead, Ray and I lived in his car. We eventually rented rooms from one of my old neighbors, Pinky. We only stayed at Pinky's for two weeks before she was evicted, so we were once again homeless.

I woke up one morning and Ray was gone. He left without saying a word. The next time I saw my attorney, I was told that Ray plead guilty and would be testifying against me on the behalf of the District of Columbia.

I resorted to staying in abandoned buildings. I did what I could to stay high during the day, and I lived in an "'abandominum" by night. I never knew there were so many homeless people. These were professional people that had allowed addiction to bring them down to nothing. There were also quite a few mentally ill individuals. The heroin and cocaine took me down to nothing. Once the vultures saw I was now vulnerable to attack, they swooped down upon me like I was a defenseless bunny. We all existed in our little world-within-a-world. I pray that I never ever have to live that way ever again.

The day before my scheduled trial date, for my drug charge with Ray, I was on the Frank's Tavern Liquor Store lot, getting high. While in a drug stupor, I was accosted and beaten by two young robbers. People still thought I had money, and they looked upon me as an easy victim. They beat me so badly that I was unable to make it to court the next day. Since I lived in an abandoned house and I didn't have any money, I never even called to courts to tell them of my predicament, so a bench warrant was issued on my behalf. I was in such bad shape, I was forced to call my sister Judy to take me to the hospital.

Judy took me to Prince George's Hospital Center in Cheverly, Maryland. I was found to have a broken leg and a broken eye socket. I was in such bad shape, Judy told the hospital staff I was suicidal and needed mental health treatment. She figured, hell, I was crazy, and at least I would be fed and out of the streets. She also figured I could get some form of drug treatment. As a result of her testimony, I was committed to the psych ward, H-400.

While in the psych ward, I saw an old friend, Sam Foggie. Sam had turned his life around, and he was now in charge of the detoxification program at the hospital. Sam put me directly under his wing. He went out of his way more than once to help me. Sam had me examined by the psychologist. After I told the doctor about all the traumas I had experienced in my life; the psychologist diagnosed me with Post Traumatic Stress Disorder (PTSD). The problem was that I didn't want to be helped; I wanted to die. Between Nita's death and the cancer, I had simply given up on life. All I wanted to do was to have as much fun as I could before the end came, but the life I was living was in no way fun.

After 14 days of being detoxed and treated with anti-depressants, I was placed in a transition house. The problem was my wisdom tooth was impacted, and the hospital no longer provided dental treatment. That was my excuse to leave. Addicts search for reasons to get high, and in my sick mind, I actually thought I could make it in society with no home, no money, and with a broken leg.

I had gotten a few visits while in the hospital, so I had maybe $35 in my pocket. I still remember hopping to the bus stop, and going back to Kenilworth. Mind you, this was the same exact area where I had been beaten and robbed. I was now on crutches, and I had no way of protecting myself. My only thought was that I needed to get to where the drugs were.

Once I got off the bus, I made a beeline for the same liquor store where I had been accosted. On the way, I saw my cruddy buddy, Tony. He had his sister's truck and was on a drug run. I showed him and Jerry that I had money, and they let me ride. We went to Lincoln Heights, where I brought both dope and coke. As soon as I took my first hit of crack, it numbed my entire body. I no longer had a toothache, but I also had nowhere to live and no more money in my pocket. Once back in Kenilworth, Tony dropped me off and went on his merry way.

Now that I have had the chance to evaluate my situation, I know everything I experienced in my addiction was no one's fault but my own. I made my bed, so I was forced to lay in it.

On June 16, 2003, I was arrested on Street in North East Washington, for sleeping in a stolen vehicle. It was raining that particular day, and I'd climbed in the car to simply get out of the rain. Not more than 30 minutes before I was arrested, a friend gave me a 10 pack of heroin, "Yao-ming". The dope was a bomb. That's one of the reasons I fell asleep; that along with the fact that my body was exhausted.

I was woken up with a gun in my face and half-dozen officers from the stolen car task force. They dragged me from the car and threw me to the ground. The lead detective claimed that they had chased me to that area, but in all actuality I was just asleep in the car. The officers arrested me and took me to the 7th District Police Station in Southeast Washington. An officer had been killed in the northeast station, and the 6th District Station was closed for the memorial service. Everyone that was arrested in the northeast that day was taken to the 7th District.

When the officers arrested me, I had all my belongings in the backseat of the car. The officers refused to allow me to give my things to a friend that was watching the entire scene. Either way, I still would have lost everything.

Somehow I managed to hide the heroin in my rectum. When the officers searched me, they never found the dope. While in the holding cell, I snorted two more bags. When I was finished, I hid one bag in my pants zipper and the rest in my ass.

When the officer's finally processed me, they noticed how high I was. The officer said, "Damn, I wish I had some of the dope you had; man you're twisted." Do you know my crazy ass handed the officer the bag I had in my zipper. I actually told the officer, "Since you have been so hospitable, this one's on me." After that move, I not only had an unauthorized use of a motor vehicle charge, but a possession of heroin charge too.

I was eventually taken Southeast Community Hospital so they could look at my leg. When I was arrested, I had crutches in my possession, but the task force officers wouldn't allow me to bring anything with me. They simply dragged me to the squad car and then into the precinct. My leg was x-rayed at the hospital, and they determined it was broken. They gave me more painkillers, put a cast on the leg, and gave me a pair of crutches. They actually had pork chops for lunch that day.

Finally, I was taken to the Superior Court to be formally charged. The Magistrate actually gave me personal recognition for the theft and the possession charges, but the Honorable Judge Kramer revoked my bail for my earlier failure to appear at trial. The only good thing that happened that day was that they'd put a cast on my leg. I now had a place to hide my dope.

I sat in the D.C. Jail until August, when I finally got a chance to go to trial. They'd offered me probation several times, but I knew I had nowhere to live, and if I accepted the probation, I was definitely going back to prison. I made up my mind early that I was going to fight this case.

Before the actual trial started, I gave my attorney several questions to ask the officer. The attorney refused to ask the questions. He claimed by law, he was bound from asking questions of ethnicity. I asked the attorney to ask the officer, "What is the major ethnic group in this area?" I wanted to prove that two white officers would stick out like a sore thumb in Northeast D.C., especially two in uniform. If I was involved in the transaction of the drugs, don't you think I would have at least warned Ray that he was being followed? I wanted to prove that I was actually in the car asleep. The attorney refused to ask my question.

The prosecutor, a young black woman, asked the exact same question that I asked my attorney to ask. From that moment on, I knew I was going to be thrown. This was a Judge trial, not a jury trial; Judge Kramer found me guilty of possession of cocaine. I gave her a sob story, and she only gave me 120 days.

I was assigned to SW-I. There were 160 men on the tier. It was separated by a wall, and they only allowed one side out at a time; for security reasons. There was simply no way 3 officers could effectively guard 160 people. My cell buddy was Fred Parker. He had lived in Kenilworth, and he was around my age, so we got along perfectly. We spent our days and nights mastering the game of Casino.

We spent a great deal of time in our cells at the D.C. Jail. They only let 80 people at a time, come out for recreation at one time. We came out at 8:30 a.m. and went in at 3:00 p.m. We didn't come out again until 5:00pm the next day, thus we were locked in (26) hours every other day. While we were in, the other side was out. The Recreation schedule simply rotated.

In September of 2003, my old friend Rick was brought on the unit. He was arrested for a possession charge on Division Avenue. He was doing his thing on Division, and they couldn't catch him, so the crooked police created a possession charge to get him off the streets for a while. The courts also offered Rick probation, but he was on parole in Maryland, and a conviction would violate his parole. Rick was also forced to go to trial. I guess the judicial system put the fix on him too because he was also found guilty. Everybody that comes before Judge Kramer simply can't be guilty.

Rick and I got close while were in SW-I. We had a chance to reminisce about old times, and we talked about my brother Ronald and Chapel Oaks in general. I told Rick about my homelessness situation, and he promised me that he would have somewhere for me to stay when I was released. Rick was released two weeks before me, and he did keep his word.

I was eventually released in November 11, 2003. My sister Judy gave me $500 of my money and wished me luck. I met Rick and his friend Tiny at the Ebony Inn. They actually took me to their home in Forestville.

Tiny was a very nice lady. She had 3 children, and she also mentored on the weekends. She worked at a Charter School in the northwest. I couldn't for the life of me tell what she saw in Rick. She allowed me to move in her house with her and her children. I will always be grateful for her hospitality. Here I couldn't go to any of my family's homes, and a total stranger invited me into hers. I will always keep Tiny in my prayers.

Eventually, Rick and Tiny started having problems because Rick was spending more time with me and Moon than with her. Moon is the slickest thief I've ever met in my life. Things that normal people would take for granted, he would see them as a hustle. Moon was short, and he was able to creep into places that normal grown people couldn't. I learned a great deal from him. He took care of me more than once. I will always be in his debt.

After Rick's marital problems, he and I ended up staying with his mother, Miss Gloria in Mitchellville, Maryland. Miss Gloria had a beautiful home. She's the nicest person I've ever met. She was the type of person that gave anyone a chance. Some of the people she let in her home, shelters would turn away. Everyone loved her and always gave her respect. If I make some money off this book, I'll definitely throw some her way.

In December of 2003, I started getting high again. I brought another car, from the auction; a Toyota Camry. I scrubbed that car for hours to get the paint to shine. I brought a nice radio and some dealer's tags. I hooked back up with Ray because I wanted him to help me out with the UUV charge that I still had pending in court. When I was arrested on the UUV charge on 57th Street, Ray was the one friend that had witnessed the entire event. I wanted him to come to court and testify that I was in the car asleep, and that I hadn't actually stolen the car.

I found Ray at the same house on 57th Street, Billy and Sharon's house. The house had no heat and no electricity. I thought I was doing Ray a favor by picking him up, getting him a room, and getting him high. Ray, like most street people, took my niceness for weakness.

Around this time, I met a young lady from Virginia named Monique. She was intelligent and nice-looking. We slipped off to get high and be together. Ray tried to make me think he was a third wheel, and he also needed some dope. My crazy ass gave him my car and the money to get the dope. That was the last time I saw Ray or my car. I had only had the car for two days. I was so upset about Ray taking the car; I went back to 57th Street and beat Billy to a pulp. I broke my hand in the process.

Depressed about my impending legal problems, along with my car being stolen, I over-indulged in crack and heroin once again. Before I knew it, I was broke and homeless again. If it wasn't for Moon taking me on a few capers, I would have slipped back to skid row. Moon did screw Monique when I left the hotel, but I had screwed one of his girls while he was in prison, so I simply chalked it off as "what comes around goes around."

When I took this last fall, I actually saw how much people hated me. They had been jealous of me for years, and since I was so low, I had to look up to see the curb; they let me know their true feelings.

Deeply depressed, I asked my old friend Bo to take me back to Prince George's Hospital so I could get some help. I was on my last leg, homeless, my hand was throbbing, and I was dope sick.

I went up to see Sam before I registered. Once Sam agreed to allow me in the program, the staff at the hospital checked my hand and leg. My hand was broken in two places, and I still had the cast on my leg from June. They admitted me in the detox on December 30, 2003. I spent the rest of 2003 in treatment. I made a promise to myself that someday Ray would pay.

In 2004, got locked up in Charles County
Thanks to two stupid women, Maryland finally got me.
I guess everything in life is for a purpose,
Because being locked up in -Maryland helped my brain resurface.

Chapter 25

2004

Charles County was a place straight out of Ernest Hemmingway Novel; a Norman Rockwell painting, children playing, elders walking dogs — it was one of the safest counties in America. This has always been a place where they "keep their Negros in check." Crimes that are simply overlooked in large counties are taken very seriously here. I wonder why: to keep the community safe, or to fill that newly-built detention center? I suspect the latter.

Why do they have so many police officers? To protect the citizens; to keep the community safe; or to fill up that new detention center; my feelings are the later. The criminal justice system today is motivated by financial gains; tickets make money for the county; arrest make money for the county; the objective is to make money

My parents always taught me to be careful of a smiling face. The biggest trick the devil ever played was people don't believe he exists. In baseball, in order to hit the pitch, you have to see it coming. If you don't see it coming, it will strike you out every time. America puts people like Pete Rose in prison for cheating. Why doesn't America hold the criminal justice system to a higher standard? There are thousands of men and women in the prisons all over America that have been simply cheated out of their freedom.

On January 2, 2004, I borrowed a car from my old friend Lusby to drop some money off to my sister Judy. All that day I experienced flash backs. At one point I was with Nita right before she hurt herself; at another point I was at T & T at the exact moment I was shot. Moon and I had made a big sting the night before, and since Judy was the only person in the world I could trust, I attempted to leave some of the money with her. I was extremely tired because I was unable to get a good night sleep. Every time I dosed off, someone stole from me. It was as if people knew I had money and were following me, waiting for me to go to sleep. I even got a motel room in an attempt to get some rest. The maid awakened me the next morning, and asked me, "What are you going to do about that window." Apparently while I was sleep, someone broke out the front window of the motel room and stole everything I had in my pockets. Thank God I had some money under the mattress, or I really would have been up the creek without a paddle.

I had been staying with an old friend named Dog in the northeast part of the city. Dog had recently had surgery, and he was renting out rooms in his home to sustain his income. He and my brother Ronald had been friends, and I felt I could trust him. Dog had every crook, thief, and derelict in Washington D.C. living in his house. The place should have been immaculate — these people could steal funk off shit — but it was a total mess. If I didn't have a ride, I was forced to stay there. I do appreciate Dog; he kept me from the elements.

This particular day, I picked up two of Dog's roomers, Marie and Black Berry. I had snuck off with Marie a few times, and Black Berry was my friend Raymond's girl. Raymond's parole officer had him placed on home arrest, so he was forced to leave Black Berry at Dog's. I was just trying to be a friend to Raymond; Black Berry has always been a snake. I can't be mad at her, because I knew she was a snake when I picked her up.

The day before, both the heat and the water at Dog's house were cut off. Since it was freezing outside, I felt sorry for Marie and Black Berry. I had a little money in my pocket, so I decided to let them ride with me to Judy's house. There they could get a meal, a shower, and get some clean clothing. I had a lot of my clothing there, and I was sure something would fit them.

My friend Barkim warned me not to take the two of them anywhere, but my hardheaded ass wouldn't listen. Barkim actually jumped out of the car at a traffic light to get away from Marie and Black Berry. I know he's still laughing at me today.

Once I got to my sister's home, she wasn't there. Instead of me waiting for her to come home, I decided to go get a cord for my phone. I had recently purchased a cell phone, and I needed a phone jack that would fit into the cigarette lighter of a car. That way, I wouldn't have to worry about the phone going dead while I was driving.

I asked my sister's neighbor where the closest Sprint store was. He told me to keep going straight out Branch Avenue until I saw the Saint Charles Mall. He said the store should be on my right.

In all my riding, it never occurred to me that I was in Charles County. I had heard stories about Charles County that went all the way back to the '60s. My brother Ronald once told me he was locked up with a man from Charles County that had received 20 years in prison for stealing a loaf of bread. This was definitely a place where I didn't want to be. Besides, I'd missed the court date in D.C. for the sleeping in the car charge on 57th Street, and there was a bench warrant out for my arrest.

I brought the phone jack and was on my way back to Judy's when Black Berry claimed she needed to use the restroom. I pulled over at the first store I saw, BJ's Wholesaler, so she could relieve herself.

Black Berry stayed in the store so long, I became suspicious. I asked Marie to go in and get her. Two minutes later, Marie came back and said she didn't see Black Berry anywhere. I got out of the car and looked around the parking lot. To my surprise, Black Berry was across the main highway, spread-eagled on a police cruiser. They had caught Black Berry stealing two ink cartridges that are used for a color printer. The pawn shop pays maybe $15.00 a piece for them. Here I had over $1000 in my pocket, and this nut's stealing ink.

Marie told me to leave her, but once again, I didn't listen. Again, it never donned on me that I was wanted or that both Black Berry and Marie were heroin addicts and there might paraphernalia in that car. I drove the car to the entrance of parking area, but traffic was stopped by a traffic light. I sat at the light, waiting for it to change so I could ask the officers what Black Berry had done. Again, it never donned on me that I was wanted.

That's when Black Berry raised up off the police car and pointed in the direction of our vehicle.

The next thing I knew, there was a police cruiser behind me, his lights flashing. Another cruiser placed his front bumper against my front fender. The officer exited his cruiser, and he attempted to knock on the passenger side window of the vehicle I was driving. At that exact moment I went into another of my flash backs. I was at T & T again. The officer that was approaching my vehicle was in plain clothing, and I imagined him to be an attacker with a gun. My only thought was to run for my life. Before he could actually knock on the window, I pulled off.

When I pulled off, I scratched the front bumper and the passenger side of the cruiser. I took the officers on a 30-minute high-speed chase. It ended when I ran out of gas and lost control of the car. I ended up in the woods. Mind you, during this entire chase, I never hit anyone. I might have scared a few people with my driving antics, but I never hit anyone.

After the crash, we were apprehended by the Charles County Police Department. The officers asked me to show them my hands. Since they had guns in my face, I cooperated fully. The driver's side door on the vehicle I was driving was extremely damaged from the crash, so it would not open. The next thing I knew, I was folded up like a $5 bill and pulled through the driver's side window.

They then proceeded to beat me like a runaway slave. Marie said, "He's not resisting arrest; why are you beating him like that?" The officers told her to shut up or she was going to get the same treatment.

The next thing I knew, I was at Fort Washington Hospital. They were treating me for head, neck, and back injuries. I was eventually released and taken to the Charles County Detention Center. When I arrived at the jail, the officers tried to get some form of confession out of me. I refused to say anything to them. In fact, I played like I didn't know where I was or who I was with. I was happy to be somewhere I could finally get some rest.

When I finally saw the commissioner, I was charged with every traffic violation possible, first and second degree assault, eluding the police, and possession of both cocaine and heroin. Mind you, I had no drugs in my possession. They found a crack stem and a hypodermic needle in Marie's purse with residue in them and charged me with possession because of that. The officer claimed I had assaulted him by hitting his car. Only in Charles County is the police cruiser an officer. They even claimed I scratched another car in the pursuit, but I'd caused no damage to the car.

The commissioner gave me a $50,000 bond. I knew I was wanted in Washington, so there was no since in me attempting to get out. I still remember telling the commissioner, "I don't care what you make my bond; I'm not getting out anyway."

From the very beginning, I knew I was in trouble. The situation started with the Public Defender's Office. Supposedly, they are bound by professional ethic to protect the defendant, but in all actualities, they are part of the same exact court defendants are fighting against. How can a person that is ignorant of the law get proper representation if the prosecutors and public defenders are on the same team? Mind you, this rule doesn't hold true for all public defenders, but enough of them participate in these "lynch mobs" to make a significant increase in the prison population.

The first thing my public defender asked me was how much time I was willing to do. I had just gone through this in Washington, and I wasn't about to be thrown to the wolves again. As soon as I was able to function normally, I made my home in the law library. I also wrote the office of the public defender in Baltimore and asked them to appoint me a pool attorney. Since all three of us were being represented by the Public Defender's Office, and I knew the state's attorney was going to trick one of my co-defendants into testifying on me. This had to be some form of conflict of interest. I've been involved with the criminal justice system since the 1980s; I should know a little something about the law.

I grew up around street people, and a common street tactic used to get the ups on a victim is to "rock them to sleep." That's when you pretend to be their friend, and once they let their guard down, you split their head. The criminal justice system uses these same tactics daily. My parents always taught me to be careful of a smiling face. The biggest trick the devil ever played was that people don't believe he exists. In baseball, in order to hit the pitch, you have to see it coming. If you don't see it coming, it will strike you out every time. Each day in America, an unsuspecting victim, that is ignorant of the law, is sent up the penitentiary river for not having proper representation. These are very evil people that use these tactics, thus you can't fight this type of evil with good; good has too many restrictions; we need an even more evil presence; someone else's greed.

Let me paint a metaphor for those of you who don't understand. First, you have a large corporation, (Charles County) within this corporation you have a business manager, (the Judge) also a sales manager, (States Attorney) and a broker. (Public Defender) All three of these entities work for the exact same corporation. (Charles County) Their job is to make money for the corporation, buying and selling commodities. The poor is that commodity. The Government pays over $20,000 a year for the confinement of an inmate. Now, the system might try to convince you that they are bound by profession ethics; people lie, cheat, and steal, just look at the politicians that have been recently arrested. They too are bound by the same ethics.

All three of these entities: Judge, Prosecutor, and Public Defender are roll players. We know how successful a team of roll players can be; especially when they all work together. Perfect example: 1960's Boston Celtics, 1980's Los Angeles Lakers, and the 1990's Chicago Bulls. These teams were simply unbeatable until distention came between the players. That when the old concept of "divide and conquer" comes into play. The only way you can beat an unbeatable team is to split them up and take them out of their positions.

When I was arrested, I had $1,045 in my pocket. I was so out of it from the beating that the reception officer got me to sign a receipt for $35. Marie, Black Berry, and I were all put in the medical unit. They knew how much money I had, so they asked me to buy them some commissary. That way, they could possibly get a nurse bring them what I had ordered for them. When the order came, I only got $35 worth of stuff. That's when I knew I was in another Macon County.

Charles County was my Negro awakening. They definitely let me know I was black. But contrary to popular thought, not all criminals are dumb. We live by our wits, so we see things that a normal law abiding citizen would not. I can spot a con a mile away. What they did wrong was to underestimate my intelligence. They place all black people in the same category; the category of fool. In the end, I would eventually bite them on the ass.

From the very beginning, I figured the only way I was going to get out of this mess was to be nuts. I told the nurses I was hearing voices and was suicidal from the door. They had me placed in the isolation unit. God works in mysterious ways, and blessings come in all sorts of packages. If it wasn't for my 73-year-old cellmate, James Kelso Savoy, waking up my brain, I might have 25 years today. He simply made me think. He gave me a complete lobotomy with a checkerboard.

Mr. Savoy didn't go that far in school, and I'm a college graduate. When he first asked me to play checkers, my ego told me there's no way this man can beat me. To my disbelief, he beat me up and down the checker board. He beat me so bad I was forced to put my pride in my back pocket and became willing to learn. He taught me to think before I made moves, back my moves up, and to think two moves ahead. I just started to apply this same concept to life. It's crazy how simple common sense disappears when you use drugs. I thank you, Mr. Savoy, for giving me the combination to the safe.

From that day on, my mind started clicking. The more I played, the better I could think. I started seeing things for what they really were. For the first time in years, I could finally see the complete picture. That's the point when I knew I had to help out those that were less fortunate than I. The problem was most of the black men in Charles County had an inferiority complex. They simply thought everything white people told them was the truth. I learned early in life that if you don't read something for yourself— holy books, and law books, etc.— it's subject to be a lie. I helped the people I could, but the majority listened to their public defenders and got screwed. I have never figured out how a man can be the worst crook in the world while in the streets, but once they are incarcerated, they won't lie to the white man in the black dress. I pray someday my brothers and sisters wake up and see the light.

As I mentioned earlier, thousands of men and women have been wrongly convicted. According to http://justicedenied.org, a number of factors contribute to the remarkable ease with which vast numbers of men, women, and increasingly children, are victimized by a wrongful conviction. One or more of the following factors are typically present in a case of wrongful conviction:

1. Overzealous prosecutors solely concerned with winning.
2. Inadequate police investigation.
3. Fabrication of evidence or doctored reports by the police and/or crime lab technicians.
4. Erroneous identification by the victim or other eyewitnesses.
5. False confession, physically or psychologically coerced
6. Inexperienced or incompetent defense lawyer.
7. Perjury by the police and/or other prosecution witnesses.
8. Inaccurate analysis of evidence by crime lab technicians.

9. Uncritical jurors who blithely accept the prosecutor's case. Tunnel vision by police and prosecutors who presume defendant's guilt to the exclusion of other suspect
10. Slanting of a judge's rulings to favor the prosecution.
11. Lack of resources that prevent the defendant from hiring investigators and/or experts to find exculpatory evidence.
12. Pressuring of witnesses to give pro-prosecution testimony.
13. Smearing of the defendant's character in the courtroom and the media for alleged or actual actions that have no relationship to the charges.
14. Critical evidence disappears, is destroyed, or the prosecution resists providing it for defense testing.
15. Prejudice against a defendant's ethnicity, religion, or political or personal ideas by the prosecutor, judge, and/or jurors.
16. Coercion of an innocent defendant to accept a plea bargain by the prosecutor's piling on of charges that will result in much longer sentence if the defendant goes to trial and loses.
17. Purchase of perjurious testimony by the prosecutor.
18. Wording of an indictment to paint an innocent person in the worst light possible in the eyes of the judge and jury.

The playing field is heavily tilted in favor of the prosecution when a defendant isn't wealthy enough to hire quality lawyers, investigators, and expert witnesses to counter the prosecutor's virtually unlimited resources.

My attorney filed a motion for me to be evaluated for my mental health. In May of 2004, I was evaluated by a state psychologist. I acted as if I had Turrets Syndrome. I made crazy faces and yelled abruptly. I told the examiner I had been smoking PCP for years, and I experience blackouts. I also pretended not to know the answers to the questions the examiner asked me concerning the courts. I was asked questions like, "what is a judge? What the Judge; what is the prosecutor and what does your Attorney do for you?" I answered vaguely to each of his questions. Eventually, he recommended that I be sent to Spring Grove Hospital for further evaluation.

I was sent to Spring Grove in June of 2004. The officer that drove me was from Washington, and I felt comfortable talking to him. I told him about me wanting to write a book, and I also recited some of my poetry to him. He actually was overwhelmed, and asked me to write a poem specifically for him. Hell, I was going to the nut house, and I had nothing but time on my hands. I figured since he was a big man in his church, if I gave him some of my work, there was a possibility I could get some exposure.

I was taken to Dayhoff A. This was the unit specifically structured for evaluations. The majority of the staff there had worked for the Crownsville Hospital, but since it had recently closed, they were all sent to Spring Grove. Closing a building and not changing the staff doesn't cure the problem, for the same neglectful acts went on at Spring Grove. There were counselors that liked to antagonize the patients and others that didn't want to do anything at all. I actually saw patients that had urinated on themselves stay in those same dirty clothing for days. The day room actually stank. When I tried to assist those patients myself, I was told to mind my business.

When I found out that there was no more law for guilty by reason of insanity," I wanted out. They now have what you call "not criminally responsible." To be found not criminally responsible, you have to admit to all the crimes you are facing, if the doctors deem you not criminally responsible, you are taken back to court and given "Not Criminally Responsible" probation. The probation is for a period of 10 years; and if at any time while on this probation you violate it, the 10 years starts over again. I met people there that had been there since 1982. One guy had used drugs continuously while on release, and each time he was taken back before the courts, the judge started the 10 years over. It was 2004, and the same man had 8 years left on his probation.

I knew from the time I heard this man's story that I wanted out. Besides, I had a detainer in Washington, and you cannot be admitted into Spring Grove if you have an open detainer. They were simply trying to get me to tell on myself; if I had of revealed any negative information; that information would have been sent directly to the Judge.

After I caused enough trouble and they realized I was not going to talk about my case, they hurriedly sent me back to jail. I still remember the social worker telling me that Mental Health Treatment wasn't for me. There was a great deal of stipulations to the treatment, and I, along with my family would have to comply with the stipulations, or I would never be released. I had to get back to jail. I was sure I could eventually get out of jail, but I could be stuck in mental health treatment for the rest of my life.

I confided in the psychologist about my fears of dying and asked her if she could have my liver tested. She had me tested on July 16, 2004 at Saint Agnes Hospital in Catonsville, Maryland. The test results hadn't come back by the time I was sent back to the jail, but she had already done her report on July 14th. She stated in her report that there was nothing wrong with my liver. This made the court think I was faking about my illness. On the 18th of July, the results confirmed that I had liver cancer, but I wasn't given the results before my trial. I actually had to sue Charles County Detention Center to get all my medical records.

The same officer that took me to Spring Grove came to get me. When we got back to the jail, I gave him a copy of I am what I am. A poem I wrote when I was simply fed up with the way people are treated because of their economic status. This was my way of flipping the script and putting them in my position. I actually wanted them to feel the pain I felt on a daily basis. Mind you, a great deal of the problems I've faced were created by me, but the victimization of my forefathers continuously echoes in my soul.

I am what I am

One day while I was angry at the system I wrote this poetry
I am what I am not by chance,
I'm just attempting to enhance;
After the more than 100th glance
Of a script that was created in my behalf.
I've found no reason to laugh
About a society
That never gave a dam about me.
One that wants to kill me,
Imprison me,
And genocide me;
I cannot change my past, And even though I fast;
I still feel sad
About a life that's gone bad
so come with me on a trip,
As I attempt to flip the script,
Bear with me, because this one's straight off my hip.
Be careful of the swirl,
As you visit my world;
I pray you don't despise;
Seeing life through my eyes;

Everything will be ok;
I experience this shit every day;
So take it on the chin;
As I finally smile and grin
About a game that only one side seems to win.
Just imagine us trading place;
Let's switch eyes, and even faces;
Middle class America you stand at about faces;
Because today is about wealth, and I have friends in high places;
Now I'm holding the cards, stacking the decks, and holding all the political aces..
Can you feel the rages?
Of all the different races;
That have been beaten, embarrassed and locked in dog cages.
I'll find ways to hinder and minimize your education;
I'll even go as far as to erase your entire historical foundation.
Would you learn to steal, or even kill, if there were no alternatives to crime, crying children, homelessness, and starvation?
Would you stand in a corner and hustle in dangerous places;
Rob, steal, and catch cases?
Now that you are behind,
I can mess with your mind,
make you think that I am kind;
Even get you to kiss my behind,
to get out of a bind.
Steal all your dreams,
And kill your self-esteem,
Do you know what I mean,
Now look at your faces,
After only the thought of us trading places;

Don't you feel manipulated?
Even though I wrote this poem in haste;
I pray it wasn't a waste;
For I've given God my case;
For only with him can I erase;
Those bad feelings of the past, and live again at last.
There's no reason to cuss, fuss,
I have nothing else to discuss;
In a world like this one only God can save us...

Once back at the jail, I was placed in unit BC. They had brought my buddy Moon in on a theft charge, and in that unit, we became even closer. Moon taught me the game of chess. He taught me how to equate chess pieces with life itself and how to strategically work my way through life. I thank God for the teachings of Moon, for without his patience, I might be doing life in prison today. From that day on, I dissected my case. I worked out angles in every perspective. My every waking moment was spent figuring out ways to get around the lies the Charles County Police Officers had told. I had nothing but time, so I became extremely prepared.

The prosecutor's office wanted me to do a considerable amount of time. They had my case placed before the Honorable Judge Robert C. Sally. Sally was known for siding with his officers and giving out disproportionately long sentences. He was intent on hiding me, and my attorney was playing along in the game.

Before they sent me to Spring Grove, I explicitly told Judge Chappell that I didn't want this attorney representing me. The attorney had simply taken too many liberties in his own hands; without informing me. My original trial date was for July 7, 2004, but my attorney allowed the judge to postpone my trial without my consent. In fact, I wasn't even taken to court that day. There is a rule in the Circuit Court, where if a man asks for a speedy trial, the court has 180 days to bring that case to trial. By the attorney allowing the court to waive my Hicks rule without me being there, this violated my speedy trial rights.

At the very next hearing, I fired my attorney. I asked the judge to appoint me a panel attorney. Since both of my co-defendants were already being represented by the Public Defender's Office, I felt it was a conflict of interest for me to have a public defender, especially since the prosecutor was attempting to have one of my co-defendants make adverse statements against me.

At that hearing, the judge actually told me he was not allowed to appoint me an attorney and said that was the duty of the Public Defender's Office. I knew that was a lie, and he also said, in so many words, that if he did appoint me one, the attorney would be one of his "good ol' boys." I simply asked to represent myself.

Unit BC was in constant disarray. I had to figure out a way to get some peace and quiet to work on my case. There was a man on my unit that I simply hated. This man threatened every white man on the tier. He took racial conflict to a new level. One day, while watching the Comedy Awards on BET, he looked at me the wrong way. I think I subconsciously wanted to hit him anyway, but after he looked at me like that, I went to my cell and put on my boots. I walked back into the day room and picked a fight. I ended up punching him on the jaw.

The incident happened so quickly that the officers had no idea who was hit or who did the hitting. They locked down the entire unit and went from cell to cell asking who the culprits were. To my surprise, everyone on the unit stuck up for me. They actually yelled from their cell doors, "I did it." It took the officers over an hour to find out my identity. The captain came on the unit and threatened one of the inmates, and that inmate told them my name.

When the incident occurred, I was wearing Timberland boots and Grant sweatpants, but while the officers were going from cell to cell, I changed clothes with another inmate. They actually charged me with wearing a disguise.

I was also charged with assault, hindering an investigation, disorderly conduct, and lying to an officer. When I went before the adjustment officer, I admitted to hitting the man, but I claimed the reason I did it was because I was hearing voices. They sentenced me to 15 days in segregation. I actually looked forward to going. It would be quiet there, and I would have the time to concentrate on my case.

When I was released from segregation, they put me in unit BE. My cell mate was Cecil Moore. He gave me a good pep talk before I was to represent myself in trial.

On October 19, 2004, I went before the Honorable Judge Sally for trial. Judy brought my gray suit, a burgundy paisley tie, and some black Stacy Adams shoes. I fit the part of an attorney. I had been over the trial thousands of times in my mind. I had also practiced my lines on every cellmate I had. When I entered the court room, I was ready to do battle.

I began my case by telling the judge that my sister had hired me an attorney, Leonard Long. I'd asked the jury for a postponement, so Mr. Long could represent me. Mr. Long had represented a few of the members of the Raful Edmonds gang, and made a name for himself by keeping his defendant from getting life, like the rest of the gang.

Judge Sally informed me that he had spoken to Mr. Long, and he had told him that Charles County doesn't give postponements to out-of-state attorneys. Judge Sally stated I'd been told I was either to take the plea offer, or prepare for trial. I chose the latter.

I also asked the judge about the court going past my Hicks date. He gave me some bullshit about how the Hicks situation had already been handled. The fix was in from the door.

The prosecutor offered me a plea bargain for theft of over $500 and reckless driving. Theft over $500 carried a maximum penalty of 15 years. If I took the plea bargain, I would be giving up my right to appeal. Besides, I smelled a rat. They weren't that prepared. Trials cost the state a considerable amount of money. Prosecutors and Public Defenders do everything in their powers to keep cases out of the trial court. Since I didn't have an attorney and I knew I was dying of cancer, why in the world would I plead guilty to 15 years, especially since I was given three or four years to live? I had in my mind from the door to fight.

When it came time for jury selection, I really got a slim picking. There were maybe nine possible black, out of 25 possible jurors, and 3 of them were police officers. When the prosecutor started getting rid of all the black jurors, I was forced to ask for a sidebar with the judge. I eventually got 5 black jurors out of the 12-person panel.

The prosecutor made his opening statement and simply bashed my integrity. When it was my turn, I put on an eloquent speech. I don't think the prosecutor took me seriously. He wasn't very prepared. I guess they simply underestimated my legal abilities. Defending my case wasn't that hard because the majority of my charges were trumped up. Today, I think I put too much emphasis on winning the assault charges. If I had put that much time into the theft charges, I wouldn't be here today.

The state's first witness was the owner of the stolen car. She had gone in a drug store on Marlboro Pike, and when she came out, her car was gone. She was naturally upset about her car being missing, but the insurance company had given her $3,500 for a vehicle that wasn't worth $100. I realize she might have had some sentimental value, but $3,500 should have compensated for her loss.

One of the reasons my attorney and I first had a falling out was because I had written the victim a letter, apologizing to her for the inconvenience she suffered. I explained to her that I was not the person that stole her vehicle. I let her know I was in the hospital at the time the car was stolen. I also explained to her that I was loaned the car, and I would pay her for her for the damages.

I mailed this letter from the jail, but the prosecutor's office got the letter before the victim. Apparently the jail was screening my mail, and when they saw I was writing to the victim, they had stopped the letter. When I arrived that morning at the Hearing, I saw the prosecutor hand my attorney a letter. When my attorney attempted to hide the letter from me, I knew whose side he was on, and I immediately fired him.

Once the trial actually began, I felt as if I was in another world. This small segment of time which the trial took could determine the outcome of the rest of my life. To the normal sane individual, representing yourself would be scary as hell, but I looked at it as a chance of a lifetime. I've been involved in the criminal justice system since 1985, and never had I actually had a true say in my defense. Even though I was facing one of the most feared judges in the State Maryland, I was prepared to stand up for human rights. The majority of the inmates in Charles County plead guilty; I simply wanted to show the other inmates that the people in courts were human too. I've been asked how I possibly thought I could win by representing myself. In all actuality, I didn't care whether I won or not — I simply wanted to fight. Besides, with the attorney they were offering me, the only chance I did have was to represent myself.

The thing that astonished me was the fact that all three of the officers involved in my case told a different story. I guess they thought I didn't have the balls to represent myself, so they never collaborated on their testimonies. They had three totally conflicting testimonies about the assault.

In trial, I was always very polite, and I spoke very articulately. The jurors could see I was educated, and I got a few brownie points for that fact alone. The thing that messed up my case was my affiliation with my two codefendants. Black Berry gave the impression that she was a poor defenseless dope fiend, and Marie actually told the court she was a prostitute. Any normal law-abiding citizen would figure I had done something wrong simply by the company I kept.

I was eventually found guilty of theft over $500, conspiracy to theft under $500, eluding the police, reckless driving, hit and run, and possession of cocaine. I was found not guilty of first-degree assault, two counts of second-degree assault, and theft under $500. I was acquitted on the possession of heroin charge. Out of all these charges, the possession charge bothered me the most. Marie actually took the stand and stated before the court that all the paraphernalia found in the car was hers, and I was still found guilty of possession. The amount of cocaine they found me guilty of possessing was equivalent to some dust.

I was given a pre-sentence investigation by the probation department in November of 2004. These people already had in their minds to send me up the road. This lady made me out to be the worst possible human being in the world. She even said I was using Nita's death as an excuse to commit crimes. The only thing she gave me any credit for was having a good education and job history, and the only reason she did that was so they could give me a $7,000 fine.

I was sentenced in December of 2004. The Honorable Judge Robert C. Sally said things to me at that sentencing hearing which still bother me to this day. My sentencing guidelines were from four to eight years, but Judge Sally saw fit to give me a fifteen-year sentence and suspend five years. As a result, I ended up with ten years in prison, and five years on probation to follow my ten year prison sentence. He cited acts of violence as a justification for going outside of the guideline range, but I wasn't found guilty of any crimes of violence.

Before he sentenced me, I asked Judge Sally for leniency because of my cancer. I told him an extended term in prison would be in fact a life sentence, and I didn't deserve life for the crimes at hand. Sally said, "I'm tired of you animals from Washington, D.C., coming down here ruining my county. I know you are sick, and I hope you die in prison."

I've seen Judge Sally give white boys four years for raping their children. One of the white boys that burned down a black neighborhood in Charles County got nine years, and he caused millions of dollars in damage. Here I got ten years for a 1989 car that was stolen while I was in the hospital, and the actual theft occurred in Prince George's County, not Charles County.

I caused so much trouble in the Charles County Detention Center by suing the jail and creating petitions they sent me to the Department of Correction on the next shipment. Besides, the correctional officers were very upset I had beaten the assault charges. I had also filed a grievance against the arresting officers, and since I beat those charges, they would now have a mark on their permanent records.

They had people in the detention center that had been waiting for months to get to DOC, and they put me ahead of all of them. I left on December 30, 2004. I would be spending the New Year in Baltimore.

Back in prison in 2005;
It's simply a miracle I'm still alive.
When I first came to prison I was the youngest one;
Look at me now: I'm an uncle, son.
Being in this place makes me sick,
and all this because I like to smoke that shit...

Chapter 26

2005

I spent New Year's at the Maryland Reception-Diagnostic & Classification Center (MRDCC) in Baltimore Maryland. The place was simply a stockyard where they directed the cattle. About 10,000 men come through that place each year, so the officers there will never be without a job. I was sent there with big Scott Adams. Big Scott had also gotten a raw deal from his attorney, and he was truly stressed about being in the system for the first time. Even though I've never been locked up in the State of Maryland before, I am no stranger to the penitentiary. I know how to work my way around the criminal justice system.

The two of us were placed on the 6th Floor. Scott only had four years, so his stay would be considerably shorter than mine. They classified Scott as pre-release; I was made medium because I had a detainer in Washington. We only stayed in that tomb for two weeks, and then it was off to the Maryland Correctional Training Center (MCTC) in Hagerstown Maryland.

They call MCTC the "New Jail" even though it was built in the 1960s. The place actually looks like a housing project to me. When we got to the Orientation unit, Unit 6, I was given a cell with no window-panes. The Cell was so cold; I was forced to sleep on the floor, under the bunk, to keep snow from falling on my face. I caught pneumonia in that cell.

There were eight other men from Washington that came to MCTC with me and Scott on the Blue Bird. They had nick names like Moe-D, Ghost, K, Little Greg, Perry, and Juvenile. For all of us, this was our first time ever being in this prison, and we were a little unsure what to expect.

I've heard some disturbing stories about the officer in Hagerstown being part of the Klu Klux Klan. There are well over 2,000 inmates in this prison, and the entire time I've been here, I've only seen maybe five black correctional officers, and never all at the same time.

The thing that bothered me the most was when I saw black men killing each other for menial things, but they allow white correctional officers say any and everything to them without giving any opposition. To this day, I cannot understand why men that break every law imaginable in society come to prison and follow all the rules and regulations. If they were following the rules in society, they wouldn't be there in the first place.

I was eventually taken to Unit 7, nicknamed Little Iraq, where I was placed on tier A. I had a lot of homies there too: Twan, De-Bo, Joe Keys, Stink, Jug Head, and Little Shawn, to name a few. They had their own little click.

Since I was now past 40, I was now considered an "uncle," so I was kept from the entire gang situation. Besides, I don't smoke cigarettes and I don't use drugs anymore; that's where convicts create a lot of problems for themselves in prison.

Since I had a detainer in Washington, I often went to the law library. I met Mr. G, an older, more distinguished convict who was very knowledgeable about the law. Mr. G helped me file a motion to have my detainer in Washington dismissed. The next month, I was taken back to Baltimore, where the Federal Marshals form Washington took me back to their jurisdiction.

When I arrived at the jail, I was taken to unit NW-3, the orientation unit. I stayed there until I was taken to the Superior Court for the District of Columbia. Once at the Court house, I was taken before the Honorable Judge Lebowitz. I had written her several times, and she was very familiar with my case. As soon as the proceedings got started, the prosecuting attorney said "D.C. no longer wished to prosecute my case.", thus the case was dismissed with prejudice. My case was dismissed on March 4, 2005, but it would take me until May 5, 2005 to get back to Maryland.

Once back at the D.C. Jail, I was really hurt to see the amount of children that were in the system. The majority of them used PCP, so their brains were fried. Some didn't know right from left, nor up from down. When you have such a diminished capacity, that makes it considerably easy for the criminal justice system to give you a slave number (DCDC Number), and send you to the plantation (Penitentiary).

The complete ignorance of these young men made me wonder about the well-being of my own teenage son. I tried several times to get in touch with him, and when I couldn't, I wrote a poem called

"Dead Beat Dad," and sent the poem to his Aunt Jean in hopes she would send it to him.

DEAD BEAT DAD

I'm what they call a deadbeat dad;
Because I dropped my seed and then ran scared,
Straight to the confines of another woman's bed;
I didn't know what I was doing, because I was just a kid,
But now as I sit here on this 3rd bid
I wonder who gets to put shit in my son's head.
Will it be keedie, Tag, or his uncle Slick?
You know the three who push coke in front the rib pit.
"Will they teach my baby how to roll a spliff?
How to bag up weed and cut up coke and shit?
I wonder who will help him with those big decisions.
I wonder from whom he'll get his vision;
Please not 50 Cent, Jay-Z, or a rapper on a mission
Or will my fiend just give him dope to sell on Nannie Helen and Division.
From the very' beginning his mom taught him to hate me.
She said, "Your daddy aint shit, he's done nothing for us lately."
So, I understand
Why you hate the older black. Man;
But I hold a lot of the secrets to the plots and plans.
I was taught the game is to sold and never told;
But that was from the years of old;
for don't you think I'd be kind of cold;
If I never exposed
You, to the Knowledge I've got.

You might never earn enough to keep from getting shot, Wheelchairs, jail cells, courts, and what not.
I thought by maybe showing you my pain,
And making it plain,
I could keep you from joining a gang;
Because 25 years ago, I did the very same thing
I thought I was a part of a big thing,
Loved to hear my glock sing,
But there're consequences for everything;
A bad decision will surely bring;
A visit to that Circuit Court,
Where they lock up young blacks just for the sport
Never in life would I ever dream,
A judge and a jury could be so mean;
Prosecutors and Public Defenders on the same team
I wrote this poem to make you more aware,
That the game these folks are praying isn't fair.
I wouldn't have written this if I didn't care;
And on my life I have to swear;
That I want to leave a legacy,
And without your young man, there was no me...

I went over in my mind thousands of times, the fact that I had let my children down. I prayed constantly that my transgressions would not befall on my children. There is an old saying, "the apple doesn't fall far from the tree." I definitely pray my tree was at the top of a hill.

While in the D.C. Jail I also saw another injustice committed by the United States Parole Commission. As we all well know, parole is a privilege not a right, but when a person is released on parole, in all actualities, that person is completing his sentence on the streets. If a man stays out of trouble for say (10) years, if that person is re-arrested, it is unethical to take all that man's street time.

They justify their actions in a Jim Crow contract called the "Expedited Cop." They tell young men that they can go home in ninety days if they sign the contract. If you read the small print at the bottom of the form, it says they are allowed to literally steal these men's street time. For example, imagine you have a 20-year sentence, did 10 years of incarceration and made parole. You stayed on parole for nine years before you got a dirty urine, which led to a formal parole violation. When you sign the expedited cop, you allow the parole board to take the entire nine years and start your parole over from scratch. Thus you have to serve 10 years of parole all over again.

When I was in unit SW-3, I did my very best to discourage the men from signing these documents. I tried to explain to them the ramifications of signing that particular document, but the instant gratification of going home in 90 days, simply clouded their judgments. I left D.C. Jail May 5, 2005, heart-broken.

When I got back to MCTC, I got a job as an academic aide at the Academic School. I worked for the language teacher, Silvia Kemp. Mrs. Kemp was one of the inspirations that led to the writing of this book. She made me see life in a totally different way. I guess I was simply moving too fast to see the flowers and the trees. With Mrs. Kemp's guidance, I gained a great deal of respect for nature and for life itself.

She was a very knowledgeable woman. She not only taught language — she taught life. The students watched a movie at the beginning of each semester and wrote a report on the movie. Since I was her aide, I watched the same movie maybe six times a day. It's amazing how much of the details of the film you miss the first time you watch it. I actually gained a better perspective on films.

In December of 2005, I was finally given minimum custody. Since my security level changed, I was freed from "Little Iraq" and placed in open housing, Unit 2.

It's been more the twenty years of disaster,
So when it comes to screwing up, I am the master.
I've suffered more than twenty years of misery and pain;
God please bring me in from the rain.
I put my common sense in a safe years ago
And lost the combination which made me slow
But I'm finally waking up slowly but surely;
And that's thanks to the love of a mother that spoiled me
And a father who said, "It's a better way,
Be content in the moment; take life from day to day."
In the game of life, they say drugs are a sin;
But in the game of drugs, no one wins.

Chapter 27

2006

Unit 2 was an adventure within itself. The entire time I'd been incarcerated in the state of Maryland, I did my time in a cell. This cell contained a double bunk, a window, a desk, a sink, and a toilet. In Unit 2, the cells did not have toilets, so when you had to use the restroom, it was in an open bathroom with no stalls or doors. There was simply no privacy. The thing that bothered me the most about the restrooms was you could only use them at certain times a day, so you had to condition your body to work on a Unit 2 clock. If I'd had a serious bladder problem, I wouldn't have made it there.

The tier officer's name was Miss Sanders. She was a nice-looking, blond-haired white woman. You could tell by her demeanor that she had been hurt in life. She was simply unbending where men were concerned. Since I've been incarcerated most of my adult life, I could understand her position. If that woman showed any fear on that unit, she would lose all control. She definitely has my respect. I pray someday she finds a husband that will get her out of the dangers of corrections.

In February of 2006, the library at MCTC had a poetry contest for Black History Month. We were instructed to write a poem about the 1963 march on Washington. We were to write a speech that might hold true under today's standards. My poem was entitled My Dream:

MY DREAM:

Dr. Martin Luther King had a dream of freedom in 1963;
42 years later freedoms still an illusion; just open your eyes and see.
There's still killing, disease, and mis-education,
And 60% of my people are falling victim to incarceration.
Half of our youths are totally insane;
Smoking and sniffing to medicate the pain;
Drugs in America are truly a curse;
Crack, E-pills, weed; PCP is the worst,
These drugs leave brilliant young mind riding dead in hearses.
Some black' go to college;
To increase their knowledge;
They become middle classes;

To escape the black masses;
But there are millions of people who are left far behind; and my poem today is to enrich all of their minds.
An entire race of people asleep so it seems;
Please wake up today and listen to my dream.
I dream,
That we will come up with cures to the addictions to heroin and crack
And President Bush will bring the troops home from Iraq.
I dream,
That the public school system will create a presentation;
To stop labeling poor children "special education",
That we will change the way the teachers teach;
And stop saying the children are far beyond reach.
I hate to see teachers show little concern;
When more than half of their class is unable to learn;
'We-as the parents must fight the good fight;To ensure our children reach new heights.
I dream,
That we won't let history repeat itself;
By remembering the past and taking care of our health.
Martin marched many a mile in hail, sleet, and rain;
I pray all that marching wasn't done in vain.
We must all work together; we can't continue to fuss;
Or once again we will be sitting at the rear of the bus.
I wonder what "Popeye's" and 'KFC' "are going to do?
Now that our scientist have revived the bird flu;
To kill off poor people; that's one hell of a gimmick
But what they've unleashed is called a pandemic.
I dream,
That the courts will follow all of the amendments;

And stop treating defendants like unwanted dependents.
How can we win when the judges are mean?
And prosecutors and public defenders are on the same team.
Bush is killing the constitution, and that is a fact;
If you think I'm lying, read the "Patriot Act".
They are bugging our homes and raising the price of stamps;
Next we'll all be living in concentration camps.
If they declare Martial Law that will kill inmates the fastest;
Because my brothers in jail they are going to gas us.
If you think there are too many people, and space is starting to fade;
Just wait until Judge Alito kills "Roe v. Wade".
Please democrats protect the Supreme Court with all the strength you can muster;
If all else fails, go filibuster;
I dream,
That home can still be a special place;
Where you grow, learn, and really feel safe.
The Nation's Capital has always been home to me;
with monuments, museums; a place of history;
Now baseballs back in Washington again;
But I wonder where they plan to build that new stadium?
In my mom's backyard, they've made it plain;
'That the city's taking her home claiming immanent domain
I dream,
That the world will work harder on global warming;
It's creating natural disasters; the South's really storming.
Earthquakes, floods, and hurricanes;
Causing people to experience tremendous strains;
Can you imagine the hardships the victims of Katrina saw?
And all New Orleans is concerned with is rebuilding for '"Mardi Gras"

People went days without water, bread, or meat;
Because FEMA doesn't give a dam if poor blacks' eat.
The media call the people refugees; boy was that mean;
Because the lower classes were never included in the American Dream;
We have a war in America can't they see;
For the "'KKK' claimed they blew up the levies;
Water washed away thousands and thousands of homes;
And the government tells senior citizens their on their own.
They give them a $2000.00 check and a clothing voucher;
And say, "Please move someplace else; we can live without cha."
How could all of this happen in such a great nation?
Freedoms only an illusion, and the South's still one big plantation.
Can you imagine how rich the Bush's have gotten?
Since the prices of oil are much higher than cotton.
I dream,
That someday my country will have much more compassion;
And stop the creation of those paid assassins;
And stop all of the fighting in the third world;
And the brutal murdering of little boys and girls;
I know this world is soon to end; God, forgive us all for our sins...

I worked with Mrs. Kemp until June of 2006. My friend Isaac recommended me to librarian, Ms. Smith, for the position of legal clerk. Working in the law library was a new experience. People like my buddy 6'9 gave me some good pointers. He is an educated man and very knowledgeable of the law; but the man I learned the most from was Mr. Ellis Douglas., aka the One.

Ellis is a legend within himself. He has litigated in the highest courts in attempts to better the conditions of the prison system. The thing that bothers both Mr. Ellis and me is the ignorance of young criminals.

They are more concerned about sports than they are their own cases. This shows through their attendance in the law library. Most of them want someone to do their work, so in the end, they end up screwed.

On November 22, 2006, I received notice from the Public Defender's Office for the appellate that my sentence has been vacated, and remanded back to the Circuit Court for Charles County for a new trial. All the sleepless nights and hard work I did on my case has worked in my favor. I just pray I was help to some of my peers while I was incarcerated. I will definitely be in church Sunday Morning.

There is an old Korean saying, "If you can walk, you can always find a way out." I never gave up on my case, and I've worked diligently for the entire time I've been incarcerated to give this time back. Now, finally all the hard work has worked out for the best.

Through all the pains and sufferings, I've experienced in my life; I always knew, I had larger calling; one that someday might assist people; and help them to realize their full potential. I pray, having read about my misfortunes, you will gain a different direction and / or purpose.

The Persian poet, Rumi, sums all this up beautifully in his poem "The Lame Goat":

You've seen a herd of goats
Going down to the water;
'The lame and dreamy goat
Brings up the rear;
There are worried faces about that one,
But ah, now they're laughing, because look
As they return
That goat is the leader!
'There are many different kinds of knowing.
The lame goat's kind is a branch

That traces back to the roots of presence.
Learn from the lame goat,
And lead the herd home...

I've always been that lame goat, but now it's my time to lead, and I promise to do my very best to lead my people out of this mental bondage we have created for ourselves. Knowledge is power, and through that knowledge, there is hope. As Popeye used to say, "Enough is enough, I can't stand no more." I am definitely tired of prison. I will do whatever it takes to be an honest, law-abiding citizen.

As a final tribute to the men here at MCTC that helped me along the way, I want to share one final poem of mine:

Thank You

As I sit in my cell;
Contemplating heaven or hell;
I reminisce on my life of crime;
I grimace, how I wasted my time;
Selling nickels and dimes;
Listening to junkie's whine; falling behind
Scarface, King of New York and Belly, all made it plain;
How Hollywood uses movies and video's to tantalizes our brains;
promising riches and fame; Am I going in sane?
Being dedicated to an unwinnable game;
The consequences are always the same;
Jails, institutions, and death;
Hustling's a fake high life drinking some Meth";
Sent me up the road for an extended rest;
you hard headed Mofo!!! Your father ,Best...

As I look up at the sky at night;
Praying only for insight;
On how to make it in spite of my plight;
I thank God I'm not here for life.
I got help from men that have spent decades away from home.
They gave me knowledge and advice when I felt alone;
They told me I needed to atone;
For leaving my children, home alone.
I was mad at the world, and everyone around me;
feeling the misery;
That lived inside me;
For not being the man my parents raised me to be.
I've only got (10) years, so why am I stressing?
I needed the rest; this time could be a blessing.
-My brothers you taught me the power of faith;
And to stop dwelling on my past, my screw ups, my case;
To be content in the moment; and to be thankful for what I have;
My life, my health, my strength; why be sad?
You taught me to work on myself to be a better person;
To learn all I can, take advantage of my time, so my situation doesn't worsen.
If I ever contemplate, committing more crimes;
'Facing more time;
Losing my mind;
Falling further behind;
I'll think of you brothers that opened up to me;

And gave me insight when I couldn't see;
Blessings come in all shapes and sizes;
And a light goes off in your head when you finally realize it;
That your world can be a better place;
Feeling sorry for yourself is only a waste.
So, today I say thank you,
For teaching me a fraction of what you knew.
I thank you brothers, and I feel your pain.
All the lessons you taught me will never go in vain...

2007, THE YEAR I FINALLY SHINE;

THE YEAR I PUT DRUGS AND CRIME FAR BEHIND.
I MUST ALWAYS REMEMBER FROM WHENCE I CAME,
OR MY SITUATIONS IN LIFE WILL ALWAYS BE THE SAME...

Chapter 28

2007

On January 2, 2007, I met with my case manager, Mr. Hoffman. He had me sign papers to be moved to the Southern Maryland Pre-Release Unit in Charlotte Hall, Maryland.

This seemed quite strange to me, because my convictions were vacated in November 2006. If anything, I should have been transferred back to the Charles County Detention Center. I've learned not to question fate. Maybe God has a purpose for me to be at the Pre-Release Center. Plus I would rather be in Southern Maryland Pre-release than in the Charles County Detention Center.

I was finally transferred to SMPRU on February 7, 2007. I was moved at 7:00 a.m. to the receiving building at MC.T.C., and sat there until

5:00 p.m. that evening. A friend form Landover, Tay, was also moved that day. He went to BCCC.

Instead of being sent directly to Southern Maryland, I was taken to Brockbridge first, and I had to wait there over night for the officers from Southern Maryland to retrieve me.They transported us in shackles, and they used a black box that goes around the handcuffs to prevent escape. That box is the most uncomfortable thing in the world. It actually crosses the hands, one over top the other. Can you imagine riding for hours in such an uncomfortable position? Can you also image an inmate designed the box?

Brockbridge was truly a warehouse. There were thousands of men that have been sentenced to less than five years, and the Department of Corrections is running out of places to put them.Thus, they put them in crowded dormitories, on top of each other. I did have the chance to see my old buddy Sweeney.They had moved him a month earlier, supposedly to Southern Maryland, but he was still sitting in Brockbridge.

I finally made it to Southern Maryland on February 8, 2007, my father's birthday. I saw people from my old neighborhood like Joe, Marco, Mike, and Zero. I always respected Zero, for he had actually conquered both the prison and hustling worlds. Zero had been out of prison for twenty years, and he had managed to buy a home, several BMWs, and a brand new 25-foot work truck. He also maintained a marriage with his wife Liza. I know Zero spent at least twenty years in prison, and in that time, he must have educated himself. I will take the knowledge I learned from him, and apply it to my life — or at least the legal parts. Z's life is a story itself, and it deserves its own book.

On February 10th they brought Greg Sharp in. It has been at least (17) years since I last saw Blackie. If you can remember, I spoke of Greg in chapter 6. I always looked up to him as an older brother. He grew a great deal while incarcerated, mentally. I actually got some good advice from him while I was there. I also forgave him for teaching me about crack. I guess there are some things in life that are best not known, for curiosity always kills the cat.

Southern Maryland Pre-Release was nothing but a scam. Once you find employment, they charge these men $170 per week to stay there. That comes to about $680 per month. Believe me, we don't have any lavish accommodations. Actually, there are only three dormitories, each containing sixty men. So in all actualities, we are also sleeping on top of each other. Then they want us to work on menial jobs at places like Burger King, junk yards, lumber yards, and small family-owned restaurants. Jobs that don't pay that much money. That way, we don't have a lot of money saved when we reach the streets. All that does is make the men do illegal things to supplement their incomes. Exploit the black market so to speak. If you ask me, I seriously feel it's a stunt to keep the men from having enough money, upon their release, to buy large quantities of narcotics. They believed we were all drug dealers and that most of the men are simply planning for their next run.

On a more positive note, SMPRU had better food than any other institution I've ever been in. We are not fenced in, and came in constant contact with nature. They have a law library, but most of the legal books are obsolete. I guess they don't want to take any chances on a Michael Moore filing a law suit against them.

It was two weeks before I saw my counselor, Mr. Woods. The first thing he asked me was, "Why did you try to run over a police officer?" I automatically thought he must be a policeman or someone who works for the Charles County court system. Woods went on to ask me how on earth I was able to make parole. I really got very negative vibes from this man. From that moment on, I watched everything I said to him.

The conversation that bothered me the most was with the black lady that monitored the law library on the weekends. I told her about the statement that Judge Sally made to me at my sentencing: "I don't want animal like you coming from Washington, D.C. ruining my county. I wish I could give your life; I hope you die in prison." This particular woman told me that the citizens of Charles County give Judge Sally a certain amount of leeway because he is keeping Charles County from turning into a P.G. county. I don't care how you put it — that type of thinking is discriminatory in nature. To hear this coming from a black woman actually hurt. I kindly answered this woman, "what happens when Judge Sally says that to your son?" She couldn't answer that question.

I immediately put together a complaint against Judge Sally with the Commission for Judicial Disabilities. They are a group of people who investigate complaints on Judges. I contacted a Mr. Steven Lemmey.

I'd first heard of them through the Yvette Cade case. Yvette Cade was the black woman that was set on fire by her estranged husband. Judge Palumbo, a P.G. county judge, dropped her protective order against her husband only days before the burning incident. Judge Palumbo also said some pretty nasty things to Ms. Cade before he dropped her order. Eventually, this particular Judge was forced to retire.

Judge Sally has been saying inappropriate things to people for decades without any type of recourse. When I filed my complaint, Mr. Lemmey told me I was the only person that had ever filed anything against Judge Sally. He says most people are afraid of him. Well, I don't have the luxury of fear. I'm dying. The American public needs to know exactly what's going on in Charles County.

On February 28, 2007, I was transported back to Charles County to await trial. Southern Maryland Pre-Release is about ten minutes from the Charles County Courthouse, but I was taken back all the way back to Brockbridge, which is in Howard County, and then had to be taken right back to Charles County, and there is supposed to be a gas shortage.

I appeared before the Honorable Judge Sally on March 2, 2007, for a Motions hearing, but apparently someone had informed him of my complaint to the Commission on Judicial Disabilities, because Sally immediately recused himself from my case. My next court date was April 6, 2007, before the Honorable Judge Henderson.

My attorney's name was Gerald Rivers. I guess he thought I was someone that was ignorant of the law, because he told me three lies in 15 minutes. The first lie was that they don't give plea bargains to inmates returning to Charles County on appeal. I immediately stood and asked Judge Sally was not giving people plea bargains when they came back on appeal, a common occurrence in Charles County? Judge Sally stated, "he had never heard of such a thing."

Next, Rivers stated "that if l went to trial again and lost the possession charge, the judge could double my sentence." I immediately showed him a copy of the Robin Collins case, Butler v. State — if a person was not found to be a subsequent offender at the first sentencing, the state doesn't get a second bite at the apple.

When Rivers lied to my sister, I knew I was not going to let him represent me in trial. He told my sister I was unable to get a bond because I had already been sentenced. When my convictions were vacated, I was eligible for bail. While sitting in Judge Sally's courtroom, I saw two cases that showed me how disproportionate Judge Sally is in his sentencing methods. Judge Sally gave a young Filipino kid five years for possession with the intent to distribute marijuana. The guy had a half-ounce of weed. Then in the next breath, he sentenced a white man with a worse record that my own to two years for possession of over 100 oxycodone. It just happens that the white man's father was a retired D.C. cop and a friend of Judge Sally's bailiff.

I read a book in prison about a prison in Germany, Stockholm. This was a place where the prisoners were treated so badly that they started to identify with their captors. (Maybe I deserved to be beaten) When I returned to Charles County this particular book came to mind.

Mind you, my convictions were vacated on November 20, 2006, so in all actualities I should have been a pre-trial inmate, (someone with a bond in general population). Instead, I was placed on a "Safe-keeper" status for 29 days in a black-and-white striped jumpsuit. During which time, I was locked in a cell for 22 hours a day, and I had no privileges. Thus, I was not allowed to get a haircut, go to the law library, or have any type of recreation other than walking around a 20x12 day room area for one hour at night. The other hour was used to clean the cells and the unit.

After being under those conditions for 22 days, I was finally taken before the Honorable Judge Henderson at 2:00 p.m. on March 22nd and was made a pre-trial inmate. Judge Henderson also gave me a $50,000 bond. It took the classification unit another week to finally move me out of there.

On March 29, 2007, I was given a green Jumpsuit that was a size too small, and I was moved to unit DI, cell 14. God works in mysterious ways, because I never had any money while I was in the Charles County Detention Center, but I had an unlimited supply of clothing and cosmetics. It seemed like every one of my cellmates who had gone home had left me all of their cosmetics.

My cell mate in DI 14, Leon Spriggs, was from Seat Pleasant, Maryland, and I know most of his family. He was also having problems with the judicial system in Charles County. He was given an illegal sentence back in 1997, and they were trying to sentence him again 10 years later. Once we were allowed to go to the law library, I gave him the case Pearson v. Stouffer. Pearson was an inmate at MCTC, and had filed a Writ against the warden of MCTC, Michael Stouffer for holding him illegally. Pearson was released immediately. They gave Leon (2) more years of probation.

The most ironic thing happened after Leon mentioned that case to his attorney. The institution claimed that the law library was broken. Tell me, how can books be broken? They claimed that there was an electrical problem, and the door to the law library wasn't functional. They have keys to the doors, so what does that have to do with electricity? It just seemed a little suspicious to me. I think they didn't want me in that law library.

In order to have a hero, you must have a villain. Thus, in order to keep their jobs, Police must arrest criminals, prosecutors must convict criminals, judges must sentence criminals, and correctional officers must watch criminal. If you stop arresting people, can you imagine the amount of people that would be out of work? The system calls this crime and justice; I call it modern day slavery.

My next court appearance was on April 6, 2007 before the Honorable Judge Henderson. Judge Henderson allowed me to fire Rivers and present two motions. Henderson denied both of my motions, and he told me a lie to discourage me from going to trial. I told the court that there was no way possible they could prove I tried to permanently deprive the owner of her vehicle. Judge Henderson told me the laws have changed and that today the prosecution doesn't have to prove that anymore. When I got back to the detention center, I found a copy of the jury's instructions from my first trial, and the instructions for theft were exactly as I'd said. The laws haven't changed in two years. Who can you trust? I would rather take my chances by myself than to deal with a crooked attorney. That's like trying to fight two nephews and a cousin, but the cousin is supposed to be on your side. The court system in Charles County is one complete unit, a gang so to speak. Fighting them is like playing Russian roulette, simply gambling on your life.

The only thing that got me through was the singing of David Watts, or as we called him, Luther. He sounds exactly like Luther Vandross. I pray he gets his act together because he is really a wasted talent. Then we had the Queen of Lincoln Heights, called Faggy Larry. Laughing at him took some of the stress off me. My new cell buddy, Ricky Thomas, got on my last nerve, but I know he meant well.

Eventually, I did get sick. My liver enzyme count went so high that it made it impossible for me to eat. I also had constant diarrhea. I went to the medical unit, and they gave me something for my stomach, but they did nothing for the impacted wisdom tooth I had in my mouth. The doctor said painkillers would only hurt my liver, so I was forced to endure the pain of a wisdom tooth along with my other problems.

My trial date was set for May 3, 2007. My sister brought me a suit in for my trial on April 27th , but she wasn't allowed to leave it. Now, they want to prejudice me before the jury. If I go to trial in prison garb, the jury automatically assumes guilt. How many tricks will these people play? Sometimes you have to rewind the tape so to speak, so you can get all the words to the song.

On May 3rd, I was taken to the holding cell at the Charles County Courthouse at 8:00 a.m., but it was over five hours later before I heard anything. They take you to trial early in the morning, so I smelled a rat.

The prosecutor came to me with a deal, an Alpha Plea, that would release me that day, and I would be on unsupervised probation until I paid off the restitution to the two different insurance companies. I thought about the book *7 Habits of Highly Effective People* by Stephen Covey. I remembered his 4th habit: Think Win/Win. I felt I could be of more help to myself and my family on the streets. Why sit in jail, especially since I'm not well, and continue to fight a losing battle alone? I decided I could help more people from the outside because I'd have more access to society.

For the first few days that I was home, I felt like a quitter, but we must choose our battles in life, and freedom is a win within itself. At least this way, I had the chance to complete my legacy, and hopefully I will work on several more projects before I die.

I wasted twenty-five years of my life trying to see how the other half-lives. I feel your pain, and I will do whatever I can to assist the underprivileged to reach greater heights in this world. I pray through reading these pages you have gained a sense that crime doesn't pay, and a good education does. Please use my life as an example of how not to live.

This book was a kind of therapy for me, because I got the chance to rewind the tape. I got to go back and correct some of my old mistakes and to bring closure to some really bad memories. There is a purpose behind these writings, for most people that lived as I did, don't get the chance to go back and rewind the tape, they die. Therefore, I conclude, "a whole lot of people prayed for me", and I feel like the world needs my testimony.

Finally, I say this to the youth of this world: Life is precious, and we don't have an endless amount of time on this earth. Please make use of that time. Find a higher power and a purpose for your life. Once you find that purpose, don't let nothing or nobody knock you from your Path. Create a plan to achieve that purpose, and set goals. Last but not least, believe in yourself, for if you believe it, you can achieve it. And once you have completed yours goals and purposes, go back and grab someone else less fortunate, and give them a helping hand. We are all in the war against drugs, poverty, mis-education, unemployment, homelessness, disease, and hopelessness together.

I have been clean from drugs and alcohol for 15 years now. In 2009, I enrolled in the University of the District of Columbia. In December of 2010, I received an Associate degree in Computer Science Technology and was inducted into Phi Theta Kappa. In December 2011, I receive a Bachelor's degree in Business Administration, (Computer Information Systems Management). I graduated Magna Cum Laude, and was inducted into Delta Mu Delta. I have been working on my MBA, and have received a diversity Scholarship to the University of West Virginia to get my PHD. My cancer is gone, and I am living a totally different life. I said once before, "someone prayed for me", but in fact, a lot of people prayed for me. The only problem I am having is society is still holding my past against me; even though I have educated myself, and change my entire perspective on life I cannot find employment in my field of study. I was forced to start a mobile car detailing company with my son. But with all the injuries I have incurred over the decades I can't work enough to make a living wage. Maybe someone reading this story can help me.

Inside The Mind of The Author

Over 20 Years of Disaster depicts my life of crime, mayhem, and drugs from the period of 1982 to 2007. I had two motivations for writing this book. First and foremost, there was Barack Obama. If a black man could be President of the United States; I knew could do anything that I put my mind to. President Obama ended all my excuses. Secondly, I read the book: *7 Habits of Highly Effective People* by Stephen Covey. This book gave me a better perspective, purpose, and direction, while providing my life with structure.

I always hid in the background because I had a fear of success. Les Brown said it best: "People prefer known hells to unknown heavens." Jail, the streets, and drugs were my known hells, so I never feared them. But having a successful life scared me to death; therefore I would always sabotage my life at the point of success.

This book is my way of giving back to society for all of the wrongs I've caused. I tried to relay my message in a manner that all generations could relate to. I gave examples for the older individual, and solved problems with poetry for the younger generation. Hopefully, reading about my life in the streets from the perspective of an active participant will provide my writing the needed creditability to change the lives of the reader.

Stay connected with Michael Kevin Moore at
www.michaelkevinmoore.com.

www.ingramcontent.com/pod-product-compliance
Lightning Source LLC
Chambersburg PA
CBHW051036160426
43193CB00010B/965
9780999465301